Duncan Hines Complete

Cake Mix Magic

Duncan Hines Complete Cake Mix Magic

300 Easy Desserts Good as Homemade

Jill Snider

Robert ROSE

For complete cataloguing information, see page 272.

Disclaimer

The recipes in this book have been carefully tested by our kitchen and our tasters. To the best of our knowledge, they are safe and nutritious for ordinary use and users. For those people with food or other allergies, or who have special food requirements or health issues, please read the suggested contents of each recipe carefully and determine whether or not they may create a problem for you. All recipes are used at the risk of the consumer.

We cannot be responsible for any hazards, loss or damage that may occur as a result of any recipe use.

For those with special needs, allergies, requirements or health problems, in the event of any doubt, please contact your medical adviser prior to the use of any recipe.

Design & Production: PageWave Graphics Inc.

Editors: Peter Matthews, Judith Finlayson and Sue Sumeraj

Proofreader: Sheila Wawanash

Recipe Editor: Jennifer MacKenzie

Indexer: Gillian Watts

Cover Photography: Colin Erricson

Associate Photographer: Matt Johannsson

Food Stylist: Kathryn Robertson

Prop Stylist: Charlene Erricson

Interior Photography: Mark T. Shapiro

Food Stylists: Kate Bush and Jill Snider

Prop Stylist: Charlene Erricson

Cover image: Chocolate Raspberry Torte (see recipe, page 68)

Image page 2: Coconut Walnut Carrot Cake (see recipe, page 90)

We acknowledge the financial support of the Government of Canada through the Book Publishing Industry Development Program (BPIDP) for our publishing activities.

Published by Robert Rose Inc.

120 Eglinton Avenue East, Suite 800, Toronto, Ontario, Canada M4P 1E2

Tel: (416) 322-6552 Fax: (416) 322-6936

www.robertrose.ca

Printed in Canada

1 2 3 4 5 6 7 8 9 TCP 19 18 17 16 15 14 13 12

FSC
www.fsc.org
MIX
Paper from
responsible sources
FSC® C011825

Introduction

Cake in some form plays an important role in the ritual of our lives — whether it is a coffee cake in the morning, a teatime treat, a lunchbox sweet, a late-night dessert or a snack at any time during the day. And, of course, a birthday party without cake just wouldn't be a proper celebration. Cake can be as plain and simple or as elegant and decadent as the occasion calls for.

In today's hectic world, there are fewer and fewer hours of free time available to bake. Consequently, people who enjoy baking have an even greater need for shortcuts that don't sacrifice quality. Anyone who bakes from scratch knows two things: baking cakes can be time-consuming and it can produce disappointing results. Although I love to bake from scratch, I'm happy to use any convenience food that saves time and still meets my high standards for quality. I call it speedy scratch baking!

A cake mix is the perfect shortcut solution, because beginning with the best always gets you off to a great start. I always have a cake mix or two and a few other ingredients on hand. It rules out the excuse that you don't have time to bake, and it's a great way to be prepared for the unexpected. Since the ingredients are already measured accurately and are consistently reliable, a mix saves preparation steps, such as measuring, sifting and creaming. Using a cake mix also greatly reduces the number of ingredients required to create a dazzling dessert. You can still add rich and flavorful ingredients, such as eggs, sour cream, butter, nuts, chocolate and fruit, that give cake the distinctive "homemade" taste no bakery cake can match.

Another benefit of cake mixes is their tolerance. Mixes are formulated to withstand minor variations such as overmixing, undermixing, oven temperature variations, measuring utensil discrepancies, different mixers and pans and a variety of added ingredients. The risk of a disaster is greatly reduced; in fact, it is almost a guarantee that you will be proud of your masterpiece. But if, by chance, something goes wrong, don't apologize. My foolproof solution is to serve it warm with a big scoop of vanilla ice cream. Everyone will be happy and none the wiser!

In *Complete Cake Mix Magic*, I've included a selection of cakes that will carry you through every occasion. The recipes are easy to follow and use ingredients you are likely to have on hand or can easily find at your local grocery store. Each chapter offers a wide variety of flavors and ingredients, and I've made suggestions for variations on the cakes and frostings to suit different tastes. I'm sure you'll think of even more combinations. With a little imagination and creativity, the possibilities are endless.

Among the many recipes, I'm sure you'll find a few that will become your favorites. I've tried to include something for every taste and occasion. Use the recipes as a starting point and add your own touches. Most of all — enjoy cake baking — the easy and delicious way!

Baking Equipment

Pans

Today's baking pans are not as standardized as they once were. They differ in size and shape from older ones and they vary from one manufacturer to another. The labeling consists of a mix of imperial and metric measurements, which is often confusing. I recommend using the pan size specified in the recipes, as using a size that is not called for can affect results. However, since cake mixes are more tolerant of variations than cakes baked from scratch, you have more latitude in terms of the pans you use. Feel free to substitute a pan that is similar in dimension and volume, but don't use pans smaller in volume, as the cake may overflow. It is usually safe to use a pan that is slightly larger than the one specified, although the cake will be shallower and will require less baking time. You can interchange shapes (e.g., round instead of square) if the volume is the same and the pan is not much deeper, shallower, longer or shorter.

To measure a pan, take the measurements on the inside, across the top. To confirm the volume of a pan, fill it with water and pour the liquid into a measuring cup.

COMMON PANS

You will need these common pans to prepare the cakes in this book:

- a 13- by 9-inch (3 L) pan
- three 8-inch (20 cm) round pans
- three 9-inch (23 cm) round pans
- a 10-inch (3 L) Bundt pan
- a 10-inch (4 L) tube pan
- an 8- to 10-inch (20 to 25 cm) springform pan
- two 8½- by 4½-inch (1.5 L) or 9- by 5-inch (2 L) loaf pans
- two muffin (cupcake) pans (12 cups each)
- a 17- by 11-inch (3 L) jellyroll pan
- a 13- by 9-inch (3 L) glass baking pan
- rimless baking sheets

I prefer good-quality, shiny metal pans for baking. They bake evenly and don't rust. If you use glass pans, decrease the oven temperature by 25°F (10°C). If using nonstick pans, follow manufacturer's directions. Most recommend reducing the temperature by 25°F (10°C), since nonstick surfaces, especially dark ones, bake faster. This adjustment is especially important for large cakes, because the edges will overbake before the center is done.

Measuring Cups and Spoons

Inaccurate measuring is one of the most common mistakes in baking. For information on how to measure, see page 10. Use dry measuring cups, which are sold in sets, to measure dry ingredients such as flour, sugar and coconut. Liquids should be measured in clear measuring cups with graduated markings. They come in a variety of sizes, ranging from 1 cup (250 mL) to 8 cups (2 L), and have a spout for easy pouring. Measuring spoons are used for both liquid and dry ingredients.

Bowls

Every kitchen needs a variety of bowls in different sizes for mixing ingredients. Have a few of each size — small, medium and large. I prefer metal or glass. Plastic does not work well for beating egg whites. Most of the batters in this book are prepared in a large mixer bowl. I refer to the bowl needed for an electric mixer as a "mixer bowl." If this isn't specified, other bowls will do (for example, when mixing a crumble topping, or fruit with sugar).

Microwave-safe bowls are ideal for melting chocolate, heating liquids, dissolving gelatin mixtures and so on. For most purposes, you'll only need one each in small and medium sizes.

Mixer

Use an electric countertop mixer or a good-quality hand mixer, not the heavy-duty commercial type, which are too powerful for normal home use. If you do a lot of baking, the countertop model is much more efficient and easier to use than a hand mixer.

Wooden Spoons

Large ones are ideal for mixing cookie dough. Smaller flat ones are useful for stirring cooked mixtures.

Sieve or Strainer

You'll need a fine sieve to sift ingredients that tend to clump, such as confectioner's (icing) sugar and cocoa. Sieves can also be used to strain liquids from fruits.

Graters, Zesters and Peelers

A coarse grater is used on vegetables such as carrots and zucchini, and often to grate chocolate. To make zest, you need a very fine grater or a zester, a gadget with tiny teeth specifically designed for this purpose. A four-sided grater with holes of different sizes, including fine, medium, coarse and one for shaving, also works well. A vegetable peeler is good for making chocolate curls.

Kitchen Shears

A sharp pair of kitchen scissors is a handy accessory. This tool makes easy work of cutting dried fruits such as apricots.

Ice Cream Scoops

Ice cream scoops help you achieve uniformity in the size and shape of your baked foods. Small ones are used for cookie dough, larger ones for muffins and cupcakes. Buy scoops that have a wire release, which removes dough easily from the scoop.

Racks

Wire racks are essential for cooling cakes. Choose stainless steel, since they have a long life and won't rust. It's a good idea to have a variety of sizes (round, square, rectangle) to suit the size of cakes you are making. Look for racks that have narrow spaces between the wires so that small items such as muffins and cookies can't slip through. To avoid rack marks on the top of your cake, keep one rack covered with a thick tea towel, pinned securely in place. When necessary, remove the towel for washing.

Knives

A long sharp serrated knife with a blade about 12 inches (30 cm) long makes cutting cakes horizontally a breeze. However, some people prefer to use dental floss for an even slice. Try both methods and pick your favorite. Electric knives are excellent for angel food cakes. A good-quality chef's knife is essential for chopping ingredients.

Saucepans

You'll need two heavy saucepans, one small and one medium, to prepare the finishing touches, such as caramelized sugar and cooked puddings, for some cakes.

Pastry Bag and Tips

These are useful for finishing cakes and are not difficult to use. All you need to make attractive decorations is a few basic tips. I prefer the disposable bags for convenience. Choose a large and a small star tip and a small round tip for writing. For simple decorating, such as writing names and drawing outlines, a plastic squeeze bottle makes an acceptable substitute.

Pastry Brush

This handy tool can be used to brush liquid glazes over warm cakes and is also ideal for removing excess crumbs from cakes and their serving plates before frosting.

Know Your Ingredients

Cake Mixes

Cake mixes contain many of the same ingredients that are required to bake cakes from scratch. The difference is, they are already measured in the correct proportion. These include flour, sugar, leavening (baking powder and baking soda), fat, salt, flavoring and coloring. When using a standard cake mix, you add eggs, oil and water. Cake mixes also contain ingredients that are not in your kitchen cupboard, such as emulsifiers, conditioners and thickeners. These are added to make the mix more tolerant so it will perform well even if a consumer doesn't follow precisely the recommended measurements and method. A little more or less water, large or small eggs, more or less oil, underbeating, overbeating — all of these can be tolerated. Of course, the mixes do perform best when the recommended measurements and method are followed.

Another advantage of cake mixes is that they have a shelf life of one year when stored unopened in a cool dry place. This makes it convenient to add cake mix to the list of staple ingredients you keep on hand. I like to have two white, chocolate and lemon cake mixes, one spice mix and one marble mix on my shelf. With these, I am ready to make any recipe in this book.

CAKE MIX FLAVORS

Be aware that cake mix flavors vary considerably among manufacturers. For instance, some white mixes have a vanilla flavor, while others taste of almond. I prefer white to yellow cake, as the flavor is not as strong. In my opinion, this makes white cake more versatile, as it can accommodate a wider range of flavors; however, this is entirely a personal preference. In most recipes, they are interchangeable. You should compare the two in a few recipes and pick your favorite. You will also find that there are several different kinds of chocolate mixes available. Again, try a few and choose your favorite. Usually they are interchangeable, and your choice will depend upon whether you prefer a stronger or milder chocolate taste.

Liquids

Water is the most common liquid used in the recipes, but there are others:

- **Milk.** I prefer 2% milk, but homogenized (whole) milk, 1% milk and skim milk will also work, although recipe results will vary slightly because of the different fat content.
- **Buttermilk.** This is made from lower-fat milk and a bacterial culture. You can find buttermilk in the dairy case of your supermarket or prepare your own: For 1 cup (250 mL) buttermilk, mix 1 tbsp (15 mL) vinegar or lemon juice and enough milk to make 1 cup (250 mL); let stand for 5 minutes, then stir.
- **Evaporated milk.** This canned product is made by evaporating milk to half its volume. It has a mild caramel taste and comes in whole and lower-fat versions.
- **Light cream.** This has a milk fat content (M.F.) of 5%.
- **Half-and-half cream.** This has 10% M.F. It can be used in recipes calling for light cream.
- **Table cream.** This has 18% M.F. It can be used in recipes calling for light or half-and-half cream.
- **Whipping cream.** This has 35% M.F. and is also called heavy cream.
- **Sour cream.** Regular sour cream is about 14% M.F.; it is also available in lower-fat and no-fat versions. Use the regular or lower-fat kind in baking. (I don't recommend the no-fat variety). In most recipes, plain yogurt can be substituted.
- **Yogurt.** This is available in plain and flavored varieties, with a range of fat contents. As with sour cream, don't use the no-fat type for baking.
- **Sweetened condensed milk.** This is evaporated milk that has been reduced further and sweetened. It is available in whole and lower-fat versions. All testing was done using the whole (or regular) variety.

Fats

It's important to use the type of fat specified in the recipe, as this has been used in testing. Sometimes a liquid is used (oil, melted butter) and sometimes solid fat (butter) is required.

- **Vegetable oil.** This is the most common fat required in cake mix recipes. It works well with the mix ingredients to give you a light, tender, moist cake. Select a light, flavorless oil such as canola, safflower, sunflower or corn oil rather than heavier varieties such as olive oil.
- **Butter and margarine.** I prefer to use lightly salted butter in baking. It has a wonderful flavor and good browning qualities. In most cases, hard margarine can be substituted. Do not use soft tub margarines or spreads, as they do not have the same consistency as butter. Hard margarines work well where there are other strong flavors, such as spices and chocolate, and where a "buttery" taste isn't as important. The exception is frostings, where unsalted butter is preferred.
- **Shortening.** Think of shortening as a solid form of vegetable oil. I use it mainly for greasing the pans rather than as an ingredient. Cooking sprays also work well for greasing pans and are especially convenient for Bundt and muffin pans. Oil or butter tends to stick and burn more easily.

Sugars

- **Granulated sugar (white).** I use regular granulated sugar in recipe testing. It is free-flowing and doesn't require sifting. You can also buy superfine or fruit sugar, but I only use this in shortbreads.
- **Confectioner's sugar.** Also referred to as icing sugar or powdered sugar, this type of sugar has been ground to a fine powder and approximately 3% cornstarch has been added to prevent lumping and crystallization during storage. (Be sure to keep the bag airtight as it can clump when stored). Confectioner's sugar is used primarily in frostings and glazes. It dissolves almost instantly in liquids, which makes it wonderful for sweetening whipping cream. When using confectioner's sugar, I prefer to measure first, then sift. I have based my recipes on this method rather than on sifting first and then measuring.
- **Brown sugar.** This is less refined than granulated sugar. The darker the color, the more molasses and moisture it contains, which intensifies the flavor. I like the golden (sometimes called yellow) variety for recipe testing, but light and dark are interchangeable. Brown sugar is used mainly in toppings, streusels and some frostings. It isn't used much in cake batters, as it makes them heavier and overly moist. (Cake mixes usually contain sufficient sugar anyway.) However, brown sugar is wonderful for use in cookies and bars, which benefit from the denser texture and caramel flavor. To measure, pack it firmly into a dry measuring cup and level off. Because of its moisture, brown sugar tends to lump. Store it airtight in a covered jar or a heavy plastic bag in a cool, dry place. If it does harden, put it in a plastic bag with a slice of apple for a few days.
- **Coarse sugar.** This is sometimes used in toppings or to coat cookies before baking, but it should not be used in batter or dough, as it does not dissolve readily.

Eggs

Eggs contribute to leavening, texture, color, flavor, volume, richness and nutritional value in cakes. In other words, they are one of the most important ingredients! All recipes in this book were tested using large eggs. One large egg measures ¼ cup (50 mL). If you're using a different size, break eggs into a measuring cup to get the correct 1 cup (250 mL) measure.

Remove eggs from the refrigerator at least 1 hour before using them so they can come to room temperature. If they are to be separated, do so when they are cold, then leave them for the hour. This will help ensure maximum volume when the whites are beaten. Even a trace of yolk in the whites will prevent them from beating into stiff peaks. Cover the separated eggs with plastic wrap to prevent them from drying out.

Use a metal or glass bowl, not plastic, for beating egg whites. Wash and dry the bowl and utensils thoroughly to be sure there is no trace of grease or the egg whites won't beat to stiff peaks. Cream of tartar helps to keep egg whites stiff.

Chocolate

Chocolate is a must-have ingredient you should never be without! Keep a supply of semi-sweet or bittersweet chocolate in a cool place. Unsweetened chocolate is not used as often, but keep a small amount on hand for some of the frostings. Chocolate is chopped, grated or melted for use in recipes.

Chocolate chips are formulated to soften but still hold their shape during baking. In general, they are used in and on top of cakes, while block chocolate (or squares) is used for melting.

White chocolate is not really chocolate but has become a popular ingredient in baking. Be sure to buy pure white chocolate (read the label and look for "pure" or "100% pure"), not the artificial kind, which won't melt properly.

Cocoa is a dry, unsweetened powder made from chocolate liquor with most of the cocoa butter removed. As cocoa tends to clump in storage, it needs to be sifted before using. As with confectioner's sugar, measure first, then sift.

MELTING CHOCOLATE

To melt chocolate, coarsely chop it and let it melt slowly in the top of a double boiler or a bowl set over hot — but not boiling — water until almost melted. Stir to finish melting completely. Don't put a lid on the pan, as condensation will cause chocolate to seize. You can also melt chocolate in a small saucepan on low heat, stirring constantly until smooth. To melt it in a microwave oven, place chopped chocolate in a microwave-safe bowl, cover tightly and heat on Medium (50%) power until almost melted (about 30 seconds to 1 minute per ounce (28 g), depending upon the quantity of chocolate and microwave power). Remove from oven and stir until completely melted.

Spices

Keep your favorite spices on hand. Buy them in small amounts and store in tightly sealed glass containers in a cool, dark place. Replace within 6 to 9 months.

Nuts

As nuts are high in fat, they tend to go rancid quickly. Store nuts in the freezer to keep them fresh. When you're ready to bake, thaw nuts and use them as directed or, for optimum flavor, toast them first: Spread nuts in a single layer on a baking sheet and bake at 350°F (180°C) for 5 to 10 minutes, stirring often, until golden and fragrant. Cool before using. Chopped nuts take less time to toast than whole nuts. For hazelnuts, rub off the skins in a tea towel while they're warm. The weight equivalent of 1 cup (250 mL) lightly toasted nuts is approximately 3½ oz (100 g).

Coconut

Like nuts, coconut is high in fat and should be stored in the freezer. I prefer flaked or shredded rather than desiccated coconut in baking. Sweetened or unsweetened is a matter of choice. Coconut also has a nicer flavor when toasted: Spread coconut in a single layer on a baking sheet and bake at 350°F (180°C) for about 5 minutes, stirring often, until light golden. Watch carefully, as coconut burns quickly.

Flavorings

Always use pure extracts, not artificial. The price is considerably more, but you use less and the flavor is well worth it.

Food Colors

The four basic liquid food colors are red, green, blue and yellow. They are usually sold in a kit, which should meet all your decorating needs.

Cream Cheese

I prefer full-fat cream cheese, but you can substitute a lower-fat variety if you prefer. For smooth blending, soften blocks of cream cheese to room temperature. Don't use tubs of soft, spreadable cheese, which are usually whipped with added liquid and are therefore not the right consistency for baking.

Fresh Fruit

- **Citrus fruit.** One medium lemon yields about ¼ cup (50 mL) juice and 2 tsp (10 mL) grated zest. Two to three medium oranges yield 1 cup (250 mL) juice and 3 tbsp (45 mL) grated zest. One medium lime yields about 2 tbsp (25 mL) juice and 1 tsp (5 mL) grated zest. To get the most juice from a citrus fruit, warm it slightly in boiling water or microwave it for about 10 seconds.
- **Apples.** One pound (500 g) or three medium apples yields about 3 cups (750 mL) sliced or diced. When cutting, sprinkle the board with lemon juice, then squeeze it on cut fruit to prevent discoloration.
- **Bananas.** One pound (500 g) or two to three large bananas yields 1 cup (250 mL) mashed.
- **Strawberries and raspberries.** One pound (500 g) contains about 4 cups (1 L) whole berries, 3 cups (750 mL) sliced or 2 cups (500 mL) crushed.

Dried Fruit

Keep raisins, dried apricots, dried cranberries and dates on hand for general baking. For special holidays, purchase candied fruit. Fruit may sink if the batter is not stiff enough. Chop fruit finely and toss it in flour to coat and help suspend the pieces in the batter.

Canned Fruit

Keep a supply of the common types of canned fruit on hand. This includes pineapple (crushed and rings), apricots, peaches, mandarin oranges and mangoes. Brands will vary in the proportion of liquid to solid fruit, as well as in the color and size of fruit pieces.

Frozen Fruit

Keep a few bags of cranberries in your freezer, as they can be hard to find out of season. Buy other frozen fruits, such as rhubarb, peaches and berries, as needed. In general, I prefer to use fresh fruit if it's available.

Cake Baking Tips and Techniques

Plan in Advance

- Read the recipe carefully, checking the ingredients, utensils and equipment required, oven temperature and baking time.
- Gather all the ingredients and equipment you need. Perform tasks such as chopping or toasting nuts, preparing fruit or grating zest. Having this out of the way ahead of time makes mixing quick and easy.
- Allow adequate time to soften butter and bring cold ingredients such as eggs to room temperature.
- Adjust the oven rack to the middle level for most cake baking. Angel food cakes are baked on the lower rack. Always check the cake mix package or recipe for specified directions. About 15 minutes before you plan to bake, preheat your oven.

Use the Right Pan, Properly Prepared

Use the pan size recommended in the recipe and prepare pans as required:

- Grease lightly with shortening or a vegetable cooking spray. Don't use butter, margarine or oil, which are more likely to stick and burn.
- If the pan also requires flouring, sprinkle the greased surface lightly with flour. Shake to distribute evenly, then shake out any excess flour.
- Pans for layer cakes can be lined with a circle of parchment paper on the bottom, which makes cake removal foolproof.
- When using springform pans, in addition to greasing, it's a good idea to place the pans on a piece of foil to catch drips that may leak out if the seal between the rim and the base is not perfect.
- For rectangular cakes that won't be served from the pan, line the pan with greased foil, leaving an overhang. The cooled cake can be removed from the pan easily, using the overhang as handles. The same technique works well for bars and squares, especially those that tend to stick to the pan. You will probably find bars and squares easier to cut after they have been removed from the pan. Lift them out of the pan in the foil and place them on a cutting board.
- For angel food cake, leave the pan ungreased so the batter crawls up, sticking to the sides as it rises during baking.
- For muffins and cupcakes, paper liners can replace greasing.

Measure Accurately

Accuracy is very important in baking, and inaccurate measuring is one of the most common mistakes.

- Use liquid (usually clear) measures for liquids. Read the measurement at eye level.
- For dry ingredients, you'll need a set of graduated measures specifically intended for dry ingredients. They have a straight rim so the ingredients can be leveled off. Spoon the ingredients into the appropriate measure and level off with a straight spatula or knife. Don't tap or pack! Brown sugar, however, should be firmly packed into the cup, then leveled off. It should hold the cup shape when turned out.
- Use measuring spoons for small amounts of both liquid and dry ingredients.
- Unless otherwise specified, dry ingredients should be measured before sifting and butter should be measured before it is melted.

Mix Properly

Mix batters in a large mixer bowl using an electric mixer. Start on low speed for about 1 minute to blend liquid and dry ingredients and prevent splattering. Then increase the speed to medium and beat for 2 minutes, or until the mixture is smooth. Scrape the bowl often during mixing.

Fill Pans Carefully

When baking layer cakes, divide the batter evenly between the pans so the layers are the same height and will bake evenly. If possible, use a kitchen scale to measure the weight of each filled pan. For most plain cakes, bang the pan firmly against the countertop after spreading the batter in the pan. This eliminates any large air bubbles. Don't do this with angel food cakes, marble cakes or cakes with a streusel filling or topping or a lot of fruit or nuts throughout.

Bake Immediately

Bake the cake as soon as it is mixed — the leavening in a mix starts to work as soon as it is moistened, and a delay in baking will result in poor volume. For proper heat distribution, pans should not touch each other or the sides of the oven during baking. If your oven won't hold three pans on a shelf, put two on the upper middle rack and one on a lower rack. Change positions halfway through baking.

Use Times as a Guideline

Use the recommended baking times as a guideline. Always set your timer for 5 minutes before the minimum time given to allow for oven variances. Ovens are often hotter than the temperature indicates, and cakes can easily be overdone, especially those that are high in sugar or baked in a dark pan. It's much safer to add more time in 5-minute segments if a cake needs more baking.

Test for Doneness

When cakes are done, a toothpick, wooden skewer or cake tester inserted in the center will come out clean. This test won't work for some cakes with "gooey" ingredients, however. Another indication that the cake is done is that the top springs back when lightly touched and the cake comes away from the sides of the pan. For lighter cakes, the color is also a good indicator — it should be a nice golden brown.

Let Cool

- Unless otherwise specified, let layer cakes cool in the pan for 10 minutes. Let deeper cakes, such as tube cakes and loaves, cool in the pan for 20 minutes. Place the cake pan on a wire rack. To remove cake from pan, run a knife around the edge (and the center of tube pans), then invert, shaking gently to remove cake.
- Bundt cakes are cooled initially in the pan, then turned out and left to finish cooling fluted side up.
- Angel food cakes are immediately turned upside down on a funnel, bottle or glass bottom and left until completely cool.
- All other cakes are inverted twice so they finish cooling in the same position (top side up) as they are baked.

Glaze or Frost as You Prefer

Glazes are often applied while cakes are warm, while butter icings and frostings are applied after they have completely cooled. There is often no right or wrong frosting or glaze for a cake. It really is a matter of personal preference. Keep both color and flavor in mind when deciding how to finish your cake. I've given several ideas for cake and frosting combinations in most recipes, but these should be used only as a guideline.

HIGH-ALTITUDE BAKING

At altitudes above 3,500 feet (1,000 m), there is less air pressure and humidity. Both of these factors can dramatically affect cake baking. Lower air pressure can cause cakes to overflow or collapse. Here are some tips to help you achieve success:

- If given a choice, use the larger pan size suggested, and don't fill pans more than half full with batter.
- Cakes tend to stick more to pans. Be sure to grease pans generously before dusting with flour.
- It helps to use eggs that are cold rather than the usual room temperature.
- Add 2 tbsp (25 mL) extra flour to toughen the cakes a little.
- Increase the oven temperature by 25°F (10°C) to set the batter before it over-rises.

Tips for Frosting Layer Cakes

- Brush loose crumbs from the sides of the cake.
- Freeze cakes for about 30 minutes. This makes them less fragile and easier to frost.
- Put a bit of frosting on the serving plate, then place cake on top. This will anchor the cake in place.
- If layers are domed, slice a bit off the top to even them off.
- To keep the serving plate clean, set four strips of waxed paper, forming a square, under the edge of the cake.
- Place the first cake layer topside down on plate.
- Spread ½ to ¾ cup (125 to 175 mL) frosting on the cake. If the filling is a jam that may bleed into the frosting, leave a ½-inch (2 cm) border around the edge. Place a second cake layer topside up over frosting. You now have the two flat surfaces together in the center so the cakes will sit evenly.
- Spread a very thin layer of frosting on the top and sides of cake. This seals the crumbs. Then cover with a second, thicker layer of frosting. You can smooth the surface with a long spatula or make swirls with a small spatula or the back of a spoon. The tines of a dinner fork can be used to make wave designs.
- Chill cake, if necessary, to firm up frosting.
- Carefully remove waxed paper strips.

Tips for Finishing Cakes

- Cakes baked in 13- by 9-inch (3 L) pans are usually glazed or frosted and served right from the pan. Pans with lids are ideal for toting desserts to get-togethers.
- When cakes are brushed with syrup while warm (usually done with tube and Bundt cakes), put the cake on a wire rack over waxed paper to catch the drips.
- Dust with confectioner's (icing) sugar for a simple yet attractive finish to plain cakes. Do this just before serving, as the moisture from the cake will quickly absorb the dusting. For an elegant or festive look, place a doily over the cake, sprinkle generously with confectioner's sugar, then remove the doily.
- Simple garnishes such as whole or chopped nuts, shaved chocolate and fresh fruit can also dress up cakes.
- For a quick glaze, microwave a ready-to-serve frosting for about 40 seconds, or just until it is warmed slightly, then stir until a shiny, thick, pourable consistency is reached. Pour over cake and leave to harden.
- Thin lines of white icing make a nice finish for coffee cakes. Mix confectioner's sugar with a little milk to make a thin drizzling consistency. Dip a large spoon into the icing and quickly move it back and forth over the cake. For a chocolate drizzle, melt chocolate and use a spoon or fork in a similar fashion.

Tips for Storing and Thawing Cakes

Storing Cakes and Other Baked Goods

- Properly wrapped, cake keeps very well. You can refrigerate most cakes for up to a week or freeze them for 4 to 6 months.
- Cool unfrosted cakes completely before freezing. Having a few plain cake layers in the freezer is a bonus. When necessary, you can thaw, fill and frost in no time.
- Chill or freeze frosted cake for about 30 minutes to harden frosting so it doesn't stick to the wrapping.
- In general, other baked goods, such as muffins, loaves, cookies and bars, freeze very well. Store them in reusable plastic freezer bags so you can easily remove just the amount you require.

- Avoid freezing desserts that contain a lot of cream. These are much better freshly prepared.

Thawing Cakes

- Thaw frosted cakes overnight in the refrigerator if the frosting contains eggs or cream. Thaw other cakes the same way, or at room temperature, for about 3 hours.
- When unfrosted cakes are going to be frosted, leave covered for about three-quarters of the thawing time, then uncover for the remaining time so they dry out slightly. This makes them easier to frost.

Single-Layer Cakes

Single-layer cakes are usually quick and easy to prepare. They are often glazed or frosted right in the pan — an ideal choice for casual entertaining, bake sales, potlucks and lunchboxes since they are easy to carry and serve. Upside-down cakes also fall into this category. They range from classic pineapple to more exotic bumbleberry.

Triple Chocolate Cake

Although this cake is easy to make, with three layers of chocolate, it's a special treat.

• Preheat oven to 350°F (180°C)
• 13- by 9-inch (3 L) cake pan, greased

SERVES 12 TO 16

CAKE

1	package (18.25 oz/515 g) white cake mix	1
2	eggs	2
1¼ cups	water	300 mL
⅓ cup	vegetable oil	75 mL
3 oz	white chocolate, melted (see page 13)	90 g

FILLING

1½ cups	semi-sweet chocolate chips	375 mL
¼ cup	butter	50 mL
¼ cup	corn syrup	50 mL
¼ cup	confectioner's (icing) sugar	50 mL

FROSTING

1	container (15 oz/450 g) ready-to-serve vanilla frosting	1
3 oz	white chocolate, melted (see page 13)	90 g
4 cups	frozen whipped topping, thawed	1 L
	Chocolate curls to garnish (optional)	

1. **Cake:** In a large mixer bowl, combine cake mix, eggs, water and oil. Beat on medium speed for 2 minutes. Gradually beat in melted chocolate. Spread batter evenly in prepared pan. Bake for 35 to 40 minutes or until a tester inserted in center comes out clean. Cool for 10 minutes in pan on a wire rack.

2. **Filling:** In a small saucepan, combine chocolate chips and butter. Heat over low heat, stirring constantly until smoothly melted. Stir in syrup and confectioner's sugar. Mix well. Spread over warm cake. Cool completely.

3. **Frosting:** In a large mixer bowl, beat together frosting and melted white chocolate until smooth and creamy. Fold in whipped topping. Spread over filling. Garnish with chocolate curls, if desired. Chill until serving. Store leftover cake in the refrigerator.

Variation: Use milk chocolate instead of semi-sweet chips in the filling.

TIPS

• To make chocolate curls, warm a chunk of chocolate slightly. Using a sharp vegetable peeler, and holding the chocolate in several layers of paper toweling to prevent its melting, pull the blade toward you.
• Baking powder starts to work when mixed with liquid, so the shorter the time before getting cake batters into the oven, the better their texture will be.

Chocolate Mayonnaise Cake

Mayonnaise adds richness to an already moist cake.

SERVES 12 TO 16		
1	package (18.25 oz/515 g) devil's food cake mix	1
3	eggs	3
1⅓ cups	milk	325 mL
1 cup	mayonnaise	250 mL
½ tsp	ground cinnamon (optional)	2 mL

TIP
- You can replace water with milk in cake mixes for added nutrition. Keep in mind that it lightens the color of darker cakes.

- **Preheat oven to 350°F (180°C)**
- **13- by 9-inch (3 L) cake pan, greased**

1. In a large mixer bowl, combine cake mix, eggs, milk, mayonnaise and cinnamon. Beat on medium speed for 2 minutes or until smooth. Spread batter evenly in prepared pan. Bake for 35 to 40 minutes or until a tester inserted in center comes out clean. Cool completely in pan on a wire rack. Frost as desired.

Variation: The hint of cinnamon is a personal preference. Omit it if it's not to your liking. You can also replace the milk with coffee or water.

Upside-Down German Chocolate Cake

The creamy top on this cake sinks during baking, then reverses to the top when served.

SERVES 12 TO 16		
1½ cups	flaked coconut	375 mL
1½ cups	chopped pecans	375 mL
1	package (18.25 oz/515 g) devil's food cake mix	1
3	eggs	3
1⅓ cups	water	325 mL
½ cup	vegetable oil	125 mL
8 oz	cream cheese, softened	250 g
½ cup	butter, melted and cooled	125 mL
3½ cups	confectioner's (icing) sugar, sifted	875 mL
	Whipped cream (optional)	

TIPS
- Don't worry if the top of the cake cracks during baking. It becomes the bottom when served.
- Serve with a dollop of whipped cream.

- **Preheat oven to 350°F (180°C)**
- **13- by 9-inch (3 L) cake pan, greased**

1. Sprinkle coconut and pecans evenly on bottom of prepared pan. Prepare cake mix with eggs, water and oil as directed on package. Pour batter over coconut and pecans.

2. In a large mixer bowl, beat cream cheese and melted butter on low speed until creamy. Gradually add confectioner's sugar, beating until smooth. Drop by spoonfuls over cake batter. Bake for 50 to 60 minutes or until a tester inserted halfway to bottom of cake comes out clean. Cool completely in pan.

3. **To serve:** Cut into serving-size pieces; turn upside down onto plate. Serve with whipped cream, if desired.

Variation: Replace some of the pecans and coconut with dried cherries.

Candy Bar Cake

A cake version of an all-time favorite, chocolate caramel pecan candy.

SERVES 12 TO 16

FILLING

1 lb	caramels (about 65)	500 g
½ cup	evaporated milk	125 mL

CAKE

1	package (18.25 oz/515 g) devil's food cake mix	1
1	package (4-serving size) chocolate instant pudding mix	1
4	eggs	4
1 cup	sour cream	250 mL
½ cup	vegetable oil	125 mL
¼ cup	water	50 mL

TOPPING

2 cups	semi-sweet chocolate chips, divided	500 mL
1¾ cups	chopped pecans, divided	425 mL
2 tbsp	butter	25 mL

TIPS

- Grease bottom and sides of cake pan very well with shortening or cooking spray. When spreading caramel, leave a border around edge. Following these steps will help keep the caramel from sticking to the pan.
- Pudding mix adds sweetness and gives a hearty but tender texture to a mix.

- **Preheat oven to 350°F (180°C)**
- **13- by 9-inch (3 L) cake pan, greased**

1. **Filling:** In a small saucepan over low heat, heat caramels and evaporated milk, stirring often until smoothly melted. Keep warm while preparing cake.

2. **Cake:** In a large mixer bowl, combine cake mix, pudding mix, eggs, sour cream, oil and water. Beat on medium speed for 2 minutes. Spread half of batter evenly in prepared pan. Bake for 15 minutes or just until set. Pour caramel mixture evenly over top.

3. **Topping:** Sprinkle 1 cup (250 mL) chocolate chips and 1 cup (250 mL) pecans over caramel layer. Carefully spread remaining cake batter over filling. Bake for 35 to 40 minutes longer. Cool for 30 minutes in pan on a wire rack before glazing. In a small saucepan over low heat, melt remaining 1 cup (250 mL) chocolate chips and butter or microwave on medium for 2 minutes, stirring until smooth. Spread over cake. Sprinkle with remaining ¾ cup (175 mL) pecans. Cool completely before cutting.

Variation: For a stronger chocolate taste, use a dark chocolate cake mix.

Chocolate Cola Cake

Some like cola with chocolate cake. Now you can enjoy it in the cake with a glass of cold milk.

SERVES 12 TO 16

CAKE

1	package (18.25 oz/515 g) white cake mix	1
1/3 cup	unsweetened cocoa powder, sifted	75 mL
2	eggs	2
1 cup	cola	250 mL
1/2 cup	milk	125 mL
1/2 cup	vegetable oil	125 mL
1 1/3 cups	miniature marshmallows	325 mL

CHOCOLATE COLA FROSTING

1/2 cup	butter	125 mL
1/3 cup	unsweetened cocoa powder, sifted	75 mL
1/3 cup	cola	75 mL
2 3/4 to 3 cups	confectioner's (icing) sugar, sifted	675 to 750 mL
3/4 cup	chopped peanuts (optional)	175 mL

- **Preheat oven to 350°F (180°C)**
- **13- by 9-inch (3 L) cake pan, greased**

1. **Cake:** In a large mixer bowl, combine cake mix, cocoa, eggs, cola, milk and oil. Beat on medium speed for 2 minutes. Fold in marshmallows. Spread batter evenly in prepared pan. Bake for 40 to 45 minutes or until top springs back when lightly touched. Cool for 1 hour in pan on a wire rack before frosting.

2. **Frosting:** In a medium saucepan, melt butter. Add cocoa and cola, stirring until smooth. Bring to a boil, stirring constantly. Remove from heat. Gradually add enough confectioner's sugar, stirring, to make a smooth spreading consistency. Stir in nuts, if desired. Spread evenly over cake. Cool completely before cutting.

Variation: The frosting is delicious with or without nuts.

TIPS
- Use cola at room temperature — not cold, as you would for drinking.
- The addition of cocoa to a white cake gives it the flavor of a chocolate cake mix. Be sure to sift the cocoa before using, since it tends to clump in storage.

Chocolate Praline Cake

The broiled topping here — or on almost any cake — makes it a guaranteed success.

SERVES 12 TO 16

1	package (18.25 oz/515 g) devil's food cake mix	1
2	eggs	2
1 1/4 cups	water	300 mL
1/3 cup	vegetable oil	75 mL
	Crunchy Broiled Topping (see recipe, page 270)	

- **Preheat oven to 350°F (180°C)**
- **13- by 9-inch (3 L) cake pan, greased**

1. In a large mixer bowl, combine cake mix, eggs, water and oil. Beat on medium speed for 2 minutes. Spread batter evenly in prepared pan. Bake for 35 to 40 minutes or until a tester inserted in center comes out clean. Cool for 5 to 10 minutes, then top with Crunchy Broiled Topping. Cool completely in pan on a wire rack before cutting.

Variation: The topping also works well on white, yellow and spice cakes.

TIP
- Broiled toppings burn quickly, so watch constantly while broiling.

Chocolate Caramel Pecan Cake

Every mouthful of this cake is wonderfully gooey, nutty and decadent.

SERVES 12 TO 16

FILLING AND TOPPING

1 cup	butter	250 mL
1 cup	packed brown sugar	250 mL
1 cup	sweetened condensed milk	250 mL
1/4 cup	corn syrup	50 mL
1 cup	milk chocolate chips or miniature semi-sweet chocolate chips	250 mL
2 cups	finely chopped pecans, divided	500 mL

CAKE

1	package (18.25 oz/515 g) devil's food cake mix	1
3	eggs	3
1 1/4 cups	water	300 mL
1/3 cup	vegetable oil	75 mL

TIP
- Be sure to stir the filling constantly while cooking, as it burns easily.

- **Preheat oven to 350°F (180°C)**
- **13- by 9-inch (3 L) cake pan, greased**

1. **Filling:** In a heavy saucepan, combine butter, brown sugar, sweetened condensed milk and corn syrup. Cook over medium heat, stirring constantly until mixture comes to a boil, then simmer for 5 minutes. Keep warm over a bowl of hot water, stirring occasionally, while preparing cake.

2. **Cake:** In a large mixer bowl, combine cake mix, eggs, water and oil. Beat at medium speed for 2 minutes. Spread half of batter in prepared pan. Bake for 15 minutes or until the center of the cake is set. Remove from oven.

3. **Topping:** Pour warm caramel mixture evenly over baked cake. Sprinkle chocolate chips and 1 cup (250 mL) of the pecans on top. Spread remaining cake batter carefully over caramel layer. Sprinkle remaining pecans on top. Bake for 25 to 35 minutes longer or until the cake springs back when lightly touched. Cool completely in pan on a wire rack.

Variation: To make a quick caramel filling, omit brown sugar and corn syrup, decrease butter to 1/2 cup (125 mL), increase sweetened condensed milk to 1 can (10 oz/300 mL). Add 75 soft caramels (20 oz/600 g). Heat in a saucepan over medium heat, stirring until caramels are melted and mixture is smooth.

Chocolate Peanut Butter and Banana Cake

Three favorites — peanut butter, banana and chocolate — all in one.

SERVES 12 TO 16		
CAKE		
1	package (18.25 oz/515 g) devil's food cake mix	1
3	eggs	3
1½ cups	mashed ripe bananas (3 to 4 large)	375 mL
½ cup	vegetable oil	125 mL
CHOCOLATE PEANUT BUTTER GLAZE		
4 oz	semi-sweet chocolate	125 g
⅔ cup	creamy peanut butter	150 mL
⅓ cup	chopped peanuts (optional)	75 mL

TIPS
- Use creamy peanut butter, not crunchy, for a smooth, satiny glaze.
- Keep this glaze in mind for other cakes and squares as well.

- **Preheat oven to 350°F (180°C)**
- **13- by 9-inch (3 L) cake pan, greased and floured**

1. **Cake:** In a large mixer bowl, combine cake mix, eggs, bananas and oil. Beat on medium speed for 2 minutes or until smooth. Spread batter evenly in prepared pan. Bake for 35 to 40 minutes or until a tester inserted in center comes out clean. Cool completely in pan on a wire rack.

2. **Glaze:** In a small saucepan over low heat, melt chocolate and peanut butter, stirring constantly until smooth. Spread evenly over cooled cake. Sprinkle nuts on top, if desired.

Variation: Omit glaze and frost with Banana Butter Frosting (see recipe, page 264).

Chocolate Chip 'n' Nut Cake

This one-step cake has the topping baked right on. No need to cool and frost later.

SERVES 12 TO 16		
1	package (18.25 oz/515 g) devil's food cake mix	1
1	package (4-serving size) chocolate instant pudding mix	1
4	eggs	4
1 cup	sour cream	250 mL
½ cup	vegetable oil	125 mL
⅓ cup	water	75 mL
2 cups	miniature semi-sweet chocolate chips, divided	500 mL
½ cup	chopped nuts (optional)	125 mL

TIP
- Cakes made with sour cream or yogurt are generally moist and keep well.

- **Preheat oven to 350°F (180°C)**
- **13- by 9-inch (3 L) cake pan, greased**

1. In a large mixer bowl, combine cake mix, pudding mix, eggs, sour cream, oil and water. Beat on medium speed for 2 minutes or until smooth. Stir in 1¼ cups (300 mL) of the chocolate chips. Spread batter evenly in prepared pan. Sprinkle remaining chocolate chips and nuts evenly over batter. Bake for 45 to 50 minutes or until a tester inserted in center comes out clean. Cool in pan on a wire rack for at least 30 minutes before cutting.

Variation: For a nice change, try using milk chocolate chips instead of semi-sweet.

Chocolate Cherry Cake

It's hard to believe the pie filling replaces the usual fat and liquid ingredients in a cake mix. But it works — very well, too!

SERVES 12 TO 16

CAKE

1	package (18.25 oz/515 g) devil's food cake mix	1
1	can (19 oz/540 mL) cherry pie filling	1
2	eggs	2

CHOCOLATE GLAZE

¾ cup	granulated sugar	175 mL
¼ cup	butter	50 mL
¼ cup	half-and-half (10%) cream	50 mL
¾ cup	semi-sweet chocolate chips	175 mL
¼ tsp	almond extract	1 mL
	Toasted sliced almonds (optional)	

- **Preheat oven to 350°F (180°C)**
- **13- by 9-inch (3 L) cake pan, greased**

1. **Cake:** In a large mixer bowl, combine cake mix, pie filling and eggs. Beat on medium speed for 2 minutes. Spread batter evenly in prepared pan. Bake for 30 to 40 minutes or until a tester inserted in center comes out clean. Cool for 30 minutes in pan on a wire rack before glazing.

2. **Glaze:** In a small saucepan, combine sugar, butter and cream. Cook, stirring constantly over medium heat until mixture comes to a boil, then boil for 1 minute. Remove from heat. Add chocolate chips and extract, stirring until smoothly melted. Spread over warm cake. Cool completely before cutting.

Variation: You either love or hate the flavor of almond extract. If you love it, you can reinforce the almond flavor in the glaze by adding ¾ tsp (4 mL) to the cake.

Cookies 'n' Cream Cake

Now kids young and old can enjoy their best-loved cookie in a cake.

SERVES 12 TO 16

CAKE

1	package (18.25 oz/515 g) white cake mix	1
3	eggs	3
1⅓ cups	water	325 mL
⅓ cup	vegetable oil	75 mL
1 cup	coarsely chopped cream-filled chocolate sandwich cookies (about twelve 2½-inch/6 cm cookies)	250 mL

FROSTING

1	container (15 oz/450 g) ready-made vanilla frosting	1
⅓ cup	coarsely chopped cream-filled chocolate sandwich cookies (about four 2½-inch/6 cm cookies)	75 mL
	Cookies, regular or minis, to garnish	

- **Preheat oven to 350°F (180°C)**
- **13- by 9-inch (3 L) cake pan, greased**

1. **Cake:** In a large mixer bowl, combine cake mix, eggs, water and oil. Beat on medium speed for 2 minutes. Stir in chopped cookies. Spread batter evenly in prepared pan. Bake for 30 to 35 minutes or until a tester inserted in center comes out clean. Cool completely in pan on a wire rack.

2. **Frosting:** Stir chopped cookies into frosting. Spread over cooled cake. Garnish with cookies.

Variation: A chocolate cake mix doesn't look as good but it tastes great.

TIPS

- To quickly chop cookies, place 6 in a food processor. Pulse several times to coarsely chop. Repeat with remaining cookies. Don't process too finely or the cake will be browner.
- Cake can be cut in half horizontally and filled with frosting, if desired.

Rainbow Dessert Cake

A colorful cake that's always popular at children's birthdays.

SERVES 12 TO 16

CAKE

1	package (18.25 oz/515 g) white cake mix	1

TOPPING

1	package (3 oz/85 g) gelatin dessert mix, any flavor	1
¾ cup	boiling water	175 mL
½ cup	cold water	125 mL
2 cups	prepared dessert topping or sweetened whipped cream	500 mL
	Rainbow-colored cake sprinkles (optional)	

TIPS

- After removing from the oven, be sure to let cake stand for no more than 20 minutes before topping.
- Start preparing gelatin mixture as soon as you put cake in the oven.
- The topping is a personal taste. You can use real whipped cream, lightly sweetened, if you prefer.

- **Preheat oven to 350°F (180°C)**
- **13- by 9-inch (3 L) cake pan, greased**

1. **Cake:** Prepare and bake cake according to package directions for 13- by 9-inch (3 L) pan. Cool for 20 minutes in pan on a wire rack.

2. **Topping:** Prepare topping as soon as you put cake into the oven. In a small bowl, add boiling water to gelatin. Stir well until gelatin crystals are completely dissolved. Stir in cold water. Set aside at room temperature. Poke deep holes about 1 inch (2.5 cm) apart through the top of cake with a fork. Slowly pour gelatin mixture evenly over surface of cake. Chill thoroughly, about 1 hour.

3. Cover cake with whipped topping. Scatter sprinkles on top, if desired. Chill until serving. Store leftover cake in the refrigerator.

Variation: Your choice of gelatin will dictate the color. We found red, green and purple to be favorites with kids.

Butterscotch Chip Cake

The double dose of butterscotch in this cake is as good as candy.

SERVES 12 TO 16

1	package (4-serving size) butterscotch instant pudding mix	1
1⅔ cups	milk	400 mL
1	package (18.25 oz/515 g) white cake mix	1
1	package (10 oz/300 g) butterscotch chips	1
1¼ cups	chopped pecans	300 mL

TIP

- Scatter the chips on the cake batter before adding the nuts. They'll sink during baking, creating a tempting pebbled top.

- **Preheat oven to 350°F (180°C)**
- **13- by 9-inch (3 L) cake pan, greased**

1. In a large mixer bowl, combine pudding mix and milk. Beat on low speed for 2 minutes. Add cake mix and beat on low speed for 1 minute longer or until smooth. Spread batter in prepared pan. Scatter butterscotch chips and then pecans on top. Bake for 35 to 45 minutes or until a tester inserted in center comes out clean. Cool for at least 30 minutes in pan on a wire rack before cutting.

Variation: Replace butterscotch chips with milk chocolate or white chocolate chips.

Chocolate Strawberry Cream Cake

This is a great dessert for a family get-together, as you can make it ahead of time.

CAKE

1	package (18.25 oz/515 g) devil's food cake mix	1
3	eggs	3
1⅓ cups	milk	325 mL
½ cup	vegetable oil	125 mL

TOPPING

1	package (10 oz/284 g) frozen sweetened sliced strawberries, thawed	1
1	package (4-serving size) vanilla instant pudding mix	1
1 cup	milk	250 mL
1 cup	whipping (35%) cream	250 mL
	Fresh strawberries	

TIPS

- Allow at least 4 hours or overnight before serving to let flavors and texture mellow.
- Use a thawed frozen cream topping in place of whipped cream for convenience.

- **Preheat oven to 350°F (180°C)**
- **13- by 9-inch (3 L) cake pan, greased**

1. **Cake:** In a large mixer bowl, combine cake mix, eggs, milk and oil. Beat on medium speed for 2 minutes. Spread batter in prepared pan. Bake for 30 to 40 minutes or until a tester inserted in center comes out clean. Cool completely in pan on a wire rack.

2. **Topping:** Purée frozen strawberries with their juices in a blender or food processor. Poke holes 1 inch (2.5 cm) apart on top of cooled cake using handle of wooden spoon. Spoon strawberry purée over top of cake, letting it soak into the holes.

3. In a large mixer bowl, combine pudding mix and milk. Beat on low speed for 2 minutes. Chill for 5 minutes to thicken. Beat cream in a separate bowl to stiff peaks. Fold into pudding mixture, gently but thoroughly. Spread over cake. Chill for 4 hours or overnight before serving. Garnish with fresh strawberries. Store leftover cake in the refrigerator.

Variation: Substitute raspberries for the strawberries.

French Apple Upside-Down Cake

Enjoy upside-down cakes with fresh fruit while it's in season; try the canned fruit versions later on. Whipped cream or ice cream is a delicious addition to this dessert.

SERVES 12 TO 16

TOPPING

4 cups	peeled, cored and sliced apples (4 to 5 large)	1 L
⅔ cup	granulated sugar	150 mL
1 tbsp	all-purpose flour	15 mL
1 tsp	ground cinnamon	5 mL
2 tbsp	butter, melted	25 mL
2 tbsp	lemon juice	25 mL

CAKE

1	package (18.25 oz/515 g) white cake mix	1
3	eggs	3
1¼ cups	water	300 mL
⅓ cup	vegetable oil	75 mL

- **Preheat oven to 350°F (180°C)**
- **13- by 9-inch (3 L) cake pan, greased**

1. **Topping:** Arrange apple slices in prepared pan. Combine sugar, flour and cinnamon. Sprinkle over apples. Combine melted butter and lemon juice. Drizzle over apples.

2. **Cake:** In a large mixer bowl, combine cake mix, eggs, water and oil. Beat on medium speed for 2 minutes. Pour batter evenly over fruit mixture. Bake for 40 to 50 minutes or until a tester inserted in center comes out clean. Let stand for 5 minutes, then turn upside down onto a large platter or a cookie sheet. Serve warm.

Variation: Try a spice or yellow cake mix another time.

TIP
- If peeling apples ahead, toss with a little lemon juice to prevent browning.

Old-Fashioned Apple Nut Cake

The apple pie filling produces a moist, flavorful cake that keeps well.

SERVES 12 TO 16

CAKE

1	can (19 oz/540 mL) apple pie filling	1
1	package (18.25 oz/515 g) white cake mix	1
½ cup	all-purpose flour	125 mL
1 tsp	baking powder	5 mL
3	eggs	3
½ cup	vegetable oil	125 mL

TOPPING

½ cup	packed brown sugar	125 mL
½ cup	all-purpose flour	125 mL
1 tsp	ground cinnamon	5 mL
¼ cup	butter, softened	50 mL
½ cup	chopped nuts	125 mL

- **Preheat oven to 350°F (180°C)**
- **13- by 9-inch (3 L) cake pan, greased**

1. **Cake:** Process apple pie filling in food processor or with a potato masher until coarsely chopped. In a large mixer bowl, combine pie filling, cake mix, flour, baking powder, eggs and oil. Beat on medium speed for 2 minutes. Spread batter evenly in prepared pan.

2. **Topping:** In a small bowl, combine brown sugar, flour and cinnamon. Cut in butter with pastry blender or fork until crumbly. Stir in nuts. Sprinkle evenly over batter. Bake for 40 to 50 minutes or until a tester inserted in center comes out clean. Cool for at least 30 minutes in pan on a wire rack before cutting.

Variation: Try a yellow cake mix in place of the white.

TIP
- If the apple pie filling is coarsely chopped first using a food processor or potato masher, it makes the cake easy to slice.

Apple Crisp Cake

This cake tastes like one of my favorite old-fashioned desserts, apple crisp.

SERVES 12 TO 16

TOPPING

⅔ cup	quick-cooking rolled oats	150 mL
½ cup	all-purpose flour	125 mL
⅓ cup	packed brown sugar	75 mL
½ tsp	ground cinnamon	2 mL
½ cup	butter	125 mL

CAKE

1	package (18.25 oz/515 g) white cake mix	1
3	eggs	3
1 cup	water	250 mL
½ cup	butter, softened	125 mL
1 tsp	ground cinnamon	5 mL
2½ cups	thinly sliced apples (3 large)	625 mL

- **Preheat oven to 350°F (180°C)**
- **13- by 9-inch (3 L) cake pan, greased**

1. **Topping:** In a medium bowl, combine oats, flour, brown sugar and cinnamon. Cut in butter with pastry blender or fork until crumbly. Set aside.

2. **Cake:** In a large mixer bowl, combine cake mix, eggs, water, butter and cinnamon. Beat on medium speed for 2 minutes. Spread batter evenly in prepared pan. Arrange apple slices evenly over batter. Sprinkle topping over apples. Bake for 40 to 45 minutes or until a tester inserted in center comes out clean. Cool completely in pan on a wire rack.

Variation: Replace 1 cup (250 mL) of the apples with fresh berries such as blueberries, raspberries or cranberries.

TIPS
- Use apples that are firm and tart, such as Granny Smith, Spies or Spartans.
- Serve cake warm with a drizzle of caramel sauce and a scoop of vanilla ice cream.

Spice Cake with Cinnamon Butter Frosting

Here's a quick and delicious way to make spice cake from a white cake mix.

SERVES 12 TO 16

1	package (18.25 oz/515 g) white cake mix	1
2½ tsp	ground cinnamon	12 mL
¾ tsp	ground nutmeg	4 mL
¼ tsp	ground cloves	1 mL
3	eggs	3
1⅓ cups	water	325 mL
⅓ cup	vegetable oil	75 mL
	Cinnamon Butter Frosting (see recipe, page 258)	

- **Preheat oven to 350°F (180°C)**
- **13- by 9-inch (3 L) cake pan, greased**

1. In a large mixer bowl, combine cake mix, cinnamon, nutmeg, cloves, eggs, water and oil. Beat on medium speed for 2 minutes. Spread batter evenly in prepared pan. Bake for 35 to 40 minutes or until a tester inserted in center comes out clean. Cool completely in pan on a wire rack. Frost with Cinnamon Butter Frosting or as desired.

TIPS
- This cake is very light and tender.
- The addition of raisins or other fruit doesn't work well as the batter isn't strong enough to support them. They will sink, creating a layer of fruit on the bottom of the cake.
- This is my favorite blend of spices, but you can adjust the spices to suit your taste.

Ginger Applesauce Spice Cake

The Ginger Cream is particularly good. Don't limit its use to this cake. Try spooning it over fresh fruit.

CAKE

1	package (18.25 oz/515 g) spice cake mix	1
3	eggs	3
1⅓ cups	unsweetened applesauce	325 mL
½ cup	butter, softened	125 mL
⅔ cup	chopped walnuts	150 mL
½ cup	finely chopped crystallized ginger	125 mL
	Confectioner's (icing) sugar	

GINGER CREAM

½ cup	granulated sugar	125 mL
½ cup	water	125 mL
1	piece (2 inches/5 cm) gingerroot, thinly sliced	1
1 cup	whipping (35%) cream	250 mL
1 tbsp	confectioner's (icing) sugar	15 mL

TIPS

- Look for crystallized ginger that is soft. It gets hard with age.
- Use unsweetened applesauce with cake mixes as there is already enough sugar in the mix.

- **Preheat oven to 350°F (180°C)**
- **10-inch (25 cm) springform pan, greased and floured**

1. **Cake:** In a large mixer bowl, combine cake mix, eggs, applesauce and butter. Beat on medium speed for 2 minutes. Stir in walnuts and ginger. Spread batter in prepared pan. Bake for 55 to 60 minutes or until a tester inserted in center comes out clean. Cool in pan on a wire rack for 15 minutes. Remove pan sides. Cool completely.

2. **Ginger Cream:** In a small saucepan, combine granulated sugar, water and ginger. Bring to a boil, stirring until sugar dissolves, then simmer over medium heat until syrupy, about 8 minutes. Strain into a bowl and refrigerate syrup until cold. Discard ginger. In a large mixer bowl, beat cream and confectioner's sugar to soft peaks. Fold in chilled syrup.

3. **To serve:** Cut into wedges and serve with a dollop of Ginger Cream.

Variations: Add ¼ cup (50 mL) minced, peeled gingerroot to batter to satisfy real ginger lovers. Fold 3 tbsp (45 mL) finely chopped crystallized ginger into the Ginger Cream.

Butter-Rum-Glazed Applesauce Cake

Better than a hot rum toddy.

SERVES 12 TO 16

CAKE

1	package (18.25 oz/515 g) white cake mix	1
3	eggs	3
1⅓ cups	unsweetened applesauce	325 mL
½ cup	butter, softened	125 mL
2 tsp	ground cinnamon	10 mL
½ tsp	ground ginger	2 mL

BUTTER-RUM GLAZE

¼ cup	butter	50 mL
2 cups	confectioner's (icing) sugar	500 mL
1 tsp	rum extract	5 mL
¼ cup	half-and-half (10%) cream	50 mL

- **Preheat oven to 350°F (180°C)**
- **13- by 9-inch (3 L) cake pan, greased**

1. Cake: In a large mixer bowl, combine cake mix, eggs, applesauce, butter, cinnamon and ginger. Beat on medium speed for 2 minutes. Spread batter in prepared pan. Bake for 40 to 45 minutes or until a tester inserted in center comes out clean. Cool for 15 minutes in pan on a wire rack.

2. Glaze: In a small saucepan, melt butter over medium heat. Cook for about 3 minutes or until starting to brown. Remove from heat. Stir in confectioner's sugar, rum extract and cream until a smooth spreadable consistency is reached. Pour over warm cake. Cool for 30 minutes. Serve warm.

Variation: Omit spices and use a spice cake mix.

TIPS
- If your applesauce has cinnamon in it, decrease the cinnamon in the recipe.
- After glazing, sprinkle warm cake with a little cinnamon.

Mix-in-the-Pan Cherry Cake

The fascinating appearance comes from swirling pie filling through the cake batter just before baking. Swirl the pie filling gently. Overmixing will result in a red cherry cake with no marbling.

SERVES 12 TO 16

¼ cup	vegetable oil	50 mL
1	package (18.25 oz/515 g) white cake mix	1
2	eggs	2
½ cup	water	125 mL
1	can (19 oz/540 mL) cherry pie filling	1

TIPS
- Sprinkle cooled cake with confectioner's (icing) sugar or serve warm with ice cream, custard or vanilla sauce.
- Soften a good quality French vanilla ice cream to a pouring consistency for an extremely easy and tasty sauce.

- **Preheat oven to 350°F (180°C)**
- **13- by 9-inch (3 L) cake pan**

1. Pour oil into pan. Tilt pan to coat bottom with oil. Sprinkle dry cake mix evenly on top. Add eggs and water. Stir all together with a fork or spoon until thoroughly blended, about 2 minutes. Scrape sides and spread batter evenly in pan. Drop spoonfuls of pie filling randomly on top. With a fork or knife, fold pie filling into batter just enough to create a marble effect. Bake for 35 to 40 minutes or until a tester inserted in center comes out clean. Cool cake for at least 30 minutes in pan on a wire rack before cutting.

Variation: Color and flavor will depend on the pie filling. Try your favorite.

Take-Along Cake

Ideal for family picnics. A one-step cake with a frosting that bakes along with the cake.

SERVES 12 TO 16		
1	package (18.25 oz/515 g) milk or Swiss chocolate cake mix	1
1 cup	miniature semi-sweet chocolate chips	250 mL
1 cup	miniature marshmallows	250 mL
¼ cup	butter, melted	50 mL
½ cup	packed brown sugar	125 mL
½ cup	chopped pecans or walnuts	125 mL

- **Preheat oven to 350°F (180°C)**
- **13- by 9-inch (3 L) cake pan, greased**

1. Prepare cake mix according to package directions. Stir in chocolate chips and marshmallows. Spread batter evenly in prepared pan. Drizzle melted butter evenly over batter. Sprinkle brown sugar and nuts on top. Bake for 40 to 50 minutes or until a tester inserted in center comes out clean. Cool for at least 30 minutes in pan on a wire rack before cutting.

Variation: Use your favorite chocolate-flavored cake mix.

TIP
- Store chocolate in a cool dry place. If storage area is warm, chocolate develops a gray coating called "bloom." Bloom has no effect on the flavor or quality of the chocolate and will disappear during baking.

Pretty Pistachio Cake

The green color can be as subtle or as bright as you like, depending upon the amount of green food coloring you add. Either way, the delicate flavor is a favorite.

SERVES 12 TO 16		
CAKE		
1	package (18.25 oz/515 g) white cake mix	1
1	package (4-serving size) pistachio instant pudding mix	1
4	eggs	4
1 cup	water	250 mL
⅔ cup	vegetable oil	150 mL
3	drops green food coloring (optional)	3
PISTACHIO CREAM TOPPING		
1	package (4-serving size) pistachio instant pudding mix	1
1 cup	milk	250 mL
1½ cups	frozen whipped topping, thawed	375 mL
	Chopped pistachios (optional)	

- **Preheat oven to 350°F (180°C)**
- **13- by 9-inch (3 L) cake pan, greased**

1. **Cake:** In a large mixer bowl, combine cake mix, pudding mix, eggs, water and oil. Beat on medium speed for 2 minutes. Stir in coloring, if desired. Spread batter evenly in prepared pan. Bake for 35 to 40 minutes or until a tester inserted in center comes out clean. Cool completely in pan on a wire rack.

2. **Topping:** In a large mixer bowl, combine pudding mix and milk. Beat on low speed for 1 minute. Let set for 2 minutes. Add whipped topping. Beat on low speed just to blend. Spread over cooled cake. Sprinkle with chopped pistachios, if desired. Chill until serving. Store leftover cake in the refrigerator.

Variations: Replace whipped topping with 1 cup (250 mL) whipping (35%) cream beaten to stiff peaks. For a different look, bake this in a tube pan for 1 hour or in two 9-inch (23 cm) round pans for 30 minutes. Put the topping between and on top of the layers.

Bumbleberry Cake

This is a great cake to make during berry season. A mixture of fresh berries nestles between a tender, light cake and a cinnamon-sugar top.

CAKE

1	package (18.25 oz/515 g) white cake mix	1
1/3 cup	granulated sugar	75 mL
8 oz	cream cheese, softened	250 g
3	eggs	3
1/2 cup	vegetable oil	125 mL
1/4 cup	water	50 mL
1 cup	fresh blueberries	250 mL
1 cup	fresh raspberries	250 mL
1 cup	fresh blackberries	250 mL

TOPPING

3/4 cup	packed brown sugar	175 mL
2/3 cup	all-purpose flour	150 mL
1 tsp	ground cinnamon	5 mL
1/3 cup	butter	75 mL

- **Preheat oven to 350°F (180°C)**
- **13- by 9-inch (3 L) cake pan, greased**

1. **Cake:** In a large mixer bowl, combine cake mix, sugar, cream cheese, eggs, oil and water. Beat on low speed for 1 minute to blend, then on medium speed for 2 minutes. Spread half of batter in prepared pan. Sprinkle berries on top. Carefully spread remaining batter over berries.

2. **Topping:** In a small bowl, combine brown sugar, flour and cinnamon. Cut in butter with pastry blender or two knives until mixture is crumbly. Sprinkle over batter. Bake for 55 to 60 minutes or until a tester inserted in center comes out clean. Cool in pan on a wire rack for at least 30 minutes before cutting. Serve warm or cool.

Variation: If you prefer, use granulated sugar instead of brown sugar in the topping.

TIPS

- Bumbleberry is a mix of different berries, often with apples.
- Choose your favorite mixture of berries or vary the taste to accommodate the season.
- In baking, always use block cream cheese at room temperature, not tubs of spreadable cream cheese.

Bumbleberry Lemon Upside-Down Cake

Bumbleberry is a mixture of fruits. Use your favorites, or what is in season.

SERVES 12 TO 16		
⅓ cup	butter	75 mL
1 cup	packed brown sugar	250 mL
1½ cups	fresh raspberries	375 mL
1½ cups	fresh blueberries	375 mL
1 cup	fresh strawberries	250 mL
1	package (18.25 oz/515 g) lemon cake mix	1
	Whipped cream (optional)	

TIP

- If you don't have a large rectangular platter, use a cookie sheet or bread board covered with foil for upside-down cakes.

- **Preheat oven to 350°F (180°C)**
- **13- by 9-inch (3 L) cake pan**

1. In cake pan, melt butter. Sprinkle brown sugar evenly on top. Scatter fruit over sugar.

2. Prepare cake mix according to package directions. Pour batter evenly over fruit. Bake for 45 to 50 minutes or until a tester inserted in center comes out clean. Let stand for 5 minutes, then turn upside down onto a large platter or a cookie sheet. Serve warm with a generous dollop of whipped cream, if desired.

Variation: Try different fruit combinations, keeping the size uniform for even cooking and the total measure to 4 cups (1 L).

Apricot Coconut Cake

This delicious cake doesn't even need a frosting — it bakes right along with the cake.

SERVES 12 TO 16		
1½ cups	apricot jam	375 mL
1 cup	flaked coconut	250 mL
¼ cup	butter, melted	50 mL
1	package (18.25 oz/515 g) white cake mix	1
3	eggs	3
⅔ cup	apricot nectar	150 mL
⅔ cup	water	150 mL
⅓ cup	vegetable oil	75 mL

TIPS

- If serving this cake for dessert, cut into large squares and top with ice cream. For afternoon tea, serve as small squares.
- You can buy cake boards in many bulk stores. They work well as large serving platters.

- **Preheat oven to 350°F (180°C)**
- **13- by 9-inch (3 L) cake pan, greased**

1. In a medium bowl, combine jam, coconut and melted butter. Mix well. Spread evenly in prepared pan.

2. In a large mixer bowl, combine cake mix, eggs, nectar, water and oil. Beat on medium speed for 2 minutes. Pour batter over jam mixture. Bake for 35 to 45 minutes or until a tester inserted in center comes out clean. Cool for 30 minutes in pan on a wire rack, then turn upside down onto a large serving plate.

Variation: Replace apricot jam with marmalade and apricot nectar with orange juice.

Peanut Butter and Banana Cake

A delicious cake with a taste that's reminiscent of the popular sandwich, this also makes a great addition to a lunchbox.

SERVES 12 TO 16		
1	package (18.25 oz/515 g) white cake mix	1
1	package (4-serving size) banana instant pudding mix	1
4	eggs	4
1½ cups	mashed ripe bananas (3 to 4 large)	375 mL
⅓ cup	vegetable oil	75 mL
½ cup	packed brown sugar	125 mL
1½ cups	peanut butter chips	375 mL

TIP
• Buy extra bananas ahead that are a bit green so they'll be ripe when you're ready to use them.

• **Preheat oven to 350°F (180°C)**
• **13- by 9-inch (3 L) cake pan, greased**

1. In a large mixer bowl, combine cake mix, pudding mix, eggs, bananas and oil. Beat on medium speed for 2 minutes. Spread half of batter in prepared pan. Sprinkle half of brown sugar and chips over batter. Repeat layers. Bake for 45 to 50 minutes or until a tester inserted in center comes out clean. Cool completely in pan on a wire rack.

Variation: If you prefer a milder banana flavor, use a vanilla instant pudding mix.

Banana Pudding Cake

Very simple and very good. Add a broiled topping, as we've done here, a banana butter icing or just leave plain.

SERVES 12 TO 16		
1	package (18.25 oz/515 g) white cake mix	1
1	package (4-serving size) vanilla instant pudding mix	1
4	eggs	4
1½ cups	mashed ripe bananas (3 to 4 large)	375 mL
⅓ cup	vegetable oil	75 mL
	Crunchy Broiled Topping (see recipe, page 270)	

TIP
• Cakes baked in this size pan are usually frosted and served from the pan. It's a wise choice if you have to transport the cake somewhere. If you want to remove the entire cake, line pan with foil, leaving side overhangs. You can lift the cooled cake out of pan easily with the foil.

• **Preheat oven to 350°F (180°C)**
• **13- by 9-inch (3 L) cake pan, greased**

1. In a large mixer bowl, combine cake mix, pudding mix, eggs, bananas and oil. Beat on medium speed for 2 minutes or until smooth. Spread batter evenly in prepared pan. Bake for 35 to 40 minutes or until a tester inserted in center comes out clean. Top with broiled topping. Cool for at least 30 minutes in pan on a wire rack before cutting.

Variation: A butterscotch or chocolate pudding makes an interesting combination with banana.

Banana Cake

This cake is delicious with a frosting such as Banana Butter Frosting (page 264), but it's also scrumptious served warm, topped with vanilla ice cream and a drizzle of caramel sauce.

SERVES 12 TO 16

1	package (18.25 oz/515 g) white cake mix	1
3	eggs	3
1⅔ cups	mashed ripe bananas (3 to 4 large)	400 mL
⅓ cup	vegetable oil	75 mL

- **Preheat oven to 350°F (180°C)**
- **13- by 9-inch (3 L) cake pan, greased**

1. In a large mixer bowl, combine cake mix, eggs, bananas and oil. Beat on medium speed for 2 minutes or until smooth. Spread batter evenly in prepared pan. Bake for 35 to 40 minutes or until a tester inserted in center comes out clean. Cool completely in pan on a wire rack. Frost as desired.

Ginger Pear Torte

Pear and ginger are a natural combination. The fresh gingerroot adds wonderful flavor!

SERVES 12 TO 16

CAKE

1	package (18.25 oz/515 g) white cake mix	1
1	package (4-serving size) vanilla instant pudding mix	1
4	eggs	4
½ cup	sour cream	125 mL
¼ cup	vegetable oil	50 mL
2 tsp	finely chopped gingerroot	10 mL
1½ tsp	ground ginger	7 mL
4	large pears, peeled and cored	4
2 tbsp	butter, melted	25 mL
⅓ cup	packed brown sugar	75 mL

GINGER CREAM TOPPING

1½ cups	whipping (35%) cream	375 mL
3 tbsp	confectioner's (icing) sugar, sifted	45 mL
½ tsp	ground ginger	2 mL

- **Preheat oven to 350°F (180°C)**
- **13- by 9-inch (3 L) cake pan, greased**

1. **Cake:** In a large mixer bowl, combine cake mix, pudding mix, eggs, sour cream, oil, gingerroot and ground ginger. Beat on medium speed for 2 minutes. Spread batter evenly in prepared pan.

2. Cut pears into ¼-inch (0.5 cm) slices. Arrange over batter, overlapping slightly as necessary. Press lightly into batter. Drizzle melted butter on top. Sprinkle brown sugar evenly over pears. Bake for 40 to 50 minutes or until set and golden. Cool in pan on a wire rack. Serve warm or cool with Ginger Cream Topping.

3. **Topping:** In a large mixer bowl, combine cream, confectioner's sugar and ginger. Beat to stiff peaks. Spoon over cake slices.

Variation: *Spicy Pear Torte:* Replace white cake with a spice cake mix and omit ground ginger in the batter.

TIP
- Use pears that are partially ripe so they'll soften during cooking but still hold their shape.

Queen Elizabeth Cake

Put a crunchy broiled topping on a moist date cake, and you've got a real winner.

SERVES 12 TO 16

CAKE

1½ cups	chopped pitted dates	375 mL
1 cup	boiling water	250 mL
1	package (18.25 oz/515 g) white cake mix	1
3	eggs	3
⅓ cup	vegetable oil	75 mL

TOPPING

2 cups	flaked coconut	500 mL
¾ cup	packed brown sugar	175 mL
6 tbsp	butter	90 mL
6 tbsp	half-and-half (10%) cream	90 mL

- **Preheat oven to 350°F (180°C)**
- **13- by 9-inch (3 L) cake pan, greased**

1. **Cake:** Put dates in a small bowl and cover with boiling water; mix and let stand until lukewarm. In a large mixer bowl, combine cake mix, eggs, oil and date mixture. Beat on medium speed for 2 minutes or until smooth. Spread batter evenly in prepared pan. Bake for 35 to 40 minutes or until a tester inserted in center comes out clean.

2. **Topping:** While cake is baking, in a saucepan, combine coconut, brown sugar, butter and cream. Bring to a boil over medium heat and boil for 1 minute, stirring often. Spread over cake as soon as it comes out of the oven. Broil 6 inches (15 cm) from the element for 2 to 3 minutes or until bubbly and golden. Cool completely in pan on a wire rack.

Variation: Substitute chopped nuts for half of the coconut in the topping.

Coconut Pecan Cake

With just a few everyday ingredients, you can make a spectacular dessert.

SERVES 12 TO 16

CAKE

1	package (18.25 oz/515 g) white cake mix	1
1	package (4-serving size) vanilla instant pudding mix	1
4	eggs	4
1 cup	sour cream	250 mL
½ cup	vegetable oil	125 mL
1½ cups	flaked coconut	375 mL
¾ cup	chopped pecans	175 mL

FROSTING

8 oz	cream cheese, softened	250 g
½ cup	butter, softened	125 mL
4 cups	confectioner's (icing) sugar, sifted	1 L
1 tsp	vanilla	5 mL
⅔ cup	chopped pecans	150 mL
⅓ cup	toasted flaked coconut	75 mL

- **Preheat oven to 350°F (180°C)**
- **13- by 9-inch (3 L) cake pan, greased**

1. **Cake:** In a large mixer bowl, combine cake mix, pudding mix, eggs, sour cream and oil. Beat on medium speed for 2 minutes. Stir in coconut and pecans. Mix well. Spread batter evenly in prepared pan. Bake for 45 to 55 minutes or until a tester inserted in center comes out clean. Cool completely in pan on a wire rack.

2. **Frosting:** In a large mixer bowl, beat cream cheese and butter until smooth. Gradually add confectioner's sugar on low speed, mixing until smooth and creamy. Add vanilla, pecans and coconut. Mix well. Spread over cooled cake. Chill until serving. Store leftover cake in the refrigerator.

Variation: Unblanched almonds or hazelnuts are also nice.

TIP
- Make this cake a day ahead to let flavors mellow.

Mississippi Mud Cake

Marshmallows are always a hit with kids, young and old.

CAKE

1	package (18.25 oz/515 g) devil's food cake mix	1
4	eggs	4
1 cup	sour cream	250 mL
½ cup	cold strong black coffee	125 mL
½ cup	vegetable oil	125 mL

TOPPING

3 cups	miniature marshmallows	750 mL
1 cup	chopped pecans	250 mL

CHOCOLATE DRIZZLE

3 oz	semi-sweet chocolate	90 g
3 tbsp	butter	45 mL

TIPS

- For optimum flavor, toast pecans (see page 14).
- If cake top is slightly domed, let marshmallows stand for a few minutes on hot cake before baking. They'll stick to the cake and stay in place.
- When melting chocolate, use squares rather than chips. Chips are formulated to keep their shape during baking, so they don't melt as smoothly as squares.

- **Preheat oven to 350°F (180°C)**
- **13- by 9-inch (3 L) cake pan, greased**

1. **Cake:** In a large mixer bowl, combine cake mix, eggs, sour cream, coffee and oil. Beat on medium speed for 2 minutes or until smooth. Spread batter evenly in prepared pan. Bake for 35 to 40 minutes or until a tester inserted in center comes out clean.

2. **Topping:** Sprinkle marshmallows and nuts over cake as soon as it comes out of oven. Bake for 5 minutes longer or until marshmallows puff. Remove from oven. Cool for 30 minutes in pan on a wire rack.

3. **Drizzle:** In a small saucepan over low heat, melt chocolate and butter or microwave on Medium for 2 minutes. Stir until smooth. Drizzle over marshmallow-nut layer. Serve warm or cool to room temperature before cutting.

Variation: Instead of pecans, try slivered almonds or chopped walnuts or hazelnuts. They also taste great.

Peach Melba Upside-Down Cake

Canned peaches are a good choice for upside-down cakes, as they keep their color and texture during baking.

SERVES 12 TO 16		
1/3 cup	butter	75 mL
1 cup	packed brown sugar	250 mL
1	can (28 oz/796 mL) sliced peaches	1
	Water	
1 cup	fresh raspberries	250 mL
1	package (18.25 oz/515 g) white cake mix	1
2	eggs	2
3 tbsp	vegetable oil	45 mL
	Whipped cream (optional)	

TIP
- If you want evenly sized slices, buy peach halves and slice them yourself. For convenience, pre-sliced peaches work well.

- **Preheat oven to 350°F (180°C)**
- **13- by 9-inch (3 L) cake pan**

1. Melt butter in cake pan. Sprinkle brown sugar evenly on top.

2. Drain peaches, reserving peach syrup. Add water to syrup to make 1 1/3 cups (325 mL) liquid; set aside. Arrange peach slices over brown sugar mixture. Scatter raspberries on top.

3. In a large mixer bowl, combine peach syrup mixture, cake mix, eggs and oil. Beat on medium speed for 2 minutes. Pour batter evenly over fruit. Bake for 45 to 50 minutes or until a tester inserted in center comes out clean. Cool for 5 minutes in pan on a wire rack, then turn upside down onto a large platter or cookie sheet. Serve warm with a generous dollop of whipped cream, if desired.

Variation: Replace raspberries with 1/2 cup (125 mL) maraschino cherry halves.

Peach of a Peach Cake

A great cake to take to your next potluck party.

SERVES 12 TO 16		
CAKE		
1	package (18.25 oz/515 g) white cake mix	1
1/4 cup	all-purpose flour	50 mL
1 tsp	baking powder	5 mL
3	eggs	3
1	can (19 oz/540 mL) peach or peach-and-passion-fruit pie filling	1
1/2 tsp	lemon extract	2 mL
1/2 cup	chopped walnuts	125 mL
TOPPING		
1/2 cup	granulated sugar	125 mL
1/2 cup	all-purpose flour	125 mL
3/4 tsp	ground cinnamon	3 mL
1/4 cup	butter, softened	50 mL

- **Preheat oven to 350°F (180°C)**
- **13- by 9-inch (3 L) cake pan, greased**

1. **Cake:** In a large mixer bowl, combine cake mix, flour, baking powder, eggs, pie filling, lemon extract and nuts. Beat on medium speed for 2 minutes or until well blended. Spread batter evenly in prepared pan.

2. **Topping:** In a small bowl, combine sugar, flour and cinnamon. With a pastry blender or a fork, cut in butter until crumbly. Sprinkle evenly over batter. Bake for 40 to 45 minutes or until a tester inserted in center comes out clean. Cool for at least 30 minutes in pan on a wire rack before cutting.

Variation: Omit lemon extract in cake, if desired.

TIP
- Use pie filling directly from can. If necessary, chop any large peach pieces.

Fruit Cocktail Cake

The taste will vary with different brands of fruit cocktail.

CAKE

1	package (18.25 oz/515 g) white cake mix	1
1	package (4-serving size) lemon instant pudding mix	1
¾ cup	flaked coconut	175 mL
4	eggs	4
⅓ cup	vegetable oil	75 mL
1	can (14 oz/398 mL) fruit cocktail, with juice	1
¼ cup	chopped maraschino cherries	50 mL

NUT TOPPING

⅔ cup	chopped pecans	150 mL
½ cup	packed brown sugar	125 mL

COCONUT TOPPING

½ cup	granulated sugar	125 mL
½ cup	butter	125 mL
½ cup	half-and-half (10%) cream	125 mL
1 cup	flaked coconut	250 mL

- **Preheat oven to 350°F (180°C)**
- **13- by 9-inch (3 L) cake pan, greased**

1. **Cake:** In a large mixer bowl, combine cake mix, pudding mix, coconut, eggs, oil and fruit cocktail with juice. Beat on medium speed for 2 minutes. Stir in cherries. Spread batter evenly in prepared pan.

2. **Nut Topping:** Combine nuts and brown sugar. Sprinkle evenly over batter. Bake for 45 to 50 minutes or until a tester inserted in center comes out clean.

3. **Coconut Topping:** (Prepare at the end of cake baking time.) In a small saucepan, combine sugar, butter and cream. Bring to a boil over medium heat, then boil for 2 minutes. Stir in coconut. Spoon blobs of topping randomly over hot cake. Cool completely in pan on a wire rack before cutting.

Variations: Use vanilla pudding mix in place of lemon.

TIPS

- Put coconut topping on in blobs. Don't try to spread it over the nuts. The blobs give the cake a unique look when cooled.
- If maraschino cherries aren't a favorite, you can leave them out.

Dump Cake

As the name implies, the ingredients for this delicious and easy-to-make cake are dumped into the pan in order.

SERVES 12 TO 16		
1	can (19 oz/540 mL) crushed pineapple, with juice	1
1	can (19 oz/540 mL) cherry pie filling	1
1	package (18.25 oz/515 g) yellow cake mix	1
1 cup	coarsely chopped almonds	250 mL
2/3 cup	butter, cut in thin slices	150 mL

- **Preheat oven to 350°F (180°C)**
- **13- by 9-inch (3 L) cake pan, greased**

1. Dump pineapple with juice into prepared pan. Spread evenly. Spoon pie filling evenly over top. Sprinkle cake mix evenly over fruit. Sprinkle nuts on top. Put butter over nuts, covering as much as possible. Bake for 45 to 55 minutes or until golden. Serve warm or cool.

TIP

- When baking in glass or dark metal pans, reduce your oven temperature by 25°F (10°C).

Pineapple Upside-Down Cake

It's always amazing when something so simple can look so beautiful. This cake certainly has passed the test of time and will always be a favorite.

SERVES 12 TO 16		
1/3 cup	butter	75 mL
1 cup	packed brown sugar	250 mL
1	can (19 oz/540 mL) pineapple rings, drained, juice reserved	1
12	maraschino cherries (optional)	12
1	package (18.25 oz/515 g) white cake mix	1
3	eggs	3
2/3 cup	reserved pineapple juice	150 mL
2/3 cup	water	150 mL
1/3 cup	vegetable oil	75 mL
	Whipped cream (optional)	

- **Preheat oven to 350°F (180°C)**
- **13- by 9-inch (3 L) cake pan**

1. Melt butter in cake pan. Sprinkle brown sugar evenly over top. Arrange drained pineapple slices over sugar. Place a cherry in center of each ring, if desired.

2. In a large mixer bowl, combine cake mix, eggs, pineapple juice, water and oil. Beat on medium speed for 2 minutes. Pour batter evenly over fruit. Bake for 45 to 50 minutes or until a tester inserted in center comes out clean. Let stand for 5 minutes, then turn upside down onto a large platter or a cookie sheet. Serve warm with a generous dollop of whipped cream, if desired.

Variation: Canned peach slices or apricot halves also look attractive on this cake.

TIP

- Although I prefer the flavor of butter in baking, you can also use hard margarine — but not the soft or diet type spreads. Tilt pan to distribute melted butter evenly over the bottom.

Pineapple Carrot Cake

Taste testers couldn't decide between this cake and Carrot Cake with Raisins (page 51) so I've included both. Top with Cream Cheese Frosting (page 265) or another favorite frosting.

SERVES 12 TO 16

1	package (18.25 oz/515 g) white cake mix	1
4	eggs	4
2 cups	grated peeled carrots	500 mL
1 cup	undrained crushed pineapple	250 mL
½ cup	vegetable oil	125 mL
¼ cup	water	50 mL
2 tsp	ground cinnamon	10 mL
¼ tsp	ground nutmeg	1 mL

TIP

- Look for crisp large carrots. They're easier to peel and grate.

- **Preheat oven to 350°F (180°C)**
- **13- by 9-inch (3 L) cake pan, greased**

1. In a large mixer bowl, combine cake mix, eggs, carrots, pineapple with juice, oil, water, cinnamon and nutmeg. Beat on low speed for 1 minute to blend, then on medium speed for 2 minutes or until well blended. Spread batter evenly in prepared pan. Bake for 35 to 40 minutes or until a tester inserted in center comes out clean. Cool completely in pan on a wire rack. Frost as desired.

Variation: A yellow cake mix gives the cake a golden color and a different flavor than white.

Triple Lemon Cake

This may not be the most attractive cake, but it definitely is the most lemony.

SERVES 12 TO 16

CAKE

1	package (18.25 oz/515 g) lemon cake mix	1
1	package (3 oz/85 g) lemon-flavored gelatin dessert mix	1
4	eggs	4
¾ cup	vegetable oil	175 mL
¾ cup	water	175 mL

GLAZE

2 cups	confectioner's (icing) sugar, sifted	500 mL
⅓ cup	lemon juice	75 mL

TIP

- If you leave this cake for 20 minutes before glazing, the glaze will harden to look like a white icing, with a bit of a crunch. Reduce the cooling time to only 10 minutes and the glaze sinks in, leaving a softer, shiny top. I'm not sure which I prefer. I love them both.

- **Preheat oven to 350°F (180°C)**
- **13- by 9-inch (3 L) cake pan, greased**

1. **Cake:** In a large mixer bowl, combine cake mix, gelatin mix, eggs, oil and water. Beat on medium speed for 4 minutes. Spread batter evenly in prepared pan. Bake for 35 to 40 minutes or until a tester inserted in center comes out clean. Cool for about 20 minutes (see tip, at left).

2. **Glaze:** Poke holes with tines of fork about 1 inch (2.5 cm) apart on top of warm cake. Whisk confectioner's sugar and lemon juice together until sugar dissolves. Pour evenly over warm cake. Cool completely in pan on a wire rack before cutting.

Variation: For a more mellow lemon flavor, try a lemon instant pudding or use the lemon gelatin with a white cake mix.

Lemon Pop Cake

The pop is in the cake; it's not the cake that "pops."

SERVES 12 TO 16		
CAKE		
1	package (18.25 oz/515 g) lemon cake mix	1
1	package (4-serving size) lemon instant pudding mix	1
4	eggs	4
⅔ cup	vegetable oil	150 mL
1 cup	lemon-lime soda	250 mL
PINEAPPLE COCONUT TOPPING		
2 cups	frozen whipped topping, thawed	500 mL
½ cup	well-drained crushed pineapple	125 mL
½ cup	toasted coconut	125 mL

- **Preheat oven to 350°F (180°C)**
- **13- by 9-inch (3 L) cake pan, greased and floured**

1. **Cake:** In a large mixer bowl, combine cake mix, pudding mix, eggs and oil. Beat on medium speed for 3 minutes. Gradually add soda, beating on low speed until smooth, then beat on medium speed for 1 minute longer. Spread batter evenly in prepared pan. Bake for 30 to 40 minutes or until a tester inserted in center comes out clean. Cool completely in pan on a wire rack.

2. **Topping:** Gently fold pineapple and coconut into whipped topping. Spread over cooled cake. Chill until serving. Store leftover cake in the refrigerator.

Variation: You can prepare the cake and freeze it. When you want a quick dessert, thaw the cake and add the topping.

Lemon Cream Dessert Cake

A refreshing light dessert to enjoy all summer long. Be sure to let cake stand for just 20 minutes after baking before pouring gelatin mixture over.

SERVES 12 TO 16		
CAKE		
1	package (18.25 oz/515 g) yellow or white cake mix	1
TOPPING		
1	package (3 oz/85 g) lemon-flavored gelatin dessert mix	1
¾ cup	boiling water	175 mL
½ cup	cold water	125 mL
1	envelope (1.3 oz/42.5 g) whipped topping mix	1
1	package (4-serving size) lemon instant pudding mix	1
1½ cups	cold milk	375 mL

TIP
- Prepare gelatin mixture as soon as you put cake in the oven. Leave gelatin mixture at room temperature while cake bakes. Chilling will make it set too quickly.

- **Preheat oven to 350°F (180°C)**
- **13- by 9-inch (3 L) cake pan, greased**

1. **Cake:** Prepare and bake cake according to package directions for 13- by 9-inch (3 L) pan. Cool for 20 minutes in pan on a wire rack.

2. **Topping:** Prepare topping as soon as you put cake into the oven. In a small bowl, add boiling water to gelatin. Stir well until gelatin crystals are completely dissolved. Stir in cold water. Set aside at room temperature. Poke deep holes about 1 inch (2.5 cm) apart through top of cake with fork. Slowly pour gelatin mixture evenly over surface of cake. Chill thoroughly, about 1 hour.

3. In a small bowl, blend topping mix, pudding mix and milk then beat on high speed for about 5 minutes or until stiff peaks form. Spread evenly over cake. Chill until serving. Store leftover cake in the refrigerator.

Variation: If you love lemon, use lemon cake mix.

Carrot Cake with Raisins

This is the choice of carrot cakes for those who like raisins and don't have a can of crushed pineapple on hand. The pudding mix gives it a different taste to Pineapple Carrot Cake (see recipe, page 48). Try them both and choose a favorite. We couldn't decide.

SERVES 12 TO 16		
1	package (18.25 oz/515 g) white cake mix	1
1	package (4-serving size) vanilla instant pudding mix	1
4	eggs	4
2 cups	grated peeled carrots	500 mL
1/3 cup	vegetable oil	75 mL
1/4 cup	water	50 mL
3/4 cup	raisins	175 mL
2 tsp	ground cinnamon	10 mL
1/2 tsp	ground nutmeg	2 mL

- **Preheat oven to 350°F (180°C)**
- **13- by 9-inch (3 L) cake pan, greased**

1. In a large mixer bowl, combine cake mix, pudding mix, eggs, carrots, oil, water, raisins, cinnamon and nutmeg. Beat on low speed for 1 minute to blend, then on medium speed for 2 minutes. Spread batter in prepared pan. Bake for 40 to 45 minutes or until a tester inserted in center comes out clean. Cool completely in pan on a wire rack. Frost as desired.

Variation: Try dried cranberries in place of raisins.

TIPS
- If raisins have dried in storage, plump them in boiling water for about 5 minutes, then drain well and pat dry.

Chocolate Nut Carrot Cake

Two favorite cakes, chocolate and carrot, are combined in this rich and tasty dessert.

SERVES 12 TO 16		
1	package (18.25 oz/515 g) devil's food cake mix	1
4 oz	cream cheese, softened	125 g
1/4 cup	granulated sugar	50 mL
3	eggs	3
1/3 cup	water	75 mL
1 tsp	ground cinnamon	5 mL
1/4 tsp	ground cloves	1 mL
2 1/2 cups	grated peeled carrots	625 mL
2/3 cup	finely chopped nuts	150 mL
	Chocolate Cream Cheese Frosting (see recipe, page 265) or Basic Cream Cheese Frosting (see recipe, page 265)	

- **Preheat oven to 350°F (180°C)**
- **13- by 9-inch (3 L) cake pan, greased**

1. In a large mixer bowl, combine cake mix, cream cheese, sugar, eggs, water, cinnamon and cloves. Beat on low speed for 1 minute, then on medium speed for 2 minutes or until smooth. Stir in carrots and nuts. Spread batter evenly in prepared pan. Bake for 40 to 50 minutes or until a tester inserted in center comes out clean. Cool completely in pan on a wire rack. Frost and decorate as desired.

TIPS
- In this recipe, use block cream cheese at room temperature, not tubs of spreadable cream cheese.
- For a double hit of chocolate, finish this cake with Chocolate Cream Cheese Frosting. Sprinkle with finely chopped nuts or shaved chocolate and decorate with small candied carrots.

Chocolate Zucchini Cake with Cranberries

Here's a great way to use up zucchini, which is often so abundant during the summer.

SERVES 12 TO 16		
1	package (18.25 oz/515 g) devil's food cake mix	1
1	package (4-serving size) chocolate instant pudding mix	1
4	eggs	4
2½ cups	grated zucchini	625 mL
⅓ cup	vegetable oil	75 mL
¼ cup	water	50 mL
1 tsp	ground cinnamon	5 mL
¼ tsp	ground nutmeg	1 mL
1 cup	dried cranberries	250 mL

- **Preheat oven to 350°F (180°C)**
- **13- by 9-inch (3 L) cake pan, greased**

1. In a large mixer bowl, combine cake mix, pudding mix, eggs, zucchini, oil, water, cinnamon and nutmeg. Beat on low speed for 1 minute to blend, then on medium speed for 2 minutes. Stir in cranberries. Spread batter in prepared pan. Bake for 40 to 45 minutes or until a tester inserted in center comes out clean. Cool completely in pan on a wire rack. Frost as desired.

Variation: Try dried cherries in place of cranberries.

TIPS
- Choose small tender zucchinis and don't peel them. The green flecks are attractive in this cake.
- This cake works well with a cream cheese frosting. Chocolate Cream Cheese Frosting (see recipe, page 265) is particularly nice.

Lemon Zucchini Cake

This cake is so moist, it's nice plain, but you can dress it up with a lemon cream cheese frosting or a lemon butter frosting.

SERVES 12 TO 16		
1	package (18.25 oz/515 g) lemon cake mix	1
1	package (4-serving size) vanilla instant pudding mix	1
4	eggs	4
2 cups	grated zucchini	500 mL
⅓ cup	vegetable oil	75 mL
⅓ cup	water	75 mL

- **Preheat oven to 350°F (180°C)**
- **13- by 9-inch (3 L) cake pan, greased**

1. In a large mixer bowl, combine cake mix, pudding mix, eggs, zucchini, oil and water. Beat on low speed for 1 minute to blend, then on medium speed for 2 minutes. Spread batter in prepared pan. Bake for 40 to 45 minutes or until a tester inserted in center comes out clean. Cool completely in pan on a wire rack.

Variation: Add ¾ cup (175 mL) dried cranberries or raisins to the batter.

TIP
- Peel the zucchini if you don't like the green flecks or don't want kids to know there are vegetables in their cake.

Multi-Layer Cakes

Multi-layer cakes take more time to complete, as the layers are filled, frosted and decorated. However, the cake portion is often very simple to make and can sometimes be prepared in advance. The cakes in this section range from simple and easy to fairly elaborate. When you pull out all the stops, the results can be spectacular, and they are usually well worth the extra time and effort. These lovely creations are just the ticket for those special occasions when you want to dazzle your guests.

Chocolate Cake with Chocolate Raspberry Frosting

Fresh raspberries and chocolate are an unbeatable combination.

SERVES 10 TO 12

CAKE

1	package (18.25 oz/515 g) devil's food cake mix	1

CHOCOLATE RASPBERRY FROSTING

1 lb	bittersweet chocolate, chopped	500 g
1⅓ cups	sour cream	325 mL
⅓ cup	seedless raspberry jam, stirred	75 mL
¼ cup	corn syrup	50 mL
2 tbsp	raspberry liqueur	25 mL
¼ cup	butter, softened	50 mL

FILLING AND TOPPING

⅓ cup	seedless raspberry jam	75 mL
2 to 3 cups	fresh raspberries	500 to 750 mL

TIPS

- Fresh raspberries always have the most flavor and bright red color when in season. You can, however, often get excellent imported raspberries year-round.
- Serve cake at room temperature, about 1 hour after it is removed from the refrigerator, so the frosting is soft and creamy.

- **Preheat oven to 350°F (180°C)**
- **Two 9-inch (23 cm) round cake pans, greased and floured**

1. **Cake:** Prepare cake mix according to package directions. Spread batter in prepared pans, dividing evenly. Bake for 30 to 35 minutes or until a tester inserted in center comes out clean. Cool for 10 minutes in pans on a wire rack, then remove and cool completely on rack. With a long sharp knife, cut cakes horizontally in half to make 4 layers.

2. **Frosting:** In the top of a double boiler, over hot water, melt chocolate, stirring constantly until smooth. (You can also melt the chocolate in a microwave oven.) Pour into a large mixer bowl. Cool to room temperature. Add sour cream, jam, corn syrup and liqueur to chocolate. Beat on medium speed until light and fluffy, about 3 minutes. Beat in butter.

3. **Assembly:** Place one cake layer, cut-side up, on a serving plate. Spread 2 tbsp (25 mL) jam on top. Spread about ¾ cup (175 mL) frosting over jam. Repeat layering twice more. Top with fourth cake layer, cut-side down. Spread remaining frosting over top and sides of cake. Arrange fresh raspberries on top of cake. Chill. Remove cake from refrigerator about 1 hour before serving. Store leftover cake in the refrigerator.

Variations: A mixture of raspberries and blackberries is nice. Replace raspberry liqueur with orange liqueur or brandy.

Double Chocolate Cake

A chocolate cake made more chocolaty with the addition of cocoa.

SERVES 10 TO 12

1	package (18.25 oz/515 g) devil's food cake mix	1
¼ cup	unsweetened cocoa powder, sifted	50 mL
4	eggs	4
1½ cups	plain yogurt	375 mL
½ cup	vegetable oil	125 mL
	White Chocolate Cream Cheese Frosting (see recipe, page 265)	
	Chocolate curls (see tip, page 20) or shaved chocolate (optional)	

TIP

- Cocoa powder tends to clump in storage. Sift it before adding it to other dry ingredients to be sure the lumps disappear in mixing.

- **Preheat oven to 350°F (180°C)**
- **Two 9-inch (23 cm) round cake pans, greased and floured**

1. In a large mixer bowl, combine cake mix, cocoa, eggs, yogurt and oil. Beat on medium speed for 2 minutes or until smooth. Spread batter in prepared pans, dividing evenly. Bake for 30 to 35 minutes or until a tester inserted in center comes out clean. Cool for 10 minutes in pans on a wire rack, then remove and cool completely on rack.

2. Prepare White Chocolate Cream Cheese Frosting. Place one cake layer top-side down on a serving plate. Spread with a generous amount of frosting. Place second cake layer top-side up over frosting. Cover top and sides of cake with remaining frosting. Decorate with chocolate curls, if desired. Chill until serving.

Variation: Add 1 tsp (5 mL) almond extract or 1 tbsp (15 mL) instant coffee powder to cake batter.

Chocolate Peanut Butter Cake

Peanut butter and chocolate are always a hit with kids young and old.

SERVES 10 TO 12

1	package (18.25 oz/515 g) devil's food cake mix	1
½ cup	creamy peanut butter	125 mL
3	eggs	3
1⅓ cups	water	325 mL
	Very Peanut Buttery Frosting (see recipe, page 263)	

DECORATION (OPTIONAL)

	Chocolate-covered peanuts, chopped peanuts or halved chocolate peanut butter cups

TIPS

- Since the cake requires a smooth peanut butter, you can always add crunch with a sprinkling of chopped peanuts over the top and sides of the frosted cake.
- Store peanuts in the freezer for maximum flavor retention.

- **Preheat oven to 350°F (180°C)**
- **Two 8-inch (20 cm) or 9-inch (23 cm) round cake pans, greased and floured**

1. In a large mixer bowl, combine cake mix, peanut butter, eggs and water. Beat on medium speed for 2 minutes. Spread batter in prepared pans, dividing evenly. Bake for 30 to 35 minutes or until a tester inserted in center comes out clean. Cool for 10 minutes in pans on a wire rack, then remove and cool completely on rack.

2. Prepare Very Peanut Buttery Frosting. Place one cake top-side down on a serving plate. Spread a generous amount (1½ cups/375 mL) of frosting over top. Place second cake top-side up over frosting. Frost top and sides of cake with remaining frosting. Decorate as desired.

Variation: Use a chocolate frosting for a different look and taste.

Chocolate Peanut Butter Tower

Here's a showstopper of a cake that will dazzle your friends.

CAKE

1	package (18.25 oz/515 g) devil's food cake mix	1
1	package (4-serving size) chocolate instant pudding mix	1
4	eggs	4
1 cup	sour cream	250 mL
½ cup	water	125 mL
1 cup	peanut butter chips	250 mL

PEANUT BUTTER CREAM CHEESE FROSTING

8 oz	cream cheese, softened	250 g
½ cup	creamy peanut butter	125 mL
4 cups	confectioner's (icing) sugar, sifted	1 L
¼ cup	whipping (35%) cream	50 mL

CHOCOLATE CREAM CHEESE FROSTING

8 oz	cream cheese, softened	250 g
½ cup	butter, softened	125 mL
3½ cups	confectioner's (icing) sugar, sifted	875 mL
⅓ cup	unsweetened cocoa powder, sifted	75 mL
¼ cup	whipping (35%) cream	50 mL

TOPPING

1 cup	chopped chocolate peanut butter cups (8 oz/250 g), divided	250 mL
¾ cup	finely chopped roasted peanuts	175 mL

TIPS
- For smooth, easy-to-spread frostings, use creamy peanut butter rather than the chunky variety.
- Don't be surprised by this batter — it is very thick.

- **Preheat oven to 350°F (180°C)**
- **Two 9-inch (23 cm) round cake pans, greased and floured**

1. **Cake:** In a large mixer bowl, combine cake mix, pudding mix, eggs, sour cream and water. Beat on low speed for 1 minute to blend, then on medium speed for 2 minutes. Stir in peanut butter chips. Spread batter in prepared pans, dividing evenly. Bake for 40 to 45 minutes or until a tester inserted in center comes out clean. Cool for 10 minutes in pans on a wire rack, then remove and cool completely on rack. With a long sharp knife, cut each cake horizontally in half to make 4 layers.

2. **Peanut Butter Cream Cheese Frosting:** In a large mixer bowl, beat cream cheese and peanut butter until light and fluffy. Gradually add confectioner's sugar and whipping cream, beating until smooth.

3. **Chocolate Cream Cheese Frosting:** In a large mixer bowl, beat cream cheese and butter until light and fluffy. Gradually add confectioner's sugar, cocoa and whipping cream, beating until smooth.

4. **Assembly:** Place one cake layer, cut-side up, on serving plate. Spread with ¾ cup (175 mL) of the peanut butter frosting. Sprinkle ¼ cup (50 mL) of the chopped peanut butter cups on top. Repeat with remaining cake layers, peanut butter frosting and peanut butter cups. Spread chocolate frosting on sides of cake. Pipe rosettes of chocolate frosting around the top edge of cake. Press chopped peanuts on side of cake. Store in the refrigerator.

Variation: For convenience, make a double quantity of one type of frosting instead of two different kinds.

Triple Chocolate Fudge Cake

The chocolate-lover's dream.

SERVES ABOUT 10 TO 12

CAKE

1	package (18.25 oz/515 g) devil's food cake mix	1
1 tbsp	instant coffee powder	15 mL
3	eggs	3
1 cup	water	250 mL
½ cup	sour cream	125 mL
⅓ cup	vegetable oil	75 mL

FILLING

½ cup	butter, softened	125 mL
3½ cups	confectioner's (icing) sugar, sifted	875 mL
½ cup	half-and-half (10%) cream	125 mL
2 oz	unsweetened chocolate, melted and cooled (see page 13)	60 g

GLAZE

4 oz	semi-sweet chocolate	125 g
2 tbsp	strong coffee	25 mL
3 tbsp	butter, softened	45 mL

TIP

- The consistency of butter icing varies with the butter temperature and the amount of beating. If the icing is too stiff, add a little more cream; if it's too soft, a little more confectioner's sugar will stiffen it.

- **Preheat oven to 350°F (180°C)**
- **Two 9-inch (23 cm) round cake pans, greased and floured**

1. **Cake:** In a large mixer bowl, combine cake mix, coffee powder, eggs, water, sour cream and oil. Beat on medium speed for 2 minutes. Spread in prepared pans, dividing evenly. Bake for 30 to 35 minutes or until a tester inserted in center comes out clean. Cool for 10 minutes in pans on a wire rack, then remove and cool completely on rack.

2. **Filling:** Beat all ingredients together on medium speed until light and fluffy. Add more confectioner's sugar or cream to make a soft, creamy spreading consistency.

3. **Assembly:** Place one cake layer top-side down on a serving plate. Spread with a generous amount of filling. Place second cake layer on top. Spread remaining filling on sides of cake, leaving top unfrosted. Chill for 30 minutes.

4. **Glaze:** In a small saucepan over low heat, melt chocolate and coffee, stirring until smooth. Remove from heat. Gradually add butter, stirring until smooth. Spread over top of cake, letting it drip down sides. Chill to set chocolate glaze.

Variation: If you don't have coffee powder, use cold strong coffee in place of water. You may prefer to omit the coffee altogether, in which case you can substitute water for coffee in the glaze.

Crunch 'n' Cream Chocolate Torte

I like to use Skor chocolate bars for this cake, but you may have another favorite.

SERVES 10 TO 12		
1	package (18.25 oz/515 g) devil's food cake mix	1
	Chocolate Whipped Cream Frosting (see recipe, page 266)	
4	toffee-crunch chocolate bars (each 1.4 oz/40 g), crushed	4

TIP
- Prepare the cake layers ahead and freeze; dessert can then be assembled as needed in just a few minutes.

- **Preheat oven to 350°F (180°C)**
- **Two 9-inch (23 cm) round cake pans, greased and floured**

1. **Cake:** Prepare and bake cake according to package directions to make two 9-inch (23 cm) round cake layers. Cool for 10 minutes in pans on a wire rack, then remove and cool completely on rack. With a long sharp knife, cut each layer horizontally in half to make 4 layers.

2. **Filling:** Prepare Chocolate Whipped Cream Frosting. Fold in three-quarters of the crushed chocolate bars.

3. **Assembly:** Place one halved cake layer on a serving plate. Spread with one-quarter of the frosting. Repeat layering with remaining cake layers and frosting. Sprinkle remaining crushed chocolate bar on top. Chill until serving. Store leftover cake in the refrigerator.

Variation: For a white filling, replace the cocoa with 1 tsp (5 mL) vanilla in the whipped cream frosting.

Chocolate Fleck Banana Layer Cake

The riper the bananas, the better the flavor of this cake.

SERVES 10 TO 12		
CAKE		
1	package (18.25 oz/515 g) white cake mix	1
4	eggs	4
1⅔ cups	mashed ripe bananas (3 to 4 large)	400 mL
⅓ cup	vegetable oil	75 mL
3 oz	semi-sweet chocolate, coarsely grated, divided	90 g
FROSTING		
	Banana Butter Frosting (see recipe, page 264)	

TIP
- The hardest part of this recipe is grating the chocolate. I prefer to do it on a hand grater because it produces a coarser result, but the food processor is easier.

- **Preheat oven to 350°F (180°C)**
- **Two 8-inch (20 cm) or 9-inch (23 cm) round cake pans, greased and floured**

1. **Cake:** In a large mixer bowl, combine cake mix, eggs, bananas and oil. Beat on medium speed for 2 minutes. Stir in two-thirds of the grated chocolate. Set remainder aside. Spread batter in prepared pans, dividing evenly. Bake for 30 to 35 minutes or until a tester inserted in center comes out clean. Cool for 10 minutes in pans on a wire rack, then remove and cool completely on rack.

2. **Frosting:** Prepare Banana Butter Frosting. Stir in reserved grated chocolate.

3. **Assembly:** Place one cake top-side down on a serving plate. Spread about ¾ cup (175 mL) frosting on top. Place remaining cake top-side up over frosting. Cover sides and top of cake with remaining frosting. Chill until serving.

Black Forest Cake

A shortcut version of an all-time favorite special-occasion cake.

SERVES 10 TO 12

CAKE

1	package (18.25 oz/515 g) devil's food cake mix	1

CHERRY FILLING

3 tbsp	granulated sugar	45 mL
3 tbsp	cornstarch	45 mL
28 oz	pitted sour cherries in syrup, well drained, juice reserved	796 mL
1¼ cups	reserved cherry juice, plus water as necessary	300 mL

WHIPPED CREAM FILLING AND TOPPING

3 cups	whipping (35%) cream	750 mL
½ cup	confectioner's (icing) sugar, sifted	125 mL
⅓ cup	cherry liqueur	75 mL
	Chocolate curls (see tip, page 20)	

TIPS

- The sour cherries in this recipe give a tart cherry filling. For a sweeter taste, a can of prepared cherry pie filling is quick and easy.
- Maraschino cherries with stems can add a colorful touch on top of the cake.

- **Preheat oven to 350°F (180°C)**
- **Three 8-inch (20 cm) or 9-inch (23 cm) round cake pans, greased and floured**

1. **Cake:** Prepare cake mix as directed on package. Spread batter in prepared pans, dividing evenly. Bake for 20 to 25 minutes or until a tester inserted in center comes out clean. Cool for 10 minutes in pans on a wire rack, then remove and cool completely on rack.

2. **Cherry Filling:** In a saucepan, mix sugar and cornstarch. Stir in cherry juice. Cook over medium heat, stirring constantly, until mixture comes to a boil and thickens. Add cherries; cook for 1 minute longer. Cool completely.

3. **Whipped Cream Filling and Topping:** Beat whipping cream and confectioner's sugar to stiff peaks.

4. **Assembly:** If top of cake is too rounded, trim to even off. Sprinkle each layer with liqueur. Place one cake layer on a serving plate. Spread half of cherry filling and one-quarter of cream over cake. Add middle cake layer. Spread with remaining cherries and one-quarter of cream. Add top cake layer. Cover top and sides of cake with remaining cream. Decorate with chocolate curls. Chill for at least 2 hours to allow flavors to mellow. Store leftover cake in the refrigerator.

Chocolate Orange Jubilee Cake

A creamy orange frosting nestled between six layers of feathery light chocolate cake.

CAKE

1	package (18.25 oz/515 g) devil's food cake mix	1
3	eggs	3
1 tbsp	grated orange zest	15 mL
⅔ cup	orange juice	150 mL
⅔ cup	water	150 mL
⅓ cup	vegetable oil	75 mL

ORANGE BUTTERCREAM FILLING AND FROSTING

1½ cups	butter, softened	375 mL
1 tbsp	grated orange zest	15 mL
2 tbsp	orange juice	25 mL
4 cups	confectioner's (icing) sugar, sifted	1 L
2	egg yolks	2
	Chocolate curls or shaved chocolate (see page 20)	
	Orange slices, candied or fresh	

TIPS

- If your oven won't hold 3 pans on one shelf, put 2 on the upper middle rack and one on a lower rack. Change positions halfway through baking.
- Icing sugar, confectioner's sugar and powdered sugar are different names for the same thing. This type of sugar has been finely ground and cornstarch has been added. Since it tends to settle and can lump during storage, for easy blending it should be sifted after measuring, before it is combined with other ingredients.

- **Preheat oven to 350°F (180°C)**
- **Three 8-inch (20 cm) or 9-inch (23 cm) round cake pans**

1. **Cake:** In a large mixer bowl, combine cake mix, eggs, orange zest, orange juice, water and oil. Beat on medium speed for 2 minutes. Spread batter in prepared pans, dividing evenly. Bake for 20 to 30 minutes or until a tester inserted in center comes out clean. Cool for 10 minutes in pans on a wire rack, then remove and cool completely on rack. With a long sharp knife, cut each layer horizontally in half to make 6 layers.

2. **Filling and Frosting:** In a large mixer bowl, beat butter, orange zest and orange juice on medium speed until creamy. Gradually add confectioner's sugar and egg yolks, beating until smooth and fluffy.

3. **Assembly:** Spread buttercream between each layer, placing one on top of the other on a serving plate. Frost sides and top of cake, reserving some for decoration. Decorate top of cake with rosettes of buttercream, chocolate curls and orange slices. Chill until serving. If using fresh orange slices, place on cake just before serving.

Chocolate Orange Marble Cake

Not only is this cake attractive, the combination of chocolate and orange liqueur is delicious.

SERVES 12 TO 16

CAKE

1	package (18.25 oz/515 g) marble cake mix	1
3	eggs	3
⅔ cup	freshly squeezed orange juice	150 mL
⅔ cup	water	150 mL
⅓ cup	vegetable oil	75 mL
1 tbsp	grated orange zest	15 mL

ORANGE FROSTING

½ cup	butter, softened	125 mL
6 cups	confectioner's (icing) sugar, sifted	1.5 L
⅓ cup	whipping (35%) cream	75 mL
⅓ cup	freshly squeezed orange juice	75 mL
1 tbsp	grated orange zest	15 mL

TIPS

- Slices of orange gumdrops look nice on this cake and a simple drizzle of melted chocolate adds a finishing touch.
- Remember to zest the orange before juicing.

- **Preheat oven to 350°F (180°C)**
- **Two 9-inch (23 cm) round cake pans, greased and floured**

1. **Cake:** In a large mixer bowl, combine large cake mix envelope, eggs, orange juice, water and oil. Beat on medium speed for 2 minutes. Spoon 2 cups (500 mL) of the batter into a small bowl and stir in pouch of chocolate mix. Stir orange zest into white batter and divide evenly between prepared pans. Drop chocolate batter by spoonfuls randomly onto white batter. Run tip of knife through batters to create a marble effect. Bake for 30 to 35 minutes or until a tester inserted in center comes out clean. Cool for 10 minutes in pans on a wire rack, then remove and cool completely on rack.

2. **Frosting:** In a large mixer bowl, beat butter on high speed until creamy. Add confectioner's sugar alternately with cream and juice, beating until smooth. Stir in orange zest.

3. **Assembly:** Place one cake top-side down on a serving plate. Spread a generous amount, about 1½ cups (375 mL), of frosting over top. Place second cake top-side up over frosting. Frost top and sides of cake with remaining frosting. Decorate as desired.

Variation: Use a chocolate frosting for another great look and taste.

Chocolate Strawberry Torte

Mix chocolate and strawberries, and you're guaranteed success.

CAKE

1	package (18.25 oz/515 g) devil's food cake mix	1

STRAWBERRY FILLING

3 tbsp	granulated sugar	45 mL
3 tbsp	cornstarch	45 mL
1	package (15 oz/425 g) frozen sliced strawberries in syrup, thawed and drained, juice reserved	1
1¼ cups	reserved strawberry juice, plus water if necessary	300 mL
1 tbsp	lemon juice	15 mL
2 cups	sliced fresh strawberries	500 mL

WHIPPED CREAM FILLING AND TOPPING

3 cups	whipping (35%) cream	750 mL
½ cup	confectioner's (icing) sugar	125 mL
⅓ cup	orange liqueur	75 mL
	Fresh strawberries	

TIPS

- When the berries are in season, leave the tops on for a colorful garnish. Halved and sliced berries also look nice.
- Freshly squeezed lemon juice has the best flavor. Use it whenever possible.

- **Preheat oven to 350°F (180°C)**
- **Three 8-inch (20 cm) or 9-inch (23 cm) round cake pans, greased and floured**

1. **Cake:** Prepare cake mix as directed on package. Spread batter in prepared pans, dividing evenly. Bake for 20 to 25 minutes or until a tester inserted in center comes out clean. Cool for 10 minutes in pans on a wire rack, then remove and cool completely on rack.

2. **Strawberry Filling:** In a saucepan, mix sugar and cornstarch. Stir in strawberry juice. Cook over medium heat, stirring constantly, until mixture comes to a boil and thickens. Add frozen berries and cook for 1 minute longer. Add lemon juice. Cool completely. Stir in sliced fresh berries.

3. **Whipped Cream Filling and Topping:** Beat whipping cream and confectioner's sugar to stiff peaks.

4. **Assembly:** If tops of cakes are too rounded, trim to even off. Sprinkle each layer with liqueur. Place one cake layer top-side down on a serving plate. Spread half of the strawberry filling and one-quarter of the cream filling over cake. Add middle cake layer. Spread with the remaining strawberry filling and one-quarter of the cream filling. Add top cake layer. Cover top and sides of cake with the remaining cream filling. Decorate with fresh strawberries. Chill for at least 2 hours to allow flavors to mellow. Store leftover cake in the refrigerator.

Variations: Replace the devil's food cake mix with a deep chocolate cake mix. Try raspberries instead of strawberries.

Chocolate Strawberry Shortcake

You don't have to spend much time in the kitchen to get rave reviews for this dessert.

CAKE

1	package (18.25 oz/515 g) devil's food cake mix	1
2	eggs	2
1¼ cups	water	300 mL
⅓ cup	vegetable oil	75 mL

FILLING AND TOPPING

3 oz	semi-sweet chocolate, chopped	90 g
1 tbsp	shortening	15 mL
2 tbsp	orange liqueur or orange juice	25 mL
2 cups	whipping (35%) cream	500 mL
¼ cup	confectioner's (icing) sugar, sifted	50 mL
3 cups	fresh strawberries	750 mL

TIPS
- Dip tips of whole strawberries in chocolate for an exquisite finish.
- If time is critical, use two-thirds of the chocolate for the drizzle and leave strawberries plain.

- **Preheat oven to 350°F (180°C)**
- **Two 9-inch (23 cm) round cake pans, greased and floured**

1. **Cake:** In a large mixer bowl, combine cake mix, eggs, water and oil. Beat on medium speed for 2 minutes. Spread batter in prepared pans, dividing evenly. Bake according to package directions. Cool for 10 minutes in pans on a wire rack, then remove and cool completely on rack. Freeze one cake for another use. With a long sharp knife, cut remaining cake horizontally in half.

2. **Filling and Topping:** In the top of a double boiler, over hot water, partially melt chocolate with shortening. (You can also do this in the microwave on medium power for 2 minutes.) Stir until smooth. Dip 7 strawberries in chocolate. Place on waxed paper and chill to set. Save remaining chocolate for the drizzle. Hull and cut remaining berries in half or thick slices. Brush each cake layer with 1 tbsp (15 mL) of the orange liqueur. In a large mixer bowl, beat whipping cream and confectioner's sugar to stiff peaks.

3. **Assembly:** Place one cake layer cut-side up on serving plate. Spread half of whipped cream on top. Scatter sliced strawberries over cream. Place second cake layer cut-side down over berries. Top with remaining whipped cream. If necessary, heat reserved chocolate mixture again to soften. Drizzle over cream. Arrange dipped strawberries on top of cake. Chill until serving. Store leftover cake in the refrigerator.

Variation: A mixture of raspberries, blueberries and strawberries also works well in this recipe.

Twin Boston Cream Pies

A good choice for a crowd, since this recipe makes two cakes.

SERVES 12 TO 16

CAKE

1	package (18.25 oz/515 g) yellow cake mix	1

FILLING

1	package (4-serving size) vanilla instant pudding mix	1
1¼ cups	milk	300 mL

CHOCOLATE GLAZE

1 cup	ready-to-serve chocolate frosting	250 mL

TIPS

- Don't be confused by the name of this recipe. Although called a "pie," it's really a cake with a vanilla custard filling and chocolate glaze.
- Although not traditional, a chocolate filling is also nice. Replace the vanilla pudding mix with a chocolate one.

- **Preheat oven to 350°F (180°C)**
- **Two 9-inch (23 cm) round cake pans, greased and floured**

1. **Cake:** Prepare and bake cake according to package directions for two 9-inch (23 cm) layers. Cool for 10 minutes in pans on a wire rack, then remove and cool completely on rack. With a long sharp knife, cut each layer horizontally in half to make 4 layers.

2. **Filling:** In a small bowl, beat pudding mix and milk for 1 minute. Let stand for 5 minutes to set.

3. **Assembly:** You'll need 2 serving plates. Place bottom cake layers on plates. Spread half of filling on each layer. Place top cake layers over filling.

4. **Glaze:** In a microwave on High, heat frosting in a microwaveable container for 30 to 40 seconds, or set frosting container in a pot of hot water to soften to a shiny, thick pouring consistency. Pour over top of cakes to cover completely and let some drizzle down the sides. Chill to set. Store leftover cake in the refrigerator.

Ribbon Torte

You can make a plain and a chocolate cake layer from one marble cake mix.

SERVES 10 TO 12

1	package (18.25 oz/515 g) fudge marble cake mix	1
3	eggs	3
1¼ cups	water	300 mL
⅓ cup	vegetable oil	75 mL
	Chocolate Pudding and Cream Frosting (see recipe, page 264)	
	Shaved chocolate or chocolate curls (see tip, page 20) (optional)	

TIP

- Chill your bowl and beaters before whipping cream to get the best volume and nice stiff peaks.

- **Preheat oven to 350°F (180°C)**
- **Two 8-inch (20 cm) or 9-inch (23 cm) round cake pans, greased and floured**

1. In a large mixer bowl, combine large cake mix packet, eggs, water and oil. Beat on medium speed for 2 minutes. Spread half of batter (about 2½ cups/625 mL) into one pan. Blend contents of small cocoa packet from cake mix into remaining batter. Mix well and spread in remaining pan. Bake as directed on package. Cool for 10 minutes in pans on a wire rack, then remove and cool completely on rack. With a long sharp knife, cut each layer horizontally in half to make 4 layers.

2. Prepare chocolate Pudding and Cream Frosting. Place one halved cake layer cut-side up on serving plate. Spread one-quarter of cream mixture on top. Repeat with remaining cake, alternating light and dark layers with cream mixture between layers and on top. Decorate with shaved chocolate or chocolate curls, if desired. Chill until serving. Store leftover cake in the refrigerator.

Chocolate Raspberry Cream Torte

What could be more decadent than this chocolate cake, topped with chocolate and raspberry cream? And it's easy to make, as well.

SERVES 10 TO 12

CAKE

1	package (18.25 oz/515 g) devil's food cake mix	1
3	eggs	3
1 cup	sour cream	250 mL
¾ cup	water	175 mL
⅓ cup	vegetable oil	75 mL
1½ cups	miniature semi-sweet chocolate chips	375 mL

CHOCOLATE GANACHE

1 cup	semi-sweet chocolate chips	250 mL
½ cup	whipping (35%) cream	125 mL
1 tbsp	butter	15 mL
1 tbsp	raspberry or orange liqueur (optional)	15 mL

RASPBERRY CREAM

1	package (10 oz/284 g) frozen raspberries in syrup, thawed	1
2 tbsp	granulated sugar	25 mL
2 tbsp	cornstarch	25 mL
½ cup	whipping (35%) cream	125 mL

TIPS

- For a Valentine's or a Mother's Day surprise, bake cakes in heart-shaped pans.
- For a dynamite presentation, garnish with fresh raspberries and chocolate leaves.

- **Preheat oven to 350°F (180°C)**
- **Two 9-inch (23 cm) round cake pans, greased and floured**

1. **Cake:** In a large mixer bowl, combine cake mix, eggs, sour cream, water and oil. Beat on medium speed for 2 minutes. Stir in chocolate chips. Spread batter in prepared pans, dividing evenly. Bake for 35 to 40 minutes or until a tester inserted in center comes out clean. Cool for 10 minutes in pans on a wire rack, then remove and cool completely on rack. Wrap and freeze one layer for another use.

2. **Chocolate Ganache:** In a small saucepan, combine chocolate chips and whipping cream. Heat on low heat, stirring often until melted and smooth. Remove from heat. Add butter and liqueur, stirring until smooth. Refrigerate for 1 to 1½ hours, stirring occasionally, until cold. Beat with wooden spoon or electric mixer on low speed until a thick, creamy spreading consistency is reached.

3. **Raspberry Cream:** To remove seeds, place raspberries in a strainer over a small saucepan. Press with back of spoon. Discard seeds. Mix sugar and cornstarch. Add to raspberry juice, stirring until smooth. Cook over medium heat, stirring constantly until mixture comes to a boil and is thickened. Boil for 1 minute. Transfer to a bowl and cover surface with plastic wrap. Chill for about 1 hour or until cold. In a large mixer bowl, beat cream to stiff peaks. Fold into raspberry mixture.

4. **Assembly:** Place cake top-side down on a serving plate. Spread with about ⅓ cup (75 mL) of chocolate ganache. Cover sides of cake with about half of remaining ganache. Pipe remainder around the top and bottom edge of cake. Spread raspberry cream on top of cake inside the chocolate border. Chill until serving. Store leftover cake in the refrigerator.

Variations: Use a dark chocolate cake mix, such as German chocolate or fudge, in place of devil's food. Replace raspberries with strawberries.

Chocolate Raspberry Torte

You can't go wrong with the combination of chocolate, whipped cream and fresh raspberries.

CAKE

1	package (18.25 oz/515 g) devil's food or dark chocolate cake mix	1

FILLING

2 cups	whipping (35%) cream	500 mL
¼ cup	confectioner's (icing) sugar, sifted	50 mL
1 cup	raspberry jam	250 mL

FROSTING

1½ cups	semi-sweet chocolate chips	375 mL
¾ cup	sour cream	175 mL
	Chocolate curls (see tip, page 20)	
	Fresh raspberries	

TIP

- Spread whipped cream on cake layers, leaving small border so side frosting doesn't get creamy.

- **Preheat oven to 350°F (180°C)**
- **Two 9-inch (23 cm) round cake pans, greased and floured**

1. **Cake:** Prepare and bake cake according to package directions to make two 9-inch (23 cm) round cake layers. Cool for 10 minutes in pans on a wire rack, then remove and cool completely on rack. With a long sharp knife, cut each layer horizontally in half to make 4 layers.

2. **Filling:** Beat whipping cream and confectioner's sugar until stiff peaks form.

3. **Frosting:** In top of a double boiler, melt chocolate chips or microwave on Medium for 2 minutes. Stir until smooth. Stir in sour cream.

4. **Assembly:** Place one halved cake layer cut-side up on a serving plate. Spread with ⅓ cup (75 mL) jam and one-third of the cream. Repeat layering, ending with top cake layer cut-side down. Frost top and sides of cake with frosting. Decorate with chocolate curls and fresh raspberries. Chill until serving. Store leftover cake in the refrigerator.

Variation: Strawberry jam and fresh strawberries are a nice variation when raspberries are an outrageous price.

Raspberry Dream Cake

An adult raspberry taste with a kid's color appeal.

SERVES 10 TO 12		
1	package (18.25 oz/515 g) white cake mix	1
1	package (3 oz/85 g) raspberry-flavored gelatin dessert mix	1
4	eggs	4
1¼ cups	plain or raspberry yogurt	300 mL
⅓ cup	vegetable oil	75 mL
	Raspberry Butter Frosting (see recipe, page 258)	
	Fresh raspberries to garnish	

TIP
- This cake freezes well without the raspberry garnish.

- **Preheat oven to 350°F (180°C)**
- **Two 9-inch (23 cm) round cake pans, greased and floured**

1. In a large mixer bowl, combine cake mix, gelatin, eggs, yogurt and oil. Beat on medium speed for 2 minutes. Spread batter in prepared pans, dividing evenly. Bake for 30 to 35 minutes or until a tester inserted in center comes out clean. Cool for 10 minutes in pans on a wire rack, then remove and cool completely on rack. With a long sharp knife, cut each layer horizontally in half to make 4 layers.

2. Prepare Raspberry Butter Frosting. Place one halved cake layer top-side down on a serving plate. Spread with one-quarter of frosting. Place bottom halved cake layer over frosting. Repeat layering with remaining frosting and cake, ending with frosting on top. Decorate top with whole raspberries. Chill until serving.

Peaches 'n' Cream Cake

Not only does the peach gelatin add a whop of flavor to this cake but the color is unique, too.

SERVES 10 TO 12		
1	can (28 oz/796 mL) peach slices, well drained	1
1	package (18.25 oz/515 g) white cake mix	1
1	package (3 oz/85 g) peach-flavored gelatin dessert mix	1
4	eggs	4
⅓ cup	vegetable oil	75 mL
	Peach Cream Cheese Frosting (see recipe, page 265)	

TIPS
- To keep layer cakes from slipping on your serving plate, spread a little frosting on the plate before putting the first cake layer down. This "glues" it to the plate.
- For this frosting, use blocks of cream cheese at room temperature, not the tubs of spreadable cream cheese.

- **Preheat oven to 350°F (180°C)**
- **Two 9-inch (23 cm) round cake pans, greased and floured**

1. In a food processor, purée peaches. You should have about 2 cups (500 mL) of purée. Measure 1¼ cups (300 mL) purée for cake and ½ cup (125 mL) for frosting. In a large mixer bowl, combine cake mix, gelatin, eggs, peach purée and oil. Beat on medium speed for 2 minutes. Spread batter in prepared pans, dividing evenly. Bake for 30 to 35 minutes or until a tester inserted in center comes out clean. Cool for 10 minutes in pans on a wire rack, then remove and cool completely on rack. With a long sharp knife, cut each layer horizontally in half to make 4 layers.

2. Prepare Peach Cream Cheese Frosting. Place one halved cake layer top-side down on a serving plate. Spread with about ⅓ cup (75 mL) frosting. Place bottom halved cake layer over frosting. Repeat layering of frosting and cake, placing last cake layer top-side up. Cover top and sides of cake with remaining frosting. Chill until serving. Store leftover cake in the refrigerator.

Apricot Cream Cake

Canned apricots have a wonderful flavor and give a summery taste to a year-round cake.

SERVES 10 TO 12		
2	cans (each 14 oz/398 mL) apricot halves, drained, ½ cup (125 mL) syrup reserved	2
1	package (18.25 oz/515 g) white cake mix	1
4	eggs	4
½ cup	butter, melted	125 mL
	Apricot Whipped Cream Frosting (see recipe, page 266)	

TIPS

- A food processor is the best way to purée the apricots. But if you don't have one, a potato masher also works well.
- A garnish of mint leaves is attractive.
- Always use large eggs in baking unless otherwise specified.
- Have all ingredients for cakes at room temperature.

- **Preheat oven to 350°F (180°C)**
- **Two 9-inch (23 cm) round cake pans, greased and floured**

1. Reserve 4 apricot halves for garnish. In a food processor, purée apricots to make 1½ cups (375 mL) purée. In a large mixer bowl, combine cake mix, eggs, apricot purée and melted butter. Beat at medium speed for 2 minutes. Spread batter in prepared pans, dividing evenly. Bake for 30 to 35 minutes or until a tester inserted in center comes out clean. Cool for 10 minutes in pans on a wire rack, then remove layers and place right-side up on rack over waxed paper. Poke holes in top of warm cakes with a fork or toothpick. Brush reserved apricot syrup over cakes, using ¼ cup (50 mL) for each layer, and let it soak in. Cool completely. With a long sharp knife, cut each layer horizontally in half to make 4 layers.

2. Prepare Apricot Whipped Cream Frosting. Place one halved cake layer on a serving plate. Spread with one-quarter of filling. Repeat layering with remaining cake and filling. Slice reserved apricot halves and arrange on top of cake. Chill until serving. Store leftover cake in the refrigerator.

Variation: Replace apricots with peaches.

Apricot Hazelnut Cake

A feathery light, nutty, not-too-sweet delight. Simple but attractive.

SERVES 10 TO 12

CAKE

1	package (18.25 oz/515 g) white cake mix	1
1 cup	ground hazelnuts	250 mL
4	eggs	4
1⅓ cups	water	325 mL
⅓ cup	vegetable oil	75 mL
	Apricot Whipped Cream Frosting (see recipe, page 266)	

GLAZE

½ cup	strained apricot jam	125 mL
¼ cup	coarsely chopped hazelnuts (optional)	50 mL

TIP
- For optimum flavor, toast hazelnuts before grinding (see page 14).

- **Preheat oven to 350°F (180°C)**
- **Two 8-inch (20 cm) round cake pans, greased and floured**

1. **Cake:** In a large mixer bowl, combine cake mix, ground hazelnuts, eggs, water and oil. Beat on medium speed for 2 minutes. Spread batter in prepared pans, dividing evenly. Bake for 30 to 35 minutes or until a tester inserted in center comes out clean. Cool for 10 minutes in pans on a wire rack, then remove and cool completely on rack. With a long sharp knife, cut each layer horizontally in half to make 4 layers.

2. **Assembly:** Prepare Apricot Whipped Cream Frosting. Place one halved cake layer on a serving plate. Spread with one-third of filling. Repeat with remaining 3 cake layers and filling, placing last cake layer top-side up.

3. **Glaze:** Warm jam if necessary to soften to a spreading consistency. Spread over top of cake, right to the edge. Garnish with a ring of chopped hazelnuts, if desired. Chill until serving. Store leftover cake in the refrigerator.

Ice Cream Loaf Cake

Here's a great dessert that you can keep in your freezer for unexpected company.

SERVES 8

CAKE

1	package (18.25 oz/515 g) white cake mix	1
1	package (4-serving size) vanilla instant pudding mix	1
4	eggs	4
½ cup	sour cream	125 mL
¼ cup	vegetable oil	50 mL

FILLING

2 cups	chocolate ice cream, softened	500 mL
2 cups	strawberry ice cream, softened	500 mL

FROSTING

2 cups	whipping (35%) cream	500 mL
¼ cup	confectioner's (icing) sugar, sifted	50 mL

- **Preheat oven to 350°F (180°C)**
- **Two 9- by 5-inch (2 L) loaf pans, greased and floured**

1. **Cake:** In a large mixer bowl, beat cake mix, pudding mix, eggs, sour cream and oil on medium speed for 2 minutes. Spread batter evenly in prepared pans. Bake for 40 to 45 minutes or until a tester inserted in center comes out clean. Cool for 20 minutes in pans on a wire rack, then remove and cool completely on rack. Freeze one cake for later use. With a long knife, cut remaining cake horizontally into 3 layers.

2. **Filling:** Place bottom cake layer on serving platter. Spread chocolate ice cream evenly on top. Spread middle cake layer with strawberry ice cream and place on top of bottom layer. Top with third cake layer. Freeze until firm.

3. **Frosting:** In a large mixer bowl, beat whipping cream and confectioner's sugar until stiff peaks form. Spread on sides and top of loaf. Freeze until firm. Remove from freezer 10 minutes before serving.

Pineapple Orange Cake

The combination of orange and pineapple is both fresh and exotically tropical in this simple yet delicious cake.

SERVES 10 TO 12		
1	package (18.25 oz/515 g) white cake mix	1
1	package (3 oz/85 g) orange-flavored gelatin dessert mix	1
4	eggs	4
1	can (14 oz/398 mL) crushed pineapple, with juice	1
1/3 cup	vegetable oil	75 mL
2	recipes Orange-Flavored Whipped Cream (see recipe, page 266)	2
	Orange slices (optional)	

- **Preheat oven to 350°F (180°C)**
- **Two 9-inch (23 cm) round cake pans, greased and floured**

1. In a large mixer bowl, combine cake mix, gelatin, eggs, pineapple with juice and oil. Beat on medium speed for 2 minutes. Spread batter in prepared pans, dividing evenly. Bake for 30 to 35 minutes or until a tester inserted in center comes out clean. Cool for 10 minutes in pans on a wire rack, then remove and cool completely on rack.

2. Prepare Orange-Flavored Whipped Cream (doubling the recipe). Place one cake layer top-side down on a serving plate. Spread half of cream mixture on top. Place remaining cake layer top-side up over cream and cover with remaining cream. Decorate with orange slices, if desired. Chill until serving. Store leftover cake in the refrigerator.

Pineapple Mandarin Cake

Sometimes the simple cakes are the best. Although easy to prepare with just a few ingredients, the flavor and appearance of this cake is wonderful.

SERVES 12 TO 16		
1	package (18.25 oz/515 g) white cake mix	1
3	eggs	3
1	can (10 oz/284 mL) mandarin oranges, drained, juice reserved	1
1	can (10 oz/284 mL) crushed pineapple, drained, juice reserved	1
1 1/3 cups	reserved mandarin orange and pineapple juice, plus water as necessary	325 mL
1/3 cup	vegetable oil	75 mL
	Lemon Butter Frosting (see recipe, page 258)	

TIP

- Be sure to buy mandarins that are whole segments, not the broken ones. The reserved fruit is used for decoration.

- **Preheat oven to 350°F (180°C)**
- **Two 9-inch (23 cm) round cake pans, greased and floured**

1. In a large mixer bowl, combine cake mix, eggs, juice mixture and oil. Beat on medium speed for 2 minutes. Spread batter in prepared pans, dividing evenly. Bake for 30 to 35 minutes or until a tester inserted in center comes out clean. Cool cakes for 10 minutes in pans, then remove to a wire rack and cool completely.

2. Prepare Lemon Butter Frosting. Place one cake layer top-side down on a serving plate. Spread with a generous amount of frosting. Put remaining cake layer top-side up over frosting. Cover top and sides of cake completely with remaining frosting. Decorate top of cake with a ring of drained mandarin segments around the outside. Fill center with well-drained pineapple. Decorate center with a few mandarins. Chill until serving. Store leftover cake in the refrigerator.

Variation: Replace lemon juice and zest with orange in the frosting.

Piña Colada Torte

The combination of flavors — pineapple, coconut and rum — immortalized in the famous cocktail is equally delicious in a cake.

SERVES 10 TO 12

CAKE

1	package (18.25 oz/515 g) white cake mix	1

PINEAPPLE FILLING

1	can (19 oz/540 mL) crushed pineapple, with juice	1
2 tbsp	granulated sugar	25 mL
2 tbsp	cornstarch	25 mL
1 tsp	lemon juice	5 mL

RUM SYRUP

⅔ cup	water	150 mL
⅓ cup	granulated sugar	75 mL
3 tbsp	rum	45 mL

COCONUT BUTTERCREAM

1 cup	butter, softened	250 mL
3½ cups	confectioner's (icing) sugar, sifted	825 mL
3 to 4 tbsp	half-and-half (10%) cream	45 to 60 mL
1 tsp	coconut extract	5 mL

GARNISH

3½ cups	shaved coconut	825 mL

TIPS

- All the parts can be prepared up to 3 days ahead and the cake can be assembled the day before.
- Light rum will not discolor the cake, but if you only have amber, the taste will still be awesome!
- Shaved coconut is attractive and makes a nice finish for cakes. It's available in South Asian grocery stores.
- Lightly toasted coconut has a sweeter flavor and a crunchy rather than chewy texture.
- The flavor of coconut extract intensifies if it's left to stand. Keep this in mind if you're preparing the cake ahead.

- **Preheat oven to 350°F (180°C)**
- **Two 8-inch (20 cm) or 9-inch (23 cm) round cake pans, greased and floured**

1. **Cake:** Prepare cake mix as directed on package. Spread batter in prepared pans, dividing evenly. Bake for 30 to 35 minutes or until a tester inserted in center comes out clean. Cool for 10 minutes in pans on a wire rack, then remove and cool completely on rack. With a long sharp knife, but cakes horizontally in half to make 4 layers.

2. **Filling:** In a saucepan, combine pineapple with juice, sugar, cornstarch and lemon juice. Cook, stirring constantly, over medium heat until mixture comes to a boil, then simmer for 3 minutes. Cool completely.

3. **Rum Syrup:** In a small saucepan, combine water and sugar. Bring to a boil, stirring until sugar is dissolved. Remove from heat. Stir in rum. Cool completely.

4. **Coconut Buttercream:** In a large mixer bowl, beat butter and half of confectioner's sugar until light and creamy. Add cream and coconut extract. Gradually add remaining confectioner's sugar, beating until smooth. Add enough cream to make a soft spreading consistency.

5. **Assembly:** Place one cake layer cut-side up on a serving plate. Brush top with some rum syrup. Spread half of pineapple filling on top. Top with another cake layer. Brush with syrup and spread ¾ cup (175 mL) buttercream on top. Top with third cake layer. Brush with syrup and spread remaining pineapple over it. Place fourth cake layer on top, cut-side down. Brush with remaining syrup. Frost top and sides with remaining buttercream. Cover with coconut, pressing into buttercream lightly. Chill until serving. Store leftover cake in the refrigerator.

Variations: Replace the shaved coconut with flaked. Add 1 tsp (5 mL) coconut extract to the cake batter for a stronger coconut taste.

Lemon Berry Cake with White Chocolate Frosting

A creamy white chocolate cream cheese frosting complements the fresh berries.

CAKE

1	package (18.25 oz/515 g) white cake mix	1
1	package (4-serving size) lemon instant pudding mix	1
4	eggs	4
¾ cup	sour cream	175 mL
¼ cup	vegetable oil	50 mL
1 cup	fresh blueberries	250 mL
1 cup	fresh raspberries	250 mL

WHITE CHOCOLATE CREAM CHEESE FROSTING

1 lb	white chocolate, chopped	500 g
1 lb	cream cheese, softened	500 g
1 cup	butter, softened	250 mL
2 tbsp	grated lemon zest	25 mL
3 tbsp	freshly squeezed lemon juice	45 mL

TIPS

- Use fresh berries in this cake. The frozen ones are too moist and will sink in the light, tender cake.
- The stiff batter keeps the berries from sinking.

- **Preheat oven to 350°F (180°C)**
- **Three 9-inch (23 cm) round cake pans, greased and floured**

1. **Cake:** In a large mixer bowl, combine cake mix, pudding mix, eggs, sour cream and oil. Beat on low speed for 1 minute to blend, then on medium speed for 2 minutes. Fold in berries, gently but thoroughly. Spread batter evenly in prepared pans. Bake for 25 to 30 minutes or until a tester inserted in center comes out clean. Cool for 10 minutes in pans on a wire rack, then remove and cool completely on rack.

2. **Frosting:** In a small saucepan or a double boiler, melt white chocolate over low heat, stirring constantly until smooth. Cool to lukewarm. In a large mixer bowl, beat cream cheese and butter on low speed until blended. Add lemon zest and lemon juice, then cooled white chocolate, beating until smooth.

3. **Assembly:** Place one cake top-side down on a serving plate. Spread about ¾ cup (175 mL) frosting on top. Repeat with second cake and frosting. Top with third cake layer, top-side up. Spread remaining frosting on top and sides of cake. Store in the refrigerator.

Variations: Use all raspberries or all blueberries. Bake cake in two 9-inch (23 cm) round cake pans and put more filling between the layers.

Lemon Cream Torte

If you like lemon, you'll love this cake.

CAKE

1	package (18.25 oz/515 g) white cake mix	1
3	eggs	3
1⅓ cups	water	325 mL
⅓ cup	vegetable oil	75 mL
1 tbsp	grated lemon zest	15 mL

FILLING

1	can (10 oz/300 mL) sweetened condensed milk	1
1 tbsp	grated lemon zest	15 mL
½ cup	lemon juice	125 mL
2 cups	whipping (35%) cream	500 mL
	Lemon slices (optional)	

TIPS

- Since the filling thickens as it is left standing, set it aside for 5 minutes before adding the cream.
- Use freshly squeezed lemon juice for the best flavor. Remember to zest the lemon before juicing.

- **Preheat oven to 350°F (180°C)**
- **Two 9-inch (23 cm) round cake pans, greased and floured**

1. **Cake:** In a large mixer bowl, combine cake mix, eggs, water, oil and lemon zest. Beat on medium speed for 2 minutes. Spread batter in prepared pans, dividing evenly. Bake for 30 to 35 minutes or until a tester inserted in center comes out clean. Cool for 10 minutes in pans on a wire rack, then remove and cool completely on rack. With a sharp knife, cut each cake horizontally in half to make 4 layers.

2. **Filling:** In a small bowl, combine sweetened condensed milk, lemon zest and lemon juice. Mix well. In a large mixer bowl, beat whipping cream to stiff peaks. Reserve 1 cup (250 mL) for garnish. Fold milk mixture into remaining whipped cream, gently but thoroughly.

3. **Assembly:** Place one cake layer, cut-side up, on serving plate. Spread with one-quarter of filling. Repeat with second and third cake layers. Top with fourth cake layer, cut-side down. Spread remaining filling on top, leaving a ½-inch (1 cm) border around edge. Pipe reserved cream around edge. Chill for at least 2 hours before serving. Garnish with lemon slices, if desired. Store in the refrigerator.

Variation: For an extra hit of lemon, use a lemon cake mix.

Lemon Poppy Seed Layer Cake

Poppy seeds add a pleasant crunch to this light, tangy, lemon-lover's cake. It's my mother's favorite cake, although she prefers it without the poppy seeds.

SERVES 10 TO 12

CAKE

1	package (18.25 oz/515 g) lemon cake mix	1
3	eggs	3
1⅓ cups	water	325 mL
⅓ cup	vegetable oil	75 mL
¼ cup	poppy seeds	50 mL

LEMON CURD FILLING

2	eggs	2
2 tbsp	grated lemon zest	25 mL
6 tbsp	freshly squeezed lemon juice	90 mL
1 cup	granulated sugar	250 mL
¼ cup	butter, softened	50 mL
	Lemon Butter Frosting (see recipe, page 258)	
	Candied lemon slices to garnish (optional)	

TIPS

- The lemon filling can be prepared several days ahead and refrigerated.
- Prepare entire cake a day ahead to let flavors mellow.
- Store poppy seeds in the freezer. Left at room temperature, they quickly develop a bitter, rancid taste.

- **Preheat oven to 350°F (180°C)**
- **Two 9-inch (23 cm) round cake pans, greased and floured**

1. **Cake:** In a large mixer bowl, combine cake mix, eggs, water and oil. Beat on medium speed for 2 minutes. Stir in poppy seeds. Spread batter in prepared pans, dividing evenly. Bake for 30 to 35 minutes or until a tester inserted in center comes out clean. Cool for 10 minutes in pans on a wire rack, then remove and cool completely on rack. With a long sharp knife, cut each layer horizontally in half to make 4 layers.

2. **Filling:** In a small saucepan, beat eggs, lemon zest, lemon juice and sugar together to blend. Add butter. Cook over low heat, stirring constantly, until smoothly thickened. Remove from heat. Cover surface with plastic wrap and cool completely. Store in covered container in the refrigerator.

3. **Assembly:** Prepare Lemon Butter Frosting. Place top half of one cake layer cut-side up on a serving plate. Spread half of lemon filling over surface. Place bottom half of cake layer, cut-side down on filling. Spread lemon frosting on center layer. Top with bottom half of remaining cake layer, cut side up. Cover with remaining filling and put remaining top cake layer in place over filling. Cover top and sides of cake with remaining frosting. Decorate with candied lemon slices, if desired. Chill overnight for optimum flavor and easy slicing.

Variation: Try it without the poppy seeds. You may agree with my mother!

Mandarin Cake

This tropical treat combines mandarin oranges, pineapple and coconut for a refreshing and delicious taste.

SERVES 10 TO 12

CAKE

1	package (18.25 oz/515 g) white cake mix	1
1	can (10 oz/284 mL) mandarin oranges, with juice	1
4	eggs	4
¾ cup	butter, melted	175 mL
⅓ cup	pineapple juice (reserved from pineapple in frosting)	75 mL

PINEAPPLE COCONUT CREAM FILLING AND TOPPING

4 cups	frozen whipped topping, thawed	1 L
1	package (4-serving size) vanilla instant pudding mix	1
¾ cup	toasted coconut	175 mL
⅔ cup	well-drained crushed pineapple, juice reserved	150 mL

TIPS

- For better flavor and a crunchy texture, toast the coconut. Spread it on a baking sheet and bake at 350°F (180°C) for 5 to 10 minutes, stirring often, until golden. Cool before using in recipes.
- Brushing fruit syrup from canned fruit over warm cakes keeps them moist. Pierce the top of the cake with a fork or a tester before brushing to help syrup soak in.

- **Preheat oven to 350°F (180°C)**
- **Two 9-inch (23 cm) round cake pans, greased and floured**

1. **Cake:** In a large mixer bowl, combine cake mix, mandarin oranges with juice, eggs and melted butter. Beat on medium speed for 2 minutes or until smooth. Spread batter in prepared pans, dividing evenly. Bake for 30 to 35 minutes or until a tester inserted in center comes out clean. Cool for 10 minutes in pans on a wire rack, then remove and cool completely on rack. Pierce top of cakes with a fork or a tester. Brush warm cakes with pineapple juice, letting it soak in. Cool completely.

2. **Filling and Topping:** In a large bowl, combine whipped topping and pudding mix. Mix gently until well blended. Fold in coconut and pineapple.

3. **Assembly:** Place one cake layer, top-side down, on serving plate. Cover with a generous layer, about 1½ cups (375 mL), of the topping. Place remaining cake, top-side up, over filling. Cover top and sides of cake with remaining topping. Chill until serving. Store leftover cake in the refrigerator.

Variation: Pineapple Cream Cheese Frosting (see recipe, page 265) works well on this cake. Garnish with toasted coconut.

Triple Raspberry Treat

With three layers of raspberry, this cake is a real treat.

CAKE

1	package (18.25 oz/515 g) white cake mix	1
3	eggs	3
1 cup	water	250 mL
1/3 cup	raspberry liqueur	75 mL
1/3 cup	vegetable oil	75 mL

FILLING AND FROSTING

1 cup	butter, softened	250 mL
4 cups	confectioner's (icing) sugar, sifted	1 L
1/3 cup	raspberry liqueur	75 mL
1/4 cup	half-and-half (10%) cream	50 mL
1 cup	raspberry jam, divided	250 mL
	Fresh raspberries to garnish (optional)	

TIPS

- Although raspberry liqueur is expensive, the flavor is so intense that a little goes a long way.
- Use homemade jam, if it's available, as it has a more intense fruit taste.
- Don't use the "light" jams or fruit spreads in this recipe, as the consistency is too soft.

- **Preheat oven to 350°F (180°C)**
- **Three 8-inch (20 cm) or 9-inch (23 cm) round cake pans, greased and floured**

1. **Cake:** In a large mixer bowl, combine cake mix, eggs, water, liqueur and oil. Beat on medium speed for 2 minutes. Spread batter in prepared pans, dividing evenly. Bake for 20 to 25 minutes or until a tester inserted in center comes out clean. Cool for 10 minutes in pans on a wire rack, then remove and cool completely on rack. With a long sharp knife, cut each layer horizontally in half to make 6 layers.

2. **Filling and Frosting:** In a large mixer bowl, beat butter until creamy. Gradually add confectioner's sugar, liqueur and cream, beating until smooth.

3. **Assembly:** Place one cake layer, cut-side up, on a serving plate. Spread with 1/3 cup (75 mL) of the jam. Top with another layer, cut-side down. Spread with 1/2 cup (125 mL) of the frosting. Repeat with remaining layers, jam and frosting, ending with a cake layer, cut-side down. Frost top and sides of cake with remaining frosting. If desired, pipe some frosting on top of cake for an attractive finish. Garnish with fresh berries. Store in the refrigerator.

Variation: Replace raspberry liqueur and jam with strawberry liqueur and jam and garnish with fresh strawberries.

Banana Spice Cake with Cinnamon Banana Frosting

The subtle spices in this cake help to bring out the banana flavor.

SERVES 10 TO 12		
1	package (18.25 oz/515 g) white cake mix	1
⅓ cup	packed brown sugar	75 mL
1 tsp	ground cinnamon	5 mL
¼ tsp	ground nutmeg	1 mL
3	eggs	3
1 cup	water	250 mL
1 cup	mashed ripe bananas (2 to 3 medium)	250 mL
½ cup	vegetable oil	125 mL
	Banana Butter Frosting (see recipe, page 264)	
¼ tsp	ground cinnamon	1 mL

TIPS

- Mashed bananas not only add flavor to cakes but keep them moist. I like to mash bananas by hand using a fork on a flat plate. If you use a food processor, stop while the mixture is still thick. Don't overprocess or the texture of the bananas will become too thin.
- To soften hard, lumpy brown sugar, put a slice of apple in the bag and leave it for a few days. For immediate results, put apple and brown sugar in a microwave-safe bowl. Cover and heat on high for 30 seconds. Remove apple and stir.

- **Preheat oven to 350°F (180°C)**
- **Two 9-inch (23 cm) round cake pans, greased and floured**

1. In a large mixer bowl, combine cake mix, brown sugar, 1 tsp (5 mL) cinnamon, nutmeg, eggs, water, bananas and oil. Beat on medium speed for 2 minutes or until smooth. Spread batter in prepared pans, dividing evenly. Bake for 30 to 35 minutes or until a tester inserted in center comes out clean. Cool for 10 minutes in pans on a wire rack, then remove and cool completely on rack.

2. Prepare Banana Butter Frosting, adding ¼ tsp (1 mL) cinnamon with the confectioner's sugar.

3. Place one cake layer top-side down on a serving plate. Spread a generous amount of frosting on top. Place second cake layer top-side up over frosting. Cover top and sides of cake with remaining frosting. Chill until serving to firm up frosting for neater slicing.

Variation: This cake is also delicious with a cream cheese frosting flavored with a hint of cinnamon.

Cranberry Orange Cake

Here's a cake with flavor that dazzles.

CAKE

1	package (18.25 oz/515 g) white cake mix	1
3	eggs	3
1 tbsp	grated orange zest	15 mL
1⅓ cups	orange juice	325 mL
⅓ cup	vegetable oil	75 mL

FROSTING

1	can (14 oz/398 mL) whole-berry cranberry sauce	1
1	package (4-serving size) vanilla pudding mix	1
1 tbsp	grated orange zest	15 mL
½ cup	orange juice	125 mL
4 cups	frozen whipped topping, thawed	1 L

TIPS

- My first choice for juice is freshly squeezed, followed by commercially prepared juice with pulp.
- After removing the zest, warm oranges slightly in the microwave to get the most juice.
- Sliced almonds are a nice garnish on this cake.

- **Preheat oven to 350°F (180°C)**
- **Two 9-inch (23 cm) round cake pans, greased and floured**

1. **Cake:** In a large mixer bowl, combine cake mix, eggs, orange zest, orange juice and oil. Beat on medium speed for 2 minutes. Spread batter in prepared pans, dividing evenly. Bake for 25 to 30 minutes or until a tester inserted in center comes out clean. Cool for 10 minutes in pans on a wire rack, then remove and cool completely on rack. With a long sharp knife, cut cakes horizontally in half to make 4 layers.

2. **Frosting:** In a large bowl, combine cranberry sauce, pudding mix, orange zest and orange juice. Mix well. Let stand for 10 minutes to thicken. Fold in whipped topping, gently but thoroughly.

3. **Assembly:** Place one cake layer, cut-side up, on a serving plate. Spread with ¾ cup (175 mL) of the frosting. Repeat with remaining cake layers and frosting, ending with a cake layer, cut-side down. Spread frosting on sides and top of cake. Chill until serving. Store leftover cake in the refrigerator.

Variation: Replace whipped topping with 2 cups (500 mL) whipping (35%) cream, slightly sweetened and beaten to stiff peaks.

Spice Cake with Blackberries

Fresh blackberries and a creamy frosting add a touch of sophistication to spice cake.

SERVES 10 TO 12

CAKE

1	package (18.25 oz/515 g) spice cake mix	1

FILLING

1½ cups	fresh blackberries	375 mL
¼ cup	granulated sugar	50 mL

FROSTING

1½	recipes Basic Cream Cheese Frosting (see recipe, page 265)	1½

GARNISH

1 cup	fresh blackberries	250 mL

TIPS

- Prepare cake the day before, for convenience. Leave the final berry garnish until you're ready to serve.
- If you can't find a spice cake mix, add 2 tsp (10 mL) ground cinnamon and ½ tsp (2 mL) each ground nutmeg and cloves to a white cake mix.

- **Preheat oven to 350°F (180°C)**
- **Three 8-inch (20 cm) or 9-inch (23 cm) round cake pans, greased and floured**

1. **Cake:** Prepare cake mix according to package directions. Spread batter in prepared pans, dividing evenly. Bake for 20 to 25 minutes or until a tester inserted in center comes out clean. Cool for 10 minutes in pans on a wire rack, then remove and cool completely on rack.

2. **Filling:** Mash berries slightly with fork. Mix with sugar. Let stand for about 30 minutes or until juices are released.

3. **Assembly:** Prepare Basic Cream Cheese Frosting as directed. Place one cake top-side down on a serving plate. Spread with 1 cup (250 mL) of frosting. Spread half of filling over frosting, leaving a ½-inch (1 cm) plain border around edge. Repeat with second cake. Top with third cake, top-side up. Spread remaining frosting over top and sides of cake. Garnish with fresh blackberries. Chill until serving. Store leftover cake in the refrigerator.

Variation: Raspberries are a tasty and attractive alternative to blackberries.

Blueberry Lemon Cake

This cake is creamy, light and lemony — how can you go wrong?

SERVES 12 TO 16

CAKE

1	package (18.25 oz/515 g) lemon cake mix	1
1	package (4-serving size) vanilla instant pudding mix	1
4	eggs	4
¾ cup	sour cream	175 mL
¼ cup	vegetable oil	50 mL
2 cups	fresh blueberries	500 mL

LEMON CREAM CHEESE FROSTING

1 lb	cream cheese, softened	500 g
¾ cup	butter, softened	175 mL
4 cups	confectioner's (icing) sugar, sifted	1 L
1 tbsp	grated lemon zest	15 mL

- **Preheat oven to 350°F (180°C)**
- **Three 9-inch (23 cm) round cake pans, greased and floured**

1. **Cake:** In a large mixer bowl, combine cake mix, pudding mix, eggs, sour cream and oil. Beat on low speed for 1 minute to blend, then on medium speed for 2 minutes. Fold in blueberries, gently but thoroughly. Spread batter evenly in prepared pans. Bake for 25 to 30 minutes or until a tester inserted in center comes out clean. Cool for 10 minutes in pans on a wire rack, then remove and cool completely on rack.

2. **Frosting:** In a bowl, beat cream cheese and butter until light and fluffy. Gradually add confectioner's sugar, beating until smooth. Stir in lemon zest.

3. **Assembly:** Place one cake top-side down on a serving plate. Spread about ¾ cup (175 mL) frosting on top. Repeat with second cake and frosting. Top with third cake layer top-side up. Spread remaining frosting on top and sides of cake. Store in the refrigerator.

Toffee Crunch Cake

Butterscotch pudding mix adds great flavor to a plain cake mix.

SERVES 12 TO 16

CAKE

1	package (18.25 oz/515 g) yellow or white cake mix	1
1	package (4-serving size) butterscotch instant pudding mix	1
3	eggs	3
1 cup	milk	250 mL
½ cup	butter, melted	125 mL
⅔ cup	toffee bits	150 mL

TOFFEE CREAM FILLING AND TOPPING

2 cups	whipping (35%) cream	500 mL
3 tbsp	packed brown sugar	45 mL
1½ cups	toffee bits	375 mL
⅔ cup	sliced almonds, toasted	150 mL

- **Preheat oven to 350°F (180°C)**
- **Two 9-inch (23 cm) round cake pans, greased and floured**

1. **Cake:** In a large mixer bowl, beat cake mix, pudding mix, eggs, milk and butter on low speed for 1 minute, then on medium speed for 2 minutes. Fold in toffee bits. Spread batter evenly in prepared pans. Bake for 30 to 35 minutes or until a tester inserted in center comes out clean. Cool for 10 minutes in pans on a wire rack, then remove and cool completely on rack.

2. **Filling and Topping:** In a medium bowl, beat whipping cream and brown sugar to stiff peaks.

3. **Assembly:** Place one cake layer top-side down on a serving plate. Spread about ¾ cup (175 mL) cream over cake. Sprinkle with ½ cup (125 mL) toffee bits. Top with second cake layer. Cover top and sides of cake with remaining cream. Combine remaining toffee bits and almonds. Press into sides and top of cake. Store in the refrigerator.

Strawberry Meringue Shortcake

A real showpiece. The almond meringue topping and cake bake together, leaving only the filling to add.

SERVES 10 TO 12

CAKE

1	package (18.25 oz/515 g) white cake mix	1
4	egg yolks	4
1⅛ cups	water	275 mL
2 tbsp	vegetable oil	25 mL

MERINGUE TOPPING

4	egg whites	4
1 cup	granulated sugar	250 mL
⅔ cup	toasted sliced almonds	150 mL

FILLING

2 cups	whipping (35%) cream	500 mL
2 tbsp	confectioner's (icing) sugar, sifted	25 mL
1 tsp	vanilla	5 mL
2 cups	fresh strawberries	500 mL

TIPS

- You'll need 3 pans for this recipe, 2 rounds for the shortcake and another for a leftover cake that the family can enjoy.
- Buy extra fruit to scatter on the plate around the cake for a stunning presentation.
- For neat, easy removal of cakes from pans, loosen edge with a knife, then turn over on a tea-towel-covered board. Remove paper and turn over right-side up on rack.

- **Preheat oven to 350°F (180°C)**
- **Two 9-inch (23 cm) round cake pans and one 8-inch (20 cm) or 9-inch (23 cm) round or square pan, greased and lined with waxed paper or parchment in bottom**

1. **Cake:** In a large mixer bowl, combine cake mix, egg yolks, water and oil. Beat on medium speed for 2 minutes. Remove 2 cups (500 mL) batter. Spread it in extra prepared round or square pan. Bake as directed and reserve for another use. Spread remaining batter evenly in prepared round pans and bake.

2. **Topping:** In a small mixer bowl, beat egg whites until frothy. Gradually add sugar, beating to stiff peaks. Carefully spread meringue over batter in round pans, sealing meringue to edge of pan. Sprinkle almonds evenly on top. Bake for 25 to 30 minutes or until crisp and golden. Meringue will puff during baking. Cool completely in pans on a wire rack. Carefully remove from pans. (See tip, at left, for technique.)

3. **Filling:** Beat cream, confectioner's sugar and vanilla together until stiff peaks form.

4. **Assembly:** Place one cake layer meringue-side down on a serving plate. Spread cream on top. Reserve a few whole berries for top. Slice remaining berries and place over cream. Put second cake layer meringue-side up over berries. Garnish top with whole berries. Chill until serving. Store leftover cake in the refrigerator.

Variation: Other fruits work well. Try raspberries, blueberries and peach slices — or any other colorful combination of fruits.

Pralines 'n' Cream Pecan Cake

If pralines 'n' cream is your favorite ice cream, here's a way to enjoy the flavor in a cake. The presentation is a knockout.

SERVES 12 TO 16

CAKE

1	package (18.25 oz/515 g) white cake mix	1
1	package (4-serving size) vanilla instant pudding mix	1
4	eggs	4
1⅓ cups	sour cream	325 mL
½ cup	vegetable oil	125 mL
1½ cups	chopped pecans	375 mL

PECAN PRALINE TOPPING

1	egg white	1
1 tbsp	water	15 mL
½ cup	packed brown sugar	125 mL
1½ cups	pecan halves	375 mL

CREAM CHEESE FROSTING

12 oz	cream cheese, softened	375 g
½ cup	butter, softened	125 mL
2 tsp	vanilla	10 mL
4 cups	confectioner's (icing) sugar, sifted	1 L

TIPS

- Make an extra batch of praline for munching on or your cake could be bare!
- Prepare pecan praline topping up to 3 days ahead.

- **Preheat oven to 350°F (180°C)**
- **Two 9-inch (23 cm) round cake pans, greased and floured**
- **Rimmed baking sheet, greased**

1. **Cake:** In a large mixer bowl, combine cake mix, pudding mix, eggs, sour cream and oil. Beat on medium speed for 2 minutes. Fold in pecans. Spread batter in prepared pans, dividing evenly. Bake for 30 to 35 minutes or until a tester inserted in center comes out clean. Cool for 10 minutes in pans on a wire rack, then remove and cool completely on rack.

2. **Topping:** Preheat oven to 300°F (150°C). In a small bowl, beat egg white and water with a fork until foamy. Add brown sugar, mixing until sugar dissolves. Add pecans, tossing to coat nuts with sugar mixture. Spread on prepared baking sheet. Bake for 25 minutes, stirring occasionally, until nuts are crisp and browned. Remove from oven. Stir to loosen nuts from sheet. Cool completely on sheet.

3. **Frosting:** In a large mixer bowl, beat cream cheese, butter and vanilla until light and fluffy. Gradually add confectioner's sugar, beating until smooth.

4. **Assembly:** Place one cake top-side down on serving plate. Spread 1½ cups (375 mL) of the frosting over cake. Top with second cake layer, top-side up. Spread remaining frosting over top and sides of cake. Arrange Pecan Praline Topping over cake, mounding slightly in center. Refrigerate until serving. Store in the refrigerator.

Variations: Try your favorite chocolate cake mix. Replace pecans with unblanched almonds. Use whole almonds in the topping.

Mocha Toffee Cake

With a layer of frosting covered by a whipped cream topping, this cake is definitely decadent — but one bite will convince you that it's worth every calorie.

CAKE

1	package (18.25 oz/515 g) devil's food cake mix	1
1 tbsp	instant coffee powder	15 mL
3	eggs	3
1 cup	water	250 mL
½ cup	sour cream	125 mL
⅓ cup	vegetable oil	75 mL

WHITE CHOCOLATE COFFEE FROSTING

½ cup	whipping (35%) cream	125 mL
4 oz	white chocolate, chopped	125 g
⅓ cup	coffee liqueur or cold strong coffee	75 mL
1 cup	butter, softened	250 mL
2 cups	confectioner's (icing) sugar, sifted	500 mL

WHIPPED CREAM TOPPING AND GARNISH

2 cups	whipping (35%) cream	500 mL
3 tbsp	confectioner's (icing) sugar, sifted	45 mL
4	toffee chocolate bars (1.4 oz/40 g each), crushed	4

TIPS

- Use cold strong coffee instead of the water and coffee powder. If you don't like the taste of coffee, you can omit it.
- Chill chocolate bars for easy crushing.
- To save time when assembling the cake, prepare cake layers ahead and freeze. Defrost for 1 hour before assembly.

- **Preheat oven to 350°F (180°C)**
- **Three 9-inch (23 cm) round cake pans, greased and floured**

1. **Cake:** In a large mixer bowl, combine cake mix, coffee powder, eggs, water, sour cream and oil. Beat on medium speed for 2 minutes. Spread in prepared pans, dividing evenly. Bake for 20 to 25 minutes or until a tester inserted in center comes out clean. Cool for 10 minutes in pans on a wire rack, then remove and cool completely on rack.

2. **Frosting:** In a small saucepan, heat whipping cream and white chocolate on low heat, stirring until melted. Remove from heat. Stir in liqueur. Refrigerate for about 45 minutes, until cool. In a large mixer bowl, beat butter and confectioner's sugar on medium speed until light and creamy. Gradually add chocolate mixture, beating until smooth.

3. **Topping:** In a large mixer bowl, beat whipping cream and confectioner's sugar to stiff peaks.

4. **Assembly:** Place one cake top-side down on serving plate. Spread with ¾ cup (175 mL) of White Chocolate Coffee Frosting. Repeat with remaining cake layers and frosting, ending with a cake layer, top-side up. Frost sides and top of cake with remaining White Chocolate Coffee Frosting. Chill for about 30 minutes, until firm. Spread Whipped Cream Topping on sides and top of cake. Press crushed candy on sides and top of cake. Store in the refrigerator.

Variation: Use water for the cake and replace the liqueur in the frosting with milk or cream.

Carrot Cake with Orange Cream Cheese Frosting

Orange adds a nice touch to the traditional mildly spiced carrot cake and plain cream cheese frosting.

SERVES 10 TO 12

1	package (18.25 oz/515 g) white cake mix	1
1	package (4-serving size) vanilla instant pudding mix	1
1½ tsp	ground cinnamon	7 mL
¼ tsp	ground nutmeg	1 mL
4	eggs	4
¾ cup	orange juice	175 mL
½ cup	vegetable oil	125 mL
3 cups	grated peeled carrots	750 mL
¾ cup	raisins	175 mL
1 tbsp	grated orange zest	15 mL
	Orange Cream Cheese Frosting (see recipe, page 265)	

- **Preheat oven to 350°F (180°C)**
- **Two 9-inch (23 cm) round cake pans, greased and floured**

1. In a large mixer bowl, combine cake mix, pudding mix, spices, eggs, orange juice and oil. Beat on medium speed for 2 minutes or until smooth. Add carrots, raisins and orange zest. Mix well. Spread batter in prepared pans, dividing evenly. Bake for 35 to 40 minutes or until a tester inserted in center comes out clean. Cool for 10 minutes in pans on a wire rack, then remove and cool completely on rack.

2. Prepare Orange Cream Cheese Frosting. Place one cake layer top-side down on a serving plate. Spread a generous amount of frosting on top. Place second cake layer top-side up over frosting. Cover top and sides of cake with remaining frosting. Chill until serving.

Coconut Walnut Carrot Cake

Coconut adds a different texture and taste to a favorite cake. The layer cake presentation is a nice look. Frost with Cream Cheese Frosting (page 265) and garnish with toasted coconut.

SERVES 12 TO 16

1	package (18.25 oz/515 g) white cake mix	1
1	package (4-serving size) vanilla instant pudding mix	1
4	eggs	4
2½ cups	grated peeled carrots	625 mL
⅓ cup	vegetable oil	75 mL
¼ cup	water	50 mL
1 tsp	ground cinnamon	5 mL
1 tsp	ground ginger	5 mL
½ tsp	ground nutmeg	2 mL
⅔ cup	chopped walnuts	150 mL
⅔ cup	flaked coconut	150 mL

- **Preheat oven to 350°F (180°C)**
- **Two 9-inch (23 cm) round cake pans, greased and floured**

1. In a large mixer bowl, combine cake mix, pudding mix, eggs, carrots, oil, water, cinnamon, ginger and nutmeg. Beat on low speed for 1 minute to blend, then on medium speed for 2 minutes. Stir in walnuts and coconut. Spread batter in prepared pans, dividing evenly. Bake for 35 to 40 minutes or until a tester inserted in center comes out clean. Cool for 10 minutes in pans on a wire rack, then remove and cool completely on rack. Fill and frost cakes as desired.

Variation: Hazelnuts, almonds or pecans can replace walnuts.

TIP

- Flaked rather than shredded coconut provides the best texture in most recipes.

Tube and Bundt Cakes

Tube cakes and Bundt cakes can suit both everyday and special occasions. Generally quick and easy to make, they lend themselves to the addition of other ingredients such as nuts, puréed vegetables and fruits. If for no other reason, they are impressive because of their shape. A burst of flavor can be added by brushing syrup on the warm cake and letting it soak in. These cakes may be served plain or finished with a simple glaze, a dusting of confectioner's sugar or a basic frosting.

Milk Chocolate Fleck Cake

This moist cake has an appealing mild chocolate taste. It's a delicious coffee-time treat.

SERVES 12 TO 16		
CAKE		
1	package (18.25 oz/515 g) white cake mix	1
1	package (4-serving size) vanilla instant pudding mix	1
4	eggs	4
1 cup	sour cream	250 mL
½ cup	vegetable oil	125 mL
7 oz	milk chocolate, coarsely grated	210 g
GLAZE (OPTIONAL)		
1 tsp	vegetable oil	5 mL
2 oz	milk chocolate, melted (see page 13)	60 g

- **Preheat oven to 350°F (180°C)**
- **10-inch (3 L) Bundt pan, greased and floured**

1. **Cake:** In a large mixer bowl, combine cake mix, pudding mix, eggs, sour cream and oil. Beat on medium speed for 2 minutes. Stir in chocolate, gently but thoroughly. Spread batter evenly in prepared pan. Bake for 50 to 60 minutes or until a tester inserted in center comes out clean. Cool for 25 minutes in pan on a wire rack, then remove from pan and place on rack. Enjoy warm or cool completely and glaze or sprinkle with confectioner's sugar.

2. **Glaze:** If desired, stir oil into melted chocolate. Drizzle over cake. Chill to set chocolate.

Variation: Use bittersweet chocolate if you prefer a stronger chocolate taste.

Chocolate Cream-Filled Bundt Cake

The combination of dark chocolate cake drizzled with a bright white glaze and filled with a creamy white center is more than visually stunning. It's also delicious.

SERVES 12 TO 16		
FILLING		
8 oz	cream cheese, softened	250 g
¼ cup	granulated sugar	50 mL
1	egg	1
1 tsp	vanilla	5 mL
CAKE		
1	package (18.25 oz/5.5 g) devil's food cake mix	1
GLAZE		
1 cup	confectioner's (icing) sugar, sifted	250 mL
¼ tsp	vanilla	1 mL
1 to 2 tbsp	water or milk	15 to 25 mL

TIP

- You can bake this cake, then freeze it before adding the finish. When ready to serve, thaw and drizzle with glaze or dust with confectioner's sugar.

- **Preheat oven to 350°F (180°C)**
- **10-inch (3 L) Bundt pan, greased and floured**

1. **Filling:** In a small mixer bowl, beat cream cheese and sugar on low speed until blended. Add egg and vanilla, beating until smooth, about 2 minutes. Set aside.

2. **Cake:** Prepare cake mix according to package directions. Pour 3 cups (750 mL) of the batter into prepared pan. Spoon filling over batter without touching sides of pan. Cover with remaining batter. Bake for 50 to 60 minutes or until a tester inserted into cake (avoiding filling) comes out clean. Cool for 30 minutes in pan on a wire rack, then remove from pan and cool completely on rack set over waxed paper.

3. **Glaze:** In a small bowl, combine confectioner's sugar and vanilla. Stir in enough water to make a smooth drizzling consistency. Drizzle over cake.

Variation: For a dark chocolate color and richer flavor, use a chocolate fudge cake mix.

Chocolate Coffee Bundt Cake

The unique buttery, sugary coffee glaze does more than keep this cake moist. It also makes it especially delicious.

SERVES 12 TO 16

GLAZE

1 cup	granulated sugar	250 mL
½ cup	butter	125 mL
½ cup	prepared black coffee	125 mL
¼ cup	coffee liqueur	50 mL

CAKE

1	package (18.25 oz/515 g) devil's food cake mix	1
1	package (4-serving size) chocolate instant pudding mix	1
4	eggs	4
½ cup	water	125 mL
¼ cup	coffee liqueur	50 mL
1 tsp	ground cinnamon	5 mL
1 cup	miniature semi-sweet chocolate chips	250 mL

TIPS

- Liqueurs can often be replaced with a non-alcoholic liquid with a similar flavor. For example, in this cake you can use strong coffee for the coffee liqueur, if you prefer. Add to saucepan along with the other ingredients.
- If desired, dust this cake with confectioner's sugar just before serving.

- **Preheat oven to 350°F (180°C)**
- **10-inch (3 L) Bundt pan, greased and floured**

1. **Glaze:** In a small saucepan, combine sugar, butter and coffee. Bring to a boil over medium heat, stirring to dissolve sugar, then boil for 3 minutes. Remove from heat. Stir in liqueur. Let cool while preparing cake.

2. **Cake:** In a large mixer bowl, combine cake mix, pudding mix, eggs, water, liqueur and cinnamon. Beat on medium speed for 2 minutes. Stir in chocolate chips. Spread batter evenly in prepared pan. Bake for 50 to 55 minutes or until a tester inserted in center comes out clean. Cool for 20 minutes in pan on a wire rack, then remove from pan and cool completely on rack set over waxed paper.

3. Poke holes over surface of warm cake with fork or toothpick. Brush half of glaze over cake, letting it soak in for about 10 minutes. Brush remaining glaze over cake. Cool completely before cutting cake.

Variation: Replace coffee liqueur with orange liqueur. Omit cinnamon and add 1 tbsp (15 mL) grated orange zest to the batter.

Decadent Chocolate Bundt Cake

Easy, moist and loaded with chocolate. What could be better?

SERVES 12 TO 16

CAKE

1	package (18.25 oz/515 g) devil's food cake mix	1
1	package (4-serving size) chocolate instant pudding mix	1
4	eggs	4
1 cup	sour cream	250 mL
½ cup	water	125 mL
1 cup	milk chocolate chips	250 mL

FROSTING

⅔ cup	milk chocolate chips, melted	150 mL
⅓ cup	sour cream	75 mL

TIP

- Whatever you put in a Bundt pan will look special. You can use a 13- by 9-inch (3 L) pan and bake for about 40 minutes if you don't have a Bundt pan.

- **Preheat oven to 350°F (180°C)**
- **10-inch (3 L) Bundt pan, greased and floured**

1. **Cake:** In a large mixer bowl, combine cake mix, pudding mix, eggs, sour cream and water. Beat on medium speed for 2 minutes. Stir in chocolate chips. Spread batter evenly in prepared pan. Bake for 50 to 60 minutes or until a tester inserted in center comes out clean. Cool for 25 minutes in pan on a wire rack, then remove cake and cool completely.

2. **Frosting:** Combine melted chocolate chips and sour cream, stirring until smooth. Spread over top of cake. Cool to let frosting set.

Variations: Replace milk chocolate chips with semi-sweet or white. For a sweeter cake, use all of the chips for the cake and frost with a ready-to-serve chocolate frosting, warmed slightly for easy spreading.

Double Chocolate Delight

This cake is rich, moist and very chocolaty. It may not last long, but if it does, it keeps very well.

SERVES 12 TO 16

1	package (18.25 oz/515 g) white cake mix	1
⅓ cup	granulated sugar	75 mL
⅓ cup	unsweetened cocoa powder, sifted	75 mL
4	eggs	4
1 cup	sour cream	250 mL
⅔ cup	vegetable oil	150 mL
1½ cups	miniature semi-sweet chocolate chips	375 mL

- **Preheat oven to 350°F (180°C)**
- **10-inch (3 L) Bundt pan, greased and floured**

1. In a large mixer bowl, combine cake mix, sugar, cocoa, eggs, sour cream and oil. Beat on low speed for 1 minute to blend, then on medium speed for 2 minutes. Stir in chocolate chips. Spread batter evenly in prepared pan. Bake for 50 to 60 minutes or until a tester inserted in center comes out clean. Cool for 25 minutes in pan on a wire rack, then remove from pan and cool completely on rack.

Variation: Replace semi-sweet chips with milk chocolate chips.

TIPS

- Always sift cocoa before using. It clumps during storage and the lumps don't come out, even during beating.
- If you really want to overdose on chocolate, a chocolate drizzle (see page 92) makes a nice finish.

Double Chocolate Rum Cake

A dense, moist chocolate cake layered with a creamy chocolate rum filling. A nice and easy dessert for entertaining.

SERVES 12 TO 16

CAKE

1	package (18.25 oz/515 g) chocolate cake mix	1
1	package (4-serving size) chocolate instant pudding mix	1
4	eggs	4
⅔ cup	water	150 mL
½ cup	vegetable oil	125 mL
⅓ cup	rum	75 mL

CHOCOLATE RUM FILLING

1	envelope (1.3 oz/42.5 g) whipped topping mix	1
1	package (4-serving size) chocolate instant pudding mix	1
1 cup	cold milk	250 mL
¼ cup	rum	50 mL
	Confectioner's (icing) sugar (optional)	

TIP

- You can use rum extract in place of real rum. For the cake, mix 1 tbsp (15 mL) rum extract and ¼ cup (50 mL) water. For the filling, mix 1½ tsp (7 mL) extract and 3 tbsp (45 mL) water.

- **Preheat oven to 350°F (180°C)**
- **10-inch (4 L) tube pan, greased and floured**

1. **Cake:** In a large mixer bowl, combine cake mix, pudding mix, eggs, water, oil and rum. Beat on medium speed for 2 minutes. Spread batter evenly in prepared pan. Bake for 55 to 60 minutes or until a tester inserted in center comes out clean. Cool for 25 minutes in pan on a wire rack, then remove cake and cool completely. With a long sharp knife, cut cake horizontally to make 3 layers.

2. **Filling:** In a small mixer bowl, combine topping mix, pudding mix, milk and rum. Beat on high speed for about 7 minutes or until fluffy. Place bottom cake layer on a serving plate. Spread half of cream mixture on top. Place middle cake layer over the cream and spread with remaining cream. Put top cake layer in place. Chill until serving. Finish with a dusting of confectioner's sugar before serving, if desired. Store leftover cake in the refrigerator.

Variation: Replace chocolate pudding with vanilla for a milder chocolate flavor.

Double Chocolate Coconut Rum Cake

Chock-full of ingredients, this rich and delicious cake is a great treat after a light meal.

SERVES 12 TO 16

CAKE

1	package (18.25 oz/515 g) devil's food cake mix	1
1	package (4-serving size) chocolate instant pudding mix	1
4	eggs	4
1 cup	sour cream	250 mL
2/3 cup	whipping (35%) cream	150 mL
1/2 cup	vegetable oil	125 mL
3 tbsp	water	45 mL
3 tbsp	rum	45 mL
1 1/2 cups	white chocolate chips	375 mL
1 cup	flaked coconut	250 mL

GLAZE

1 2/3 cups	confectioner's (icing) sugar	400 mL
2 tbsp	butter, softened	25 mL
2 tbsp	milk	25 mL
1 tbsp	rum (approx.)	15 mL
	Coconut to garnish (optional)	

- **Preheat oven to 350°F (180°C)**
- **10-inch (3 L) Bundt pan or 10-inch (4 L) tube pan, greased and floured**

1. **Cake:** In a large mixer bowl, combine cake mix, pudding mix, eggs, sour cream, whipping cream, oil, water and rum. Beat on low speed for 1 minute to blend, then on medium speed for 2 minutes. Stir in white chocolate chips and coconut. Spread batter evenly in prepared pan. Bake for 50 to 55 minutes or until a tester inserted in center comes out clean. Cool for 20 minutes in pan on a wire rack, then place on rack set over waxed paper.

2. **Glaze:** In a mixer bowl, combine confectioner's sugar, butter and milk. Beat on low speed, adding enough rum to make a smooth spreadable consistency. Spread on top and sides of warm cake. Sprinkle coconut over glaze, if desired. Cool completely before cutting cake.

TIPS

- If you're feeling adventurous, try using shaved coconut, which is usually sold in South Asian grocery stores, in this recipe. It has a different texture than flaked coconut. A light toasting looks attractive on the white frosting.
- The soft glaze will melt slightly when applied to the warm cake. The waxed paper will catch any drips.

Pistachio Fudge Marble Cake

The unusual combination of a pale green cake with chocolate swirls is both attractive and delicious.

SERVES 12 TO 16

CAKE

1	package (18.25 oz/515 g) fudge marble cake mix	1
1	package (4-serving size) pistachio instant pudding mix	1
4	eggs	4
1 cup	water	250 mL
⅓ cup	vegetable oil	75 mL
5	drops green food coloring (optional)	5

FROSTING

1	package (4-serving size) pistachio instant pudding mix	1
2	envelopes (each 1.3 oz/ 42.5 g) whipped topping mix	2
1¼ cups	cold milk	300 mL
	Green food coloring (optional)	
	Chocolate curls (see tip, page 20) or shaved chocolate (optional)	

- **Preheat oven to 350°F (180°C)**
- **10-inch (4 L) tube pan, greased and floured**

1. **Cake:** In a large mixer bowl, combine large cake mix packet, pudding mix, eggs, water and oil. Beat on medium speed for 2 minutes. Stir in food coloring, if desired. Transfer 1 cup (250 mL) batter to another bowl and stir in small cocoa packet from cake mix. Spread half of green batter in prepared pan. Drizzle half of chocolate batter on top. Repeat layers with remaining batters. Run tip of knife through batters to create a marble effect. Bake for 45 to 50 minutes or until a tester inserted in center comes out clean. Cool for 30 minutes in pan on a wire rack, then remove and cool completely.

2. **Frosting:** In a large mixer bowl, combine pudding mix, whipped topping mixes and milk. Beat on high speed until stiff peaks form, about 3 minutes. Beat in coloring, if desired. Spread frosting on top and sides of cake. Decorate with chocolate, if desired. Chill until serving. Store leftover cake in the refrigerator.

TIPS

- For a potluck party, bake the cake in a 13- by 9-inch (3 L) pan for 35 minutes and serve individual pieces with a spoonful of the frosting on top.
- Use the green food coloring to suit your taste. The pudding by itself will give a hint of green. Added coloring will create more vibrancy.

Chocolate Macaroon Ring Cake

The macaroon filling sinks during baking to produce an attractive white swirl.

SERVES 12 TO 16		
FILLING		
2	egg whites	2
½ tsp	almond extract	2 mL
½ cup	granulated sugar	125 mL
½ cup	flaked coconut	125 mL
¼ cup	all-purpose flour	50 mL
CAKE		
1	package (18.25 oz/515 g) devil's food cake mix	1
2	egg yolks	2
1	whole egg	1
1 cup	water	250 mL
⅓ cup	vegetable oil	75 mL
GLAZE		
1 cup	confectioner's (icing) sugar, sifted	250 mL
4 tsp	milk	20 mL
1 tsp	vegetable oil	5 mL

- **Preheat oven to 350°F (180°C)**
- **10-inch (4 L) tube pan, greased and floured**

1. **Filling:** In a small mixer bowl, on high speed, beat egg whites and almond extract until frothy. Gradually add sugar, beating to soft peaks. Stir in coconut and flour, mixing gently but thoroughly.

2. **Cake:** In a large mixer bowl, combine cake mix, egg yolks, whole egg, water and oil. Beat on medium speed for 2 minutes. Pour half of batter into prepared pan. Spoon filling over batter without allowing it to touch sides of pan. Cover with remaining batter. Bake for 55 to 65 minutes or until a tester inserted in center comes out clean. Cool for 25 minutes in pan on a wire rack, then remove cake and cool completely.

3. **Glaze:** Combine all glaze ingredients, adding enough milk to make a smooth consistency. Spread glaze over top of cake, letting it drip down the sides.

Variation: Replace almond extract with vanilla.

TIP
- Flaked coconut works best for macaroons. Sweetened or unsweetened is a matter of taste.

Banana Split Cake

A banana split without the ice cream.

SERVES 12 TO 16		
1	package (18.25 oz/515 g) white cake mix	1
3	eggs	3
1 cup	water	250 mL
1 cup	mashed ripe bananas (2 or 3 large)	250 mL
1¼ cups	chopped, drained maraschino cherries	300 mL
⅔ cup	miniature semi-sweet chocolate chips	150 mL

TIP
- A chocolate glaze (see recipes, page 268) is nice for company, but a sprinkling of confectioner's sugar does just fine for family.

- **Preheat oven to 350°F (180°C)**
- **10-inch (3 L) Bundt pan pan, greased and floured**

1. In a large mixer bowl, combine cake mix, eggs, water and bananas. Beat on low speed for 1 minute to blend, then on medium speed for 2 minutes. Gently fold in cherries and chocolate chips. Spread batter evenly in prepared pan. Bake for 50 to 55 minutes or until a tester inserted in center comes out clean. Cool for 25 minutes in pan on a wire rack, then remove and cool completely on rack.

Variation: For chocolate lovers, a chocolate cake mix tastes great, although it isn't as attractive.

Lemon Poppy Seed Ring

The lemon glaze soaks into the warm cake, making it moist and extra lemony.

SERVES 12 TO 16

CAKE

1	package (18.25 oz/515 g) lemon cake mix	1
1	package (4-serving size) vanilla instant pudding mix	1
4	eggs	4
1 cup	lemon or plain yogurt	250 mL
1/3 cup	vegetable oil	75 mL
1/4 cup	poppy seeds	50 mL
2 tsp	grated lemon zest	10 mL

LEMON GLAZE

3/4 cup	granulated sugar	175 mL
1/3 cup	lemon juice	75 mL

TIPS
- Mix glaze ingredients ahead. If necessary, heat gently to dissolve sugar.
- You can always use sour cream in place of yogurt in cake baking.

- **Preheat oven to 350°F (180°C)**
- **10-inch (4 L) tube pan, greased and floured**

1. **Cake:** In a large mixer bowl, combine cake mix, pudding mix, eggs, yogurt, oil, poppy seeds and lemon zest. Beat on medium speed for 2 minutes. Spread batter evenly in prepared pan. Bake for 50 to 60 minutes or until a tester inserted in center comes out clean. Cool for 20 minutes in pan on a wire rack, then remove from pan and place on rack set over waxed paper.

2. **Glaze:** In a small saucepan, over low heat, combine sugar and lemon juice, stirring until sugar is dissolved. Poke holes over the surface of warm cake with a fork or toothpick. Brush glaze over cake, letting it soak in. Cool completely before cutting cake.

Variations: Although we love the poppy seed crunch, this cake is also nice plain. It also works well with 1/2 cup (125 mL) finely chopped almonds instead of the poppy seeds.

Lemon Pistachio Cake

The combination may sound strange, but this cake not only looks great, it tastes great, too. The lemon glaze isn't necessary, but it finishes the cake off nicely.

SERVES 12 TO 16

1	package (18.25 oz/515 g) lemon cake mix	1
1	package (3 oz/85 g) lemon-flavored gelatin dessert mix	1
4	eggs	4
1 1/4 cups	water	300 mL
1/2 cup	vegetable oil	125 mL
3/4 cup	finely chopped pistachios	175 mL
	Lemon Glaze (see recipe, page 267) (optional)	

- **Preheat oven to 350°F (180°C)**
- **10-inch (3 L) Bundt pan or 10-inch (4 L) tube pan, greased and floured**

1. In a large mixer bowl, combine cake mix, gelatin mix, eggs, water and oil. Beat on medium speed for 2 minutes. Stir in nuts. Spread batter evenly in prepared pan. Bake for 50 to 60 minutes or until a tester inserted in center comes out clean. Cool for 25 minutes in pan on a wire rack, then remove cake and cool completely. Drizzle with lemon glaze, if desired.

TIPS
- Measure confectioner's sugar, then sift it before mixing with other ingredients to ensure lumps are removed.
- One medium lemon should yield about 3 tbsp (45 mL) juice.

Butterscotch Swirl

Here's a treat for those who prefer the flavor of butterscotch to chocolate.

SERVES 12 TO 16

CAKE

1	package (4-serving size) butterscotch instant pudding mix, divided	1
1	package (18.25 oz/515 g) white cake mix	1
2	eggs	2
1⅓ cups	water	325 mL
¼ cup	butter, softened	50 mL
½ cup	packed brown sugar	125 mL
2 tbsp	all-purpose flour	25 mL

GLAZE

¼ cup	butter	50 mL
3 tbsp	reserved butterscotch instant pudding mix (see Step 1)	45 mL
2 tbsp	corn syrup	25 mL
2 tbsp	milk	25 mL
1 cup	confectioner's (icing) sugar, sifted	250 mL

- **Preheat oven to 350°F (180°C)**
- **10-inch (4 L) tube pan, greased and floured**

1. **Cake:** Reserve 3 tbsp (45 mL) of the pudding mix for the glaze. In a large mixer bowl, combine remaining pudding mix, cake mix, eggs, water and butter. Beat on medium speed for 2 minutes. Reserve 1 cup (250 mL) of the batter. Spread remaining batter evenly in prepared pan. Add brown sugar and flour to reserved batter. Mix well. Spoon over batter in pan. Run tip of knife through batters to create a marble effect. Bake for 40 to 50 minutes or until a tester inserted in center comes out clean. Cool for 25 minutes in pan on a wire rack, then remove from pan and place on rack set over waxed paper.

2. **Glaze:** In a small saucepan, over low heat, stir butter, reserved pudding mix, corn syrup and milk until butter is melted and mixture is smooth. Remove from heat. Stir in confectioner's sugar. Quickly spoon warm glaze over warm cake. Let glaze set before cutting cake.

TIPS
- Dark brown and golden brown sugar are interchangeable. The dark has a stronger flavor, while golden has a more appealing color.
- To ease cleanup when using a glaze, which unlike frosting tends to drip, set the wire rack over waxed paper.

Apple Cranberry Spice Cake

Cinnamon, apples and cranberries are a natural combination in this cake.

SERVES 12 TO 16

1	package (18.25 oz/515 g) spice cake mix	1
3	eggs	3
1 cup	unsweetened applesauce	250 mL
½ cup	butter, softened	125 mL
¼ cup	water	50 mL
1 cup	diced peeled apples	250 mL
1 cup	dried cranberries	250 mL

TIP
- Spy, Spartan and Golden Delicious are great apples for baking.

- **Preheat oven to 350°F (180°C)**
- **10-inch (3 L) Bundt pan or 10-inch (4 L) tube pan, greased and floured**

1. In a large mixer bowl, combine cake mix, eggs, applesauce, butter and water. Beat on low speed for 1 minute to blend, then on medium speed for 2 minutes. Stir in diced apples and cranberries. Spread batter evenly in prepared pan. Bake for 55 to 65 minutes or until a tester inserted in center comes out clean. Cool for 25 minutes in pan on a wire rack, then remove cake and cool completely.

Variation: Replace cranberries with dried cherries or raisins.

Chocolate Cranberry Ring

Here's a festive cake you can enjoy year-round. Try it with blueberries too!

SERVES 12 TO 16

CAKE

1	package (18.25 oz/515 g) white cake mix	1
1	package (4-serving size) vanilla instant pudding mix	1
4	eggs	4
1⅓ cups	sour cream	325 mL
½ cup	vegetable oil	125 mL
½ tsp	ground cinnamon	2 mL
1 cup	fresh or frozen, thawed cranberries	250 mL
1 cup	semi-sweet chocolate chips	250 mL
½ cup	sliced almonds	125 mL

GLAZE

¾ cup	granulated sugar	175 mL
3 tbsp	orange liqueur or juice	45 mL
3 tbsp	lemon juice	45 mL

- **Preheat oven to 350°F (180°C)**
- **10-inch (4 L) tube pan, greased and floured**

1. **Cake:** In a large mixer bowl, combine cake mix, pudding mix, eggs, sour cream, oil and cinnamon. Beat on medium speed for 2 minutes. Fold in cranberries, chocolate chips and almonds. Spread batter evenly in prepared pan. Bake for 45 to 55 minutes or until a tester inserted in center comes out clean. Cool for 20 minutes in pan on a wire rack, then remove from pan and place on rack set over waxed paper.

2. **Glaze:** In a small saucepan, combine sugar, liqueur and lemon juice. Bring to a boil and simmer for 1 minute, until sugar is dissolved. Poke holes over surface of warm cake with fork or toothpick. Brush warm glaze over the top and sides of warm cake. Repeat until all the glaze is used up. Cool completely before cutting cake.

Variation: Omit the glaze and dust with confectioner's sugar just before serving.

TIPS
- If using frozen cranberries, thaw and pat dry before folding into the batter.
- For an interesting color, use unblanched almonds.

Sherry Cake

This traditional Portuguese cake is perfect to serve with a cup of coffee or with ice cream for a special dessert.

CAKE

1	package (18.25 oz/515 g) white cake mix	1
1	package (4-serving size) vanilla instant pudding mix	1
4	eggs	4
¾ cup	cream sherry	175 mL
½ cup	vegetable oil	125 mL
¼ cup	butter, melted	50 mL
2 tsp	ground nutmeg	10 mL
¼ cup	granulated sugar	50 mL
1 tsp	ground cinnamon	5 mL

GLAZE

1 cup	confectioner's (icing) sugar, sifted	250 mL
2 tbsp	milk	25 mL
½ tsp	vanilla	2 mL

- **Preheat oven to 350°F (180°C)**
- **10-inch (4 L) tube pan, greased and floured**

1. **Cake:** In a large mixer bowl, combine cake mix, pudding mix, eggs, sherry, oil, melted butter and nutmeg. Beat on medium speed for 2 minutes. In a separate bowl, combine sugar and cinnamon. Spread a third of batter in prepared pan. Sprinkle half the sugar mixture on top. Add another third of the batter and the remaining sugar mixture. Cover with remaining batter. Bake for 45 to 50 minutes or until a tester inserted in center comes out clean. Cool for 25 minutes in pan on a wire rack, then remove from pan and cool completely on rack set over waxed paper.

2. **Glaze:** In a bowl, combine confectioner's sugar, milk and vanilla, mixing until smooth. Drizzle over cooled cake. Let glaze set before cutting cake.

Variation: Try making this with a yellow cake mix.

TIPS
- You can't go wrong with a bottle of sherry in your cupboard. It's nice to brush on fruitcake and to use as an ingredient in other cakes such as this.
- This may seem like a lot of sherry, but the flavor is pleasantly mellow and not overpowering.
- Although considerably more expensive, real vanilla is worth the money. Its flavor can't be matched.

Orange Chiffon Cake

Feathery light and not too sweet. It's nice with a thin orange glaze or fresh fruit.

SERVES 12 TO 16

CAKE

5	egg whites	5
½ tsp	cream of tartar	2 mL
1	package (18.25 oz/515 g) white cake mix	1
3	egg yolks	3
½ cup	frozen orange juice concentrate, thawed	125 mL
½ cup	water	125 mL
½ cup	vegetable oil	125 mL

ORANGE GLAZE

2 cups	confectioner's (icing) sugar, sifted	500 mL
3 tbsp	orange juice	45 mL

TIP

- You don't grease the pan for chiffon or angel food cakes, because the batter crawls up the pan sides, giving the cake its height.

- **Preheat oven to 325°F (160°C)**
- **10-inch (4 L) tube pan, ungreased**

1. **Cake:** In a small mixer bowl, on high speed, beat egg whites and cream of tartar until stiff peaks form. Set aside. In a large mixer bowl, combine cake mix, egg yolks, orange juice concentrate, water and oil. Beat on medium speed for 2 minutes. Fold egg whites into batter gently but thoroughly. Pour batter carefully into ungreased pan. Bake for 45 to 55 minutes or until a tester inserted in center comes out clean. Remove pan from oven and immediately turn upside down, placing center tube of pan on an upside-down glass or cup. Cool for 1 hour. Run a long sharp knife around edge of pan and center ring to loosen cake. Remove cake. Place right-side up on a wire rack to cool completely.

2. **Glaze:** Stir together confectioner's sugar and enough orange juice to create a soft, smooth consistency. Spread over top and sides of cake. Leave for 30 minutes to let glaze set before cutting.

Variation: For plain chiffon cake, replace juice with water.

Light and Lemony Feather Cake

Refreshingly light and tart, this cake tastes delicious plain or topped with fresh blueberries and a yogurt sauce or whipped cream.

SERVES 12 TO 16

5	egg whites	5
½ tsp	cream of tartar	2 mL
1	package (18.25 oz/515 g) white cake mix	1
3	egg yolks	3
½ cup	frozen lemonade concentrate, thawed	125 mL
½ cup	water	125 mL
½ cup	vegetable oil	125 mL
1 tbsp	grated lemon zest	15 mL

TIPS

- Separate the egg yolks from the whites carefully. A trace of yolk in the whites will prevent them from beating to stiff peaks.
- Cream of tartar or 1 tsp (5 mL) lemon juice helps keep beaten egg whites stiff.

- **Preheat oven to 325°F (160°C)**
- **10-inch (4 L) tube pan, ungreased**

1. In a small mixer bowl, beat egg whites and cream of tartar on high speed until stiff peaks form. Set aside. In a large mixer bowl, combine cake mix, egg yolks, lemonade concentrate, water and oil. Beat on medium speed for 2 minutes. Gently but thoroughly fold egg whites and lemon zest into batter. Pour carefully into pan. Bake for 45 to 55 minutes or until a tester inserted in center comes out clean. Remove from oven and immediately turn upside down, placing center tube of pan on an upside-down glass or cup. Cool for 1 hour. Run a long sharp knife around edge of pan and center ring to loosen cake. Remove cake and place right-side up on a wire rack to cool completely.

Variations: For an extra hit of lemon, use a lemon cake mix. The white cake mix gives a more subtle taste. You can also top with a lemon glaze (see recipe, page 267).

Tropical Pound Cake

A moist, tender pound cake that varies in flavor with the nectar used.

SERVES 12 TO 16

CAKE

1	package (18.25 oz/515 g) yellow cake mix	1
1	package (3 oz/85 g) lemon-flavored gelatin dessert mix	1
6	eggs	6
¾ cup	vegetable oil	175 mL
¾ cup	apricot nectar	175 mL
GLAZE		
2 cups	confectioner's (icing) sugar	500 mL
¾ cup	apricot nectar or orange juice	175 mL
	Juice and grated zest of 1 lemon	

- **Preheat oven to 350°F (180°C)**
- **10-inch (4 L) tube pan, greased and floured**

1. **Cake:** In a large mixer bowl, combine cake mix, gelatin mix, eggs, oil and nectar. Beat on low speed for 1 minute to blend, then on medium speed for 2 minutes. Spread batter evenly in prepared pan. Bake for 40 to 50 minutes or until a tester inserted in center comes out clean. Cool for 10 minutes in pan on a wire rack.

2. **Glaze:** In a medium bowl, combine confectioner's sugar, nectar, lemon zest and lemon juice, mixing thoroughly until smooth. Pour over warm cake. Let stand for 1 hour in pan on rack, then remove cake and cool completely on rack.

Variation: Any tropical nectar will work well. Try mango or passion fruit in place of the apricot.

Decadent Chocolate Almond Cake

Easy to make and loaded with chocolate — what could be better than this delicious, moist cake?

SERVES 12 TO 16

CAKE

1	package (18.25 oz/515 g) devil's food cake mix, divided	1
4	toffee-crunch chocolate bars (each 1.4 oz/40 g), chopped	4
½ cup	chopped almonds	125 mL
1	package (4-serving size) chocolate instant pudding mix	1
4	eggs	4
1 cup	sour cream	250 mL
¼ cup	water	50 mL
¼ cup	almond liqueur	50 mL

GLAZE

3 tbsp	butter	45 mL
¼ cup	almond liqueur	50 mL
1 tbsp	granulated sugar	15 mL

- **Preheat oven to 350°F (180°C)**
- **10-inch (4 L) tube pan, greased and lined with parchment paper**

1. **Cake:** In a small bowl, sprinkle 2 tbsp (25 mL) of the cake mix over chocolate bars and almonds. Toss to thoroughly coat. Set aside. In a large mixer bowl, combine remaining cake mix, pudding mix, eggs, sour cream, water and liqueur. Beat on medium speed for 2 minutes. Stir in chocolate bar mixture. Mix well. Spread batter evenly in prepared pan. Bake for 50 to 60 minutes or until a tester inserted in center comes out clean. Cool for 20 minutes in pan on a wire rack, then remove from pan and place on rack set over waxed paper.

2. **Glaze:** In a small saucepan, combine butter, liqueur and sugar. Bring to a boil, then simmer for 1 minute, stirring, until sugar is dissolved and glaze is slightly thickened. Brush glaze over warm cake. Cool completely.

Variation: Replace almonds with hazelnuts.

TIPS

- Chocolate bars tend to stick at the point where they come in contact with a pan. To avoid problems when removing the cake, line the bottom and sides of the pan with parchment paper.
- For a grand finale, serve this cake with a dollop of whipped cream flavored with almond liqueur.
- Use blanched or unblanched almonds, as you prefer.

Apricot Almond Cake

Apricot baby food gives great color and flavor to cakes with no work involved for the cook!

SERVES 12 TO 16

CAKE

1	package (18.25 oz/515 g) white cake mix	1
4	eggs	4
1 cup	sour cream	250 mL
1 cup	apricot baby food	250 mL
1 cup	finely chopped almonds	250 mL

APRICOT CREAM TOPPING

1 cup	whipping (35%) cream	250 mL
2 tbsp	confectioner's (icing) sugar, sifted	25 mL
½ cup	apricot baby food	125 mL

TIP

- You can keep unfrosted cake in the refrigerator for about 5 days or about 3 months in the freezer.

- **Preheat oven to 350°F (180°C)**
- **10-inch (3 L) Bundt pan or 10-inch (4 L) tube pan, greased and floured**

1. **Cake:** In a large mixer bowl, combine cake mix, eggs, sour cream and baby food. Beat on low speed for 1 minute to blend, then on medium speed for 2 minutes. Fold in almonds. Spread batter evenly in prepared pan. Bake for 40 to 50 minutes or until a tester inserted in center comes out clean. Cool for 25 minutes in pan on a wire rack, then remove cake and cool completely.

2. **Topping:** In a small bowl, beat cream and confectioner's sugar together until stiff peaks form. Fold in apricot baby food gently but thoroughly. Serve with slices of cake.

Variation: Replace apricot baby food with peach or plum.

Cherry Almond Cake

A good alternative to the traditional holiday fruitcake. This festive cake is a colorful addition to any tray and makes a welcome gift for the hard-to-buy-for people.

SERVES 12 TO 16

1	package (18.25 oz/515 g) white cake mix	1
1	package (4-serving size) vanilla instant pudding mix	1
4	eggs	4
1 cup	sour cream	250 mL
½ cup	vegetable oil	125 mL
2 cups	candied red cherries, halved	500 mL
⅔ cup	coarsely chopped blanched almonds	150 mL

TIPS

- Chill cake for easy slicing.
- For gift giving, wrap cooled cake tightly in plastic wrap and store in the refrigerator. Add a pretty bow, a gift tag and a card with the recipe on it.

- **Preheat oven to 350°F (180°C)**
- **10-inch (4 L) tube pan, greased and floured**

1. In a large mixer bowl, combine cake mix, pudding mix, eggs, sour cream and oil. Beat on medium speed for 2 minutes. Stir in cherries and almonds gently but thoroughly. Spread batter evenly in prepared pan. Bake for 50 to 60 minutes or until tester inserted in center comes out clean. Cool for 25 minutes in pan on a wire rack, then remove cake and cool completely. Store at least overnight to let flavors mellow. For longer storage, keep refrigerated and cut as needed.

Variations: All red or all green cherries looks good, but a combination is attractive too. Or substitute candied pineapple for half the cherries.

Lime Daiquiri Cake

This cake is a delicious excuse to make Lime Cream, which is one of my favorite toppings.

SERVES 12 TO 16

CAKE

1	package (18.25 oz/515 g) white cake mix	1
3	eggs	3
⅔ cup	water	150 mL
⅓ cup	rum	75 mL
⅓ cup	vegetable oil	75 mL
1 tbsp	grated lime zest	15 mL
¼ cup	lime juice	50 mL
1 to 3	drops green food coloring (optional)	1 to 3

GLAZE

½ cup	granulated sugar	125 mL
⅓ cup	lime juice	75 mL
¼ cup	rum	50 mL

LIME CREAM (OPTIONAL)

½ cup	granulated sugar	125 mL
1	egg, beaten	1
1½ tsp	grated lime zest	7 mL
3 tbsp	lime juice	45 mL
2 tbsp	butter, softened	25 mL
1 cup	whipping (35%) cream	250 mL

- **Preheat oven to 350°F (180°C)**
- **10-inch (3 L) Bundt pan or 10-inch (4 L) tube pan, greased and floured**

1. **Cake:** In a large mixer bowl, combine cake mix, eggs, water, rum, oil, lime zest and lime juice. Beat on medium speed for 2 minutes. Stir in coloring, if desired. Spread batter evenly in prepared pan. Bake for 45 to 55 minutes or until a tester inserted in center comes out clean. Cool for 20 minutes in pan on a wire rack, then invert onto rack over waxed paper.

2. **Glaze:** In a small saucepan, over medium heat, combine sugar, lime juice and rum. Cook, stirring, just until sugar dissolves. Poke holes in warm cake with fork or toothpick. Brush glaze over cake, letting it soak in. Cool completely. Serve with Lime Cream or whipped cream.

3. **Lime Cream:** If desired, in a small saucepan, combine sugar, egg, lime zest and lime juice. Cook, stirring constantly, over medium heat until thickened. Add butter, stirring until melted. Cool thoroughly. In a mixer bowl, on high speed, beat cream to stiff peaks. Fold into lime mixture. Serve a dollop of Lime Cream on top of glazed cake.

Variation: Use sweetened whipped cream as the topping, if desired.

TIPS

- One medium lime will yield about 2 tbsp (25 mL) juice and 1 tsp (5 mL) grated zest. To get the maximum amount of juice, squeeze the lime when it is at room temperature or even slightly warm.
- Use the Lime Cream topping as a dip for fresh strawberries and cherries. It can be prepared a day ahead.

Cranberry Almond Lemon Cake

Don't limit this wonderful cake to the traditional cranberry season. Keep a bag of frozen berries on hand to enjoy it year-round.

SERVES 12 TO 16

1	package (18.25 oz/515 g) white cake mix	1
1	package (4-serving size) lemon instant pudding mix	1
4	eggs	4
1⅓ cups	sour cream	325 mL
½ cup	vegetable oil	125 mL
½ tsp	ground nutmeg	2 mL
1¼ cups	fresh or frozen, thawed cranberries (see tip, below)	300 mL
¾ cup	sliced almonds	175 mL
	Confectioner's (icing) sugar for dusting (optional)	

- **Preheat oven to 350°F (180°C)**
- **10-inch (4 L) tube pan, greased and floured**

1. In a large mixer bowl, combine cake mix, pudding mix, eggs, sour cream, oil and nutmeg. Beat on medium speed for 2 minutes. Fold in cranberries and almonds. Spread batter in prepared pan. Bake for 45 to 55 minutes or until a tester inserted in center comes out clean. Cool for 25 minutes in pan on a wire rack, then remove cake and cool completely. Dust with confectioner's sugar before serving, if desired.

Variation: For an interesting color, use unblanched almonds.

TIP
- If using frozen cranberries, thaw and pat dry before folding into batter.

Cranberry White Chocolate Orange Cake

Creamy white chocolate and tart red cranberries are a perfect pair.

SERVES 12 TO 16

CAKE

1	package (18.25 oz/515 g) white cake mix	1
1	package (4-serving size) vanilla instant pudding mix	1
4	eggs	4
1⅓ cups	sour cream	325 mL
½ cup	vegetable oil	125 mL
1 tbsp	grated orange zest	15 mL
1 cup	fresh or frozen, thawed cranberries	250 mL
4 oz	white chocolate, chopped	125 g

GLAZE

3 oz	white chocolate, chopped	90 g
2 tbsp	orange juice	25 mL

- **Preheat oven to 350°F (180°C)**
- **10-inch (4 L) tube pan, greased and floured**

1. **Cake:** In a large mixer bowl, combine cake mix, pudding mix, eggs, sour cream, oil and orange zest. Beat on medium speed for 2 minutes. Fold in cranberries and white chocolate. Spread batter in prepared pan. Bake for 60 to 65 minutes or until a tester inserted in center comes out clean. Cool for 25 minutes in pans on a wire rack, then remove from pan and cool completely on rack set over waxed paper.

2. **Glaze:** In a saucepan over low heat, melt white chocolate and orange juice (or melt in the microwave on medium for 1½ minutes). Stir until smooth. Drizzle over cooled cake. Let chocolate set before cutting cake.

Variation: Replace cranberries with blueberries.

TIP
- If using frozen cranberries, thaw and pat dry before folding into batter.

Tequila Orange Sunrise

A popular drink in edible form.

SERVES 12 TO 16

CAKE

1	package (18.25 oz/515 g) white cake mix	1
1	package (4-serving size) vanilla instant pudding mix	1
4	eggs	4
½ cup	tequila	125 mL
½ cup	water	125 mL
½ cup	vegetable oil	125 mL
¼ cup	frozen orange juice concentrate, thawed	50 mL

ORANGE GLAZE

1 cup	confectioner's (icing) sugar, sifted	250 mL
1 tbsp	frozen orange juice concentrate, thawed	15 mL

- **Preheat oven to 350°F (180°C)**
- **10-inch (3 L) Bundt pan or 10-inch (4 L) tube pan, greased and floured**

1. **Cake:** In a large mixer bowl, combine cake mix, pudding mix, eggs, tequila, water, oil and orange juice concentrate. Beat for 2 minutes on medium speed. Spread batter evenly in prepared pan. Bake for 45 to 50 minutes or until a tester inserted in center comes out clean. Cool for 25 minutes in pan on a wire rack, then remove cake and cool completely.

2. **Glaze:** Combine confectioner's sugar and orange juice concentrate, mixing until smooth. Add a little more confectioner's sugar or liquid if necessary to make a thick pouring consistency. Drizzle over cooled cake.

Variation: Replace tequila with an orange or peach liqueur.

TIP
- You can replace the orange juice concentrate and water with ¾ cup (175 mL) orange juice, but the flavor will be milder.

Creamy Orange Cake

This cake is memorable for both its bright orange color and its creamy orange taste.

SERVES 12 TO 16

CAKE

1	package (18.25 oz/515 g) white cake mix	1
1	package (3 oz/85 g) orange-flavored gelatin dessert mix	1
1	envelope (1.3 oz/42.5 g) whipped topping mix	1
4	eggs	4
¾ cup	mayonnaise	175 mL
1 tbsp	grated orange zest	15 mL
¾ cup	orange juice	175 mL

GLAZE

1 cup	confectioner's (icing) sugar, sifted	250 mL
1 tsp	grated orange zest	5 mL
1 tbsp	orange juice	15 mL

- **Preheat oven to 350°F (180°C)**
- **10-inch (3 L) Bundt pan or 10-inch (4 L) tube pan, greased and floured**

1. **Cake:** In a large mixer bowl, combine cake mix, gelatin mix, topping mix, eggs, mayonnaise, orange zest and orange juice. Beat on low speed for 1 minute to blend, then on medium speed for 2 minutes. Spread batter evenly in prepared pan. Bake for 40 to 50 minutes or until a tester inserted in center comes out clean. Cool for 25 minutes in pan on a wire rack, then remove from pan and place on rack set over waxed paper to cool.

2. **Glaze:** In a bowl, combine confectioner's sugar, orange zest and orange juice, mixing until smooth. Drizzle over cooled cake. Let glaze set before cutting cake.

Variation: Try pineapple-orange gelatin for a more mellow flavor.

Hazelnut Rum Cake

A novel way to enjoy your cocktail.

SERVES 12 TO 16

CAKE

1	package (18.25 oz/515 g) yellow cake mix	1
1	package (4-serving size) vanilla instant pudding mix	1
4	eggs	4
⅔ cup	water	150 mL
½ cup	vegetable oil	125 mL
⅓ cup	rum	75 mL
¾ cup	chopped hazelnuts	175 mL

GLAZE

⅓ cup	butter	75 mL
2 tbsp	water	25 mL
⅔ cup	granulated sugar	150 mL
⅓ cup	rum	75 mL

TIPS

- You can use dark, light or amber rum. The taste is similar but the color will vary slightly.
- Regular brandy or apricot brandy taste great too.
- For a non-alcoholic version, replace rum with apple juice.
- Cakes baked in this size are usually frosted and served from the pan, which makes them easy to transport. If you want to remove the entire cake from the pan, line it with foil, leaving an overhang on the sides. You'll be able to lift the cooled cake out easily.

- **Preheat oven to 350°F (180°C)**
- **10-inch (3 L) Bundt pan or 10-inch (4 L) tube pan, greased and floured**

1. **Cake:** In a large mixer bowl, combine cake mix, pudding mix, eggs, water, oil and rum. Beat on medium speed for 2 minutes. Stir in nuts. Spread batter evenly in prepared pan. Bake for 55 to 65 minutes or until a tester inserted in center comes out clean. Cool for 20 minutes in pan on a wire rack, then remove cake and place on rack over waxed paper.

2. **Glaze:** In a small saucepan, melt butter. Add water and sugar. Bring mixture to a boil over medium heat, then simmer for 5 minutes, stirring constantly, until thickened. Remove from heat. Stir in rum. Poke holes over surface of warm cake with a fork or toothpick. Brush glaze over cake, letting it soak in. Cool completely before cutting.

Variation: Instead of hazelnuts, try unblanched almonds or pecans. Both complement the flavor of rum.

Peach and Blueberry Pudding Cake

An easy-to-make cake that tastes as good as it looks. It's nice plain or with whipped cream for special occasions.

SERVES 12 TO 16		
1	package (18.25 oz/515 g) white cake mix	1
1	package (4-serving size) vanilla instant pudding mix	1
4	eggs	4
½ cup	sour cream	125 mL
¼ cup	vegetable oil	50 mL
1 cup	diced peaches	250 mL
1 cup	blueberries	250 mL

TIP
- If using fresh peaches that are very juicy, decrease sour cream to ⅓ cup (75 mL).

- **Preheat oven to 350°F (180°C)**
- **10-inch (3 L) Bundt pan, greased and floured**

1. In a large mixer bowl, combine cake mix, pudding mix, eggs, sour cream and oil. Beat on low speed for 1 minute to blend, then on medium speed for 2 minutes. Fold in peaches and blueberries gently but thoroughly. Spread batter evenly in prepared pan. Bake for 55 to 60 minutes or until a tester inserted in center comes out clean. Cool for 25 minutes in pan on a wire rack, then remove cake and cool completely.

Variation: Replace blueberries with raspberries.

Fuzzy Navel Cake

Here's a version of a fuzzy navel, a cocktail that combines peach schnapps and orange juice. It lets you have your drink and eat it, too.

SERVES 12 TO 16		
CAKE		
1	package (18.25 oz/515 g) white cake mix	1
1	package (3 oz/85 g) peach-flavored gelatin dessert mix	1
4	eggs	4
¾ cup	orange liqueur	175 mL
1 tbsp	grated orange zest	15 mL
½ cup	orange juice	125 mL
½ cup	vegetable oil	125 mL
GLAZE (OPTIONAL)		
1 cup	confectioner's (icing) sugar, sifted	250 mL
¼ cup	orange juice	50 mL
2 tbsp	orange liqueur	25 mL

- **Preheat oven to 350°F (180°C)**
- **10-inch (3 L) Bundt pan, greased and floured**

1. **Cake:** In a large mixer bowl, combine cake mix, gelatin mix, eggs, liqueur, orange zest, orange juice and oil. Beat on medium speed for 2 minutes. Spread batter evenly in prepared pan. Bake for 45 to 55 minutes or until a tester inserted in center comes out clean. Cool for 20 minutes in pan on a wire rack, then remove from pan and invert on rack over waxed paper.

2. **Glaze:** If desired, in a small bowl, combine confectioner's sugar, orange juice and liqueur, mixing until smooth. Poke holes over surface of warm cake with fork or toothpick. Brush glaze over cake, letting it soak in. Cool completely before cutting cake.

Variation: Orange juice can replace orange liqueur, if desired.

TIPS
- Use shortening or cooking spray to grease cake pans. With oil and butter, the cakes tend to stick and burn.
- Place cake over waxed paper to catch the drips when glazing.

Hummingbird Cake

The name of this recipe has been around for years, and there are many different versions, except that they all contain pineapple and banana.

SERVES 12 TO 16		
1	package (18.25 oz/515 g) white cake mix	1
1	package (4-serving size) vanilla instant pudding mix	1
4	eggs	4
⅔ cup	well-drained crushed pineapple, juice reserved	150 mL
1 cup	reserved pineapple juice, plus water as necessary	250 mL
½ cup	vegetable oil	125 mL
1 tsp	ground cinnamon	5 mL
½ cup	finely chopped pecans	125 mL
½	ripe banana, diced	½
⅓ cup	chopped maraschino cherries	75 mL

- **Preheat oven to 350°F (180°C)**
- **10-inch (3 L) Bundt pan or 10-inch (4 L) tube pan, greased and floured**

1. In a large mixer bowl, combine cake mix, pudding mix, eggs, drained pineapple, pineapple juice, oil and cinnamon. Beat on low speed for 1 minute to blend, then on medium speed for 2 minutes. Stir in pecans, banana and cherries. Spread evenly in prepared pan. Bake for 45 to 55 minutes or until a tester inserted in center comes out clean. Cool for 25 minutes in pan on a wire rack, then remove cake and cool completely. Dust with confectioner's sugar or drizzle with a vanilla glaze (see page 267), if desired.

Variation: Use banana cream instant pudding for a more pronounced banana flavor.

TIP
- A dusting of confectioner's sugar before serving (or a white icing drizzle) finishes off this cake beautifully.

Piña Colada Cake

A favorite drink is also a favorite cake. It's hard to beat the flavor of a blend of pineapple, coconut and rum.

SERVES 12 TO 16		
CAKE		
1	package (18.25 oz/515 g) white cake mix	1
1	package (4-serving size) vanilla instant pudding mix	1
4	eggs	4
½ cup	coconut milk	125 mL
⅓ cup	rum	75 mL
⅓ cup	vegetable oil	75 mL
⅔ cup	well-drained crushed pineapple	150 mL
COCONUT GLAZE		
¾ cup	coconut milk	175 mL
2 tbsp	rum	25 mL

- **Preheat oven to 350°F (180°C)**
- **10-inch (3 L) Bundt pan or 10-inch (4 L) tube pan, greased and floured**

1. **Cake:** In a large mixer bowl, combine cake mix, pudding mix, eggs, coconut milk, rum and oil. Beat on medium speed for 2 minutes. Stir in crushed pineapple. Spread batter evenly in prepared pan. Bake for 45 to 55 minutes or until a tester inserted in center comes out clean. Cool for 20 minutes in pan on a wire rack, then remove cake and invert onto wire rack over waxed paper.

2. **Glaze:** Combine coconut milk and rum. Poke holes in warm cake with a fork or toothpick. Brush glaze over cake, letting it soak in. Cool completely before cutting.

TIPS
- Whatever rum you prefer — light, dark or amber — is fine.
- Dried pineapple chunks are a nice garnish and keep well.

Hawaiian Dream Cake

The tropical taste will make winter's long, cold nights seem easier to endure.

SERVES 12 TO 16

CAKE

1	package (18.25 oz/515 g) lemon cake mix	1
4	eggs	4
1 cup	crushed pineapple, with juice	250 mL
½ cup	vegetable oil	125 mL
½ cup	toasted flaked coconut	125 mL

PINEAPPLE CREAM CHEESE FROSTING

4 oz	cream cheese, softened	125 g
¼ cup	butter, softened	50 mL
2 cups	confectioner's (icing) sugar, sifted	500 mL
3 tbsp	well-drained crushed pineapple	45 mL
	Toasted coconut (optional)	

- **Preheat oven to 350°F (180°C)**
- **10-inch (4 L) tube pan, greased and floured**

1. Cake: In a large mixer bowl, combine cake mix, eggs, pineapple with juice and oil. Beat on medium speed for 2 minutes. Stir in coconut. Spread batter evenly in prepared pan. Bake for 45 to 55 minutes or until a tester inserted in center comes out clean. Cool for 25 minutes in pan on a wire rack, then remove cake and cool completely.

2. Frosting: In a large mixer bowl, on medium speed, beat cream cheese and butter together to blend. Gradually add confectioner's sugar, beating until smooth and creamy. Fold in pineapple. Spread over cooled cake. Sprinkle with coconut, if desired.

Variation: Omit coconut if desired.

TIP
- Toast coconut for a nutty flavor. Spread out in a shallow pan and bake at 350°F (180°C) for about 10 minutes, stirring often until golden. Cool completely.

Chocolate Pineapple Carrot Cake

A decadent twist on an all-time favorite.

SERVES 12 TO 16

1	package (18.25 oz/515 g) devil's food cake mix	1
2 tsp	ground cinnamon	10 mL
¼ tsp	ground nutmeg	1 mL
3	eggs	3
½ cup	vegetable oil	125 mL
1 cup	crushed pineapple, with juice	250 mL
¼ cup	water	50 mL
2 cups	grated peeled carrots	500 mL
	Chocolate Cream Cheese Frosting (see recipe, page 265)	

- **Preheat oven to 350°F (180°C)**
- **10-inch (3 L) Bundt pan, greased and floured**

1. In a large mixer bowl, combine cake mix, spices, eggs, oil, pineapple with juice, water and carrots. Beat on low speed for 1 minute to blend, then on medium speed for 2 minutes. Spread in prepared pan. Bake for 45 to 55 minutes or until a tester inserted in center comes out clean. Cool for 25 minutes in pan on a wire rack, then remove cake and cool completely.

2. Prepare Chocolate Cream Cheese Frosting. Spread on top of cake.

Variation: Replace grated carrot with zucchini.

TIP
- Brands of crushed pineapple vary considerably. Choose one that has coarse rather than fine pineapple pieces and not too much juice.

Pineapple Banana Cake

A quick-to-make, moist tropical cake.

SERVES 12 TO 16

CAKE

1	package (18.25 oz/515 g) white cake mix	1
3	eggs	3
1½ cups	mashed ripe bananas (3 to 4 large)	375 mL
½ cup	well-drained crushed pineapple	125 mL
⅓ cup	vegetable oil	75 mL
1 cup	chopped walnuts (optional)	250 mL

PINEAPPLE BUTTER FROSTING (OPTIONAL)

¼ cup	butter, softened	50 mL
⅓ cup	well-drained crushed pineapple, juice reserved	75 mL
3 cups	confectioner's (icing) sugar, sifted	750 mL
2 to 3 tbsp	reserved pineapple juice	25 to 45 mL

- **Preheat oven to 350°F (180°C)**
- **10-inch (4 L) tube pan, greased and floured**

1. **Cake:** In a large mixer bowl, combine cake mix, eggs, bananas, pineapple and oil. Beat on medium speed for 2 minutes. Stir in nuts. Spread batter in prepared pan. Bake for 55 to 65 minutes or until a tester inserted in center comes out clean. Cool for 25 minutes in pan on a wire rack, then remove cake and cool completely.

2. **Frosting:** If desired, in a large bowl, beat butter and pineapple together until smooth. Gradually add confectioner's sugar and pineapple juice, beating to a soft spreading consistency. Spread over cooled cake.

Variation: Frost or simply sprinkle with confectioner's sugar.

TIP
- You can bake the batter for one tube cake in two 9- by 5-inch (2 L) loaf pans for approximately the same time. It's nice to enjoy one and freeze one to enjoy later.

Chocolate Zucchini Cake

Moist, with lots of rich chocolate flavor, this cake is delicious with or without frosting.

SERVES 12 TO 16

1	package (18.25 oz/515 g) devil's food cake mix	1
3	eggs	3
¾ cup	water	175 mL
⅓ cup	vegetable oil	75 mL
½ tsp	ground cinnamon	2 mL
1½ cups	grated zucchini	375 mL
1 cup	semi-sweet chocolate chips	250 mL
½ cup	chopped nuts	125 mL

TIP
- When baking cakes, don't use grated zucchini that has been frozen. It is too wet for the batter and will result in soggy, dense cakes.

- **Preheat oven to 350°F (180°C)**
- **10-inch (4 L) tube pan, greased and floured**

1. In a large mixer bowl, combine cake mix, eggs, water, oil and cinnamon. Beat on low speed for 1 minute to blend, then on medium speed for 2 minutes. Stir in zucchini, chocolate chips and nuts. Mix well. Spread batter evenly in prepared pan. Bake for 50 to 60 minutes or until a tester inserted in center comes out clean. Cool for 25 minutes in pan on a wire rack, then remove from pan and cool completely on rack. Frost as desired.

Variations: Omit chocolate chips or replace with additional chopped nuts. For a special treat, top with Chocolate Cream Cheese Frosting (see recipe, page 265) or a Chocolate Butter Frosting (see recipe, page 260).

Spicy Zucchini Cake with Brown Sugar Fudge Frosting

It's hard to decide which is best — the cake or the frosting.

CAKE

1	package (18.25 oz/515 g) spice cake mix	1
1	package (4-serving size) vanilla instant pudding mix	1
4	eggs	4
1 cup	sour cream	250 mL
¼ cup	vegetable oil	50 mL
2½ cups	grated zucchini	625 mL
¾ cup	chopped nuts	175 mL

BROWN SUGAR FUDGE FROSTING

½ cup	packed brown sugar	125 mL
¼ cup	butter	50 mL
2 tbsp	half-and-half (10%) cream	25 mL
1 cup	confectioner's (icing) sugar, sifted	250 mL

TIPS

- Don't peel the zucchini — the skins are tender and the green fleck is interesting in the cake.
- Use medium zucchini. The overgrown ones are seedy and quite wet.
- The frosting hardens quickly on cooling, so use immediately after mixing. If necessary, rewarm on low heat to soften.

- **Preheat oven to 350°F (180°C)**
- **10-inch (4 L) tube pan, greased and floured**

1. **Cake:** In a large mixer bowl, combine cake mix, pudding mix, eggs, sour cream and oil. Beat on medium speed for 2 minutes. Stir in zucchini and nuts, mixing well. Spread batter evenly in prepared pan. Bake for 60 to 65 minutes or until a tester inserted in center comes out clean. Cool for 25 minutes in pan on a wire rack, then remove cake and cool completely.

2. **Frosting:** In a medium saucepan, combine brown sugar and butter. Bring to a boil over medium heat, then simmer for 2 minutes, stirring constantly. Carefully stir in cream. Return mixture to a boil, then remove from heat. Cool slightly. Put confectioner's sugar into a large mixer bowl. Pour warm brown sugar mixture on top. Beat on low speed just until smooth and creamy, about 2 minutes. Quickly spread on top and partially down sides of cake. Cool to let frosting set before cutting.

Variations: Substitute grated carrot for the zucchini. For a layer cake, bake in 2 round pans and frost with Cream Cheese Frosting (see recipe, page 265).

Angel food cakes have a unique texture: they are extremely moist, and light as a feather. The cakes can be enhanced with other ingredients, such as fresh fruit for a refreshingly light dessert like Raspberry Angel Trifle, or with cream and chocolate for a heavenly but decadent concoction like Tiramisu.

Lemon Angel Torte

A tart lemon cream filling between layers of angel food cake makes for a mouthwatering dessert.

SERVES 12 TO 16		
CAKE		
1	package (16 oz/450 g) white angel food cake mix	1
1 tbsp	grated lemon zest	15 mL
LEMON CREAM FILLING AND TOPPING		
1 cup	whipping (35%) cream	250 mL
1 tbsp	confectioner's (icing) sugar	15 mL
1	can (19 oz/540 mL) lemon pie filling	1
	Lemon twists (optional)	

TIPS

- If you prefer, or can't find canned lemon pie filling, prepare a cooked lemon pie filling. Cool before using.
- An electric knife is ideal to slice angel food and chiffon cakes.
- Chill the cake for at least 4 hours before serving to allow the flavors to blend.

- **Preheat oven to 325°F (160°C)**
- **10-inch (4 L) tube pan, ungreased**

1. **Cake:** Add lemon zest to cake mix and prepare, bake and cool according to package directions. With electric knife or long sharp serrated knife, cut cake horizontally into 3 layers.

2. **Filling:** In a large mixer bowl, beat cream and confectioner's sugar to stiff peaks. Fold in pie filling, gently but thoroughly. Place one cake layer, cut-side up, on serving plate. Spread 1 cup (250 mL) of the filling on cake. Repeat with remaining cake layers and filling, ending with cake layer, cut-side down. Spread remaining filling on sides and top of cake. Chill for at least 4 hours before serving. Garnish with lemon twists, if desired. Store leftover cake in the refrigerator.

Variation: Crushed hard lemon candies sprinkled on top of the cake add a nice crunch to the lemon cream.

Pink Coconut Cake

A simple decoration makes this cake special.

SERVES 10		
CAKE		
1	package (16 oz/450 g) white angel food cake mix	1
2/3 cup	flaked coconut	150 mL
TOPPING		
2 cups	whipping (35%) cream	500 mL
1/4 cup	confectioner's (icing) sugar, sifted	50 mL
2/3 cup	flaked coconut	150 mL
5	drops red food coloring	5

TIP

- You can change the color of coconut and make it pastel or bright, depending on the amount of color used.

- **Preheat oven to 325°F (160°C)**
- **10-inch (4 L) tube pan, ungreased**

1. **Cake:** Prepare cake mix according to package directions. Fold in coconut. Bake and cool as directed.

2. **Topping:** In a large mixer bowl, beat whipping cream and confectioner's sugar to stiff peaks. Place cake upside-down on a serving plate. Frost completely with cream. Shake coconut and food coloring in tightly covered jar until coconut is evenly tinted a delicate pink. Mark top and sides of cake into 10 equal wedges and side panels. Sprinkle pink coconut over alternate wedges on top and side panels. Each serving will have coconut on either the top or the side. Chill until serving. Store leftover cake in the refrigerator.

Variation: Use toasted coconut instead of plain in both the cake and topping.

Crunchy Chocolate Toffee Angel Cake

Opposites attract — try light-as-a-feather angel food cake covered with decadent crunchy chocolate bars for a great taste sensation.

SERVES 12 TO 16

CAKE

1	package (16 oz/450 g) white angel food cake mix	1

FILLING AND TOPPING

3 cups	whipping (35%) cream	750 mL
6	toffee-crunch chocolate bars (each 1.4 oz/40 g)	6

TIPS

- Freeze chocolate bars before crushing. Leave in package and hit with mallet to crush.
- Chill bowl and beater before whipping cream to get maximum volume.

- **Preheat oven to 325°F (160°C)**
- **10-inch (4 L) tube pan, ungreased**

1. **Cake:** Prepare, bake and cool cake according to package directions. With an electric knife or long sharp serrated knife, cut cake horizontally into 2 or 3 layers.

2. **Filling and Topping:** In a large mixer bowl, beat cream to stiff peaks. Finely crush 5 of the chocolate bars. Chop the last bar into larger pieces. Fold the finely crushed bars into the whipped cream. Place one cake layer cut-side up on serving plate. Spread with 1 cup (250 mL) of the cream. Repeat with remaining cake layers and cream, ending with a cake layer, cut-side down. Spread remaining cream over sides and top of cake. Sprinkle coarsely chopped bar on top. Chill until serving. Store leftover cake in the refrigerator.

Variation: Add 3 tbsp (45 mL) sifted unsweetened cocoa powder to dry cake mix for a chocolate cake.

Coffee Chocolate Swirl Angel Cake

Enjoy a feathery light coffee angel food cake with chocolate swirls throughout.

SERVES 12 TO 16

2 tbsp	unsweetened cocoa powder, sifted	25 mL
2 tbsp	cold water	25 mL
1	package (16 oz/450 g) white angel food cake mix	1
1⅓ cups	cold, strong coffee	325 mL
	Chocolate Whipped Cream Frosting (see recipe, page 266) or coffee-flavored whipped cream (see Flavored Whipped Creams, page 266)	

TIPS

- Angel food cakes keep very well. You can prepare them 1 or 2 days ahead and frost the day you're going to serve them.
- A chocolate drizzle over the cream frosting is nice.

- **Preheat oven to 325°F (160°C)**
- **10-inch (4 L) tube pan, ungreased**

1. In a small bowl, mix cocoa and water until smooth; set aside.

2. In a large mixer bowl, combine cake mix and coffee. Beat on low speed for 30 seconds to blend, then on medium speed for 1 minute. Drizzle chocolate mixture over batter. Fold in gently 2 to 3 times; don't overmix. Pour into pan. Don't cut through batter. Bake and cool as directed on package.

3. Frost with Chocolate Whipped Cream Frosting.

Variation: Omit coffee if desired.

Coffee Almond Angel Dessert

This is definitely the dessert to choose if you're trying to impress.

CAKE

1	package (16 oz/450 g) white angel food cake mix	1
2 tbsp	instant coffee powder	25 mL
½ tsp	almond extract	2 mL

FROSTING

2 cups	whipping (35%) cream	500 mL
¼ cup	confectioner's (icing) sugar, sifted	50 mL
1 tbsp	instant coffee powder	15 mL
½ tsp	almond extract	2 mL

SUGARED ALMOND GARNISH

1½ cups	sliced almonds	375 mL
⅓ cup	granulated sugar	75 mL
2 tbsp	water	25 mL

TIPS

- When making the sugared almonds, use a baking sheet with sides or a jellyroll pan so you can stir them easily. Nonstick sheets work well.
- Prepare sugared almonds 1 or 2 days ahead. Store in a cookie tin at room temperature.
- Chocolate drizzle makes this cake even more sophisticated.

- **Preheat oven to 325°F (160°C)**
- **10-inch (4 L) tube pan, ungreased**
- **Large rimmed baking sheet, greased**

1. **Cake:** Add coffee powder and almond extract to cake mix and prepare, bake and cool according to package directions.

2. **Frosting:** In a large mixer bowl, combine whipping cream, confectioner's sugar, coffee powder and almond extract. Beat to stiff peaks. Spread on top and sides of cake.

3. **Sugared Almonds:** Preheat oven to 350°F (180°C). In a small bowl, combine almonds, sugar and water. Stir well to thoroughly coat nuts. Spread on prepared baking sheet. Bake for 12 to 15 minutes, stirring often, until golden. Remove from oven. Immediately loosen from baking sheet, then cool completely in pan on a wire rack. Break into clusters. Press nuts over top and sides of cake. Refrigerate until serving. Store leftover cake in the refrigerator.

Variation: Omit almond extract or replace with vanilla, if desired.

Peachy Angel Dessert

This versatile make-ahead dessert is ideal for potluck parties.

SERVES 12 TO 16

CAKE

1	package (16 oz/450 g) white angel food cake mix	1

FILLING

8 oz	cream cheese, softened	250 g
1 cup	confectioner's (icing) sugar, sifted	250 mL
2 cups	whipping (35%) cream	500 mL
¼ cup	peach schnapps liqueur	50 mL
1	can (19 oz/540 mL) peach pie filling	1

TIP

- If it's more convenient, you can prepare the cake a few days ahead.

- **Preheat oven to 325°F (160°C)**
- **10-inch (4 L) tube pan, ungreased**
- **13- by 9-inch (3 L) cake pan, ungreased**

1. **Cake:** Prepare, bake and cool cake according to package directions. Tear into bite-size pieces. Set aside.

2. **Filling:** In a large mixer bowl, beat cream cheese and confectioner's sugar until light and fluffy. In a separate bowl, beat whipping cream and liqueur to stiff peaks. Fold cream mixture into cheese mixture, gently but thoroughly. Add cake pieces. Stir well to evenly coat cake with filling. Spoon into rectangle cake pan. Press down lightly. Spread pie filling over top. Chill until serving. Store leftover dessert in the refrigerator.

Variation: Use your favorite pie filling and choose a complementary liqueur.

Orange Angel Cream Cake

Refreshingly light and creamy, is easy to enjoy this cake even after a hearty meal.

SERVES 12 TO 16

CAKE

1	package (16 oz/450 g) white angel food cake mix	1
1 cup	water	250 mL
1 tbsp	grated orange zest	15 mL
⅓ cup	orange juice	75 mL
2 or 3	drops orange or yellow food coloring (optional)	2 or 3

ORANGE CREAM FILLING AND TOPPING

2 cups	whipping (35%) cream	500 mL
2 tbsp	confectioner's (icing) sugar, sifted	25 mL
2 tsp	grated orange zest	10 mL
	Mandarin orange segments (optional)	

TIP

- Prepare cake ahead, keeping last-minute preparation for your dinner to a minimum.

- **Preheat oven to 325°F (160°C)**
- **10-inch (4 L) tube pan, ungreased**

1. **Cake:** In a large mixer bowl, combine cake mix, water, orange zest, orange juice and food coloring, if using. Beat on low speed for 30 seconds, then on medium speed for 1 minute. Pour into ungreased pan. Bake according to package directions. With an electric knife or a long sharp, serrated knife, cut cake horizontally to make 3 layers.

2. **Filling and Topping:** Beat whipping cream and confectioner's sugar to stiff peaks. Fold in orange zest. Spread cream between layers and on top of cake. Garnish with mandarins, if desired. Chill until serving. Store leftover cake in the refrigerator.

Variation: Replace orange zest with lemon zest and half the juice with lemon juice.

Peachy Angel Dessert ▶

Tiramisu Angel Torte

Traditionally made with ladyfingers, this angel food version is lighter than the classic Italian dessert.

- **Preheat oven to 325°F (160°C)**
- **10-inch (4 L) tube pan, ungreased**

SERVES 12 TO 16

CAKE

1	package (16 oz/450 g) white angel food cake mix	1

FILLING AND FROSTING

8 oz	cream cheese, softened	250 g
2 cups	whipping (35%) cream, divided	500 mL
⅔ cup	confectioner's (icing) sugar, sifted	150 mL
½ cup	almond liqueur, divided	125 mL
3 tbsp	unsweetened cocoa powder, sifted	45 mL
1 tbsp	instant espresso powder	15 mL
3 oz	bittersweet chocolate, coarsely grated	90 g
1 cup	toasted sliced almonds	250 mL
	Chocolate curls (see tip, page 20) or shaved chocolate (optional)	

TIPS

- For an even richer flavor, substitute traditional mascarpone cheese for the cream cheese.
- If desired, substitute 1 tbsp (15 mL) coffee powder for the espresso powder.
- Grate chocolate in a food processor, for convenience. If using a hand grater, buy a chocolate bar that is slightly bigger than the quantity required to avoid scraping your knuckles.

1. Cake: Prepare cake according to package directions. With a long sharp serrated knife, cut cake horizontally into 3 layers.

2. Filling and Frosting: In a large mixer bowl, beat cream cheese until smooth. Add 1 cup (250 mL) of cream, confectioner's sugar, 2 tbsp (25 mL) of liqueur, cocoa and coffee powder. Beat until smooth. In a separate bowl, beat remaining cream to stiff peaks. Fold into cheese mixture.

3. Assembly: Place bottom cake layer, cut-side up, on a serving plate. Sprinkle with 2 tbsp (25 mL) of liqueur. Spread with 1 cup (250 mL) of filling. Sprinkle with half of chocolate. Repeat layer. Top with third cake layer, cut-side down. Sprinkle with liqueur. Cover top and sides with remaining filling. Press almonds onto sides. Decorate top with chocolate curls. Chill until serving. Store in the refrigerator.

Variations: Use ¼ cup (50 mL) coffee liqueur or crème de cacao with an equal quantity of amaretto. Use semi-sweet chocolate in place of bittersweet.

Apricot Almond Angel Roll

It's hard to believe this light, creamy dessert roll starts with an angel food cake mix.

CAKE

1	package (16 oz/450 g) white angel food cake mix	1

FILLING

1½ cups	whipping (35%) cream	375 mL
2 tbsp	confectioner's (icing) sugar, sifted	25 mL
½ tsp	almond extract	2 mL
1	can (14 oz/398 mL) apricot halves, drained and coarsely chopped	1
½ cup	toasted slivered almonds	125 mL

TIPS

- The mix makes more batter than you need for the roll, so use the extra to bake a small cake to enjoy at any time. It is nice with berries and whipped cream.
- Use an electric knife or serrated bread knife to cut angel food cake.

- **Preheat oven to 350°F (180°C)**
- **15- by 10-inch (38 by 25 cm) jellyroll pan, greased, lined with parchment or waxed paper and greased again**
- **8-inch (2 L) square cake pan, ungreased and lined with parchment or waxed paper**

1. **Cake:** Prepare cake mix according to package directions. Remove 3 cups (750 mL) batter and spread it in prepared square pan. Spread remaining batter evenly in jellyroll pan. Bake cakes for about 20 minutes or until set, golden and top springs back when lightly touched. Cool for 10 minutes in pan on a wire rack, then invert cakes onto tea towels sprinkled with confectioner's sugar. Remove pans and paper. Store square cake for another use. Starting from short side, loosely roll up jellyroll in the tea towel. Cool completely.

2. **Filling:** In a small mixer bowl, beat cream, confectioner's sugar and extract together until stiff peaks form. Remove half and set aside for topping. Fold apricot pieces into remaining cream.

3. **Assembly:** Unroll cake carefully. Spread with apricot cream mixture. Re-roll and place on a serving dish, seam-side down. Frost cake completely with reserved cream. Sprinkle almonds on top. Chill until serving. Store leftover cake in the refrigerator.

Variation: Replace apricots with peaches or fresh strawberries.

Raspberry Angel Trifle

This delicious cake is sure to become a tradition for special occasions such as Christmas and Mother's Day.

SERVES 12 TO 16

CAKE

1	package (16 oz/450 g) white angel food cake mix	1

CUSTARD

4	egg yolks	4
¼ cup	granulated sugar	50 mL
¾ cup	all-purpose flour	175 mL
3 cups	milk	750 mL

FILLING

2 cups	whipping (35%) cream	500 mL
¼ cup	orange liqueur	50 mL
3 cups	fresh raspberries	750 mL

GARNISH

3 tbsp	toasted sliced almonds	45 mL
1 oz	semi-sweet chocolate, melted (optional)	30 g

TIPS

- You can use frozen berries in place of fresh. Keep in mind they will be juicy, so the pudding will be pinkish and the texture much moister.
- Prepare custard and cake the day before the trifle is to be served.
- Store leftover egg whites in a covered container in the refrigerator for up to 4 days.

- **Preheat oven to 325°F (160°C)**
- **10-inch (4 L) tube pan, ungreased**
- **Trifle bowl or large glass serving bowl**

1. **Cake:** Prepare, bake and cool cake according to package directions. Cut cake in half. Reserve half in freezer for your next dessert request. Tear remaining half into bite-size pieces. Set aside.

2. **Custard:** In a large saucepan, combine egg yolks, sugar, flour and milk. Cook over medium heat, stirring constantly until thickened, about 5 minutes. Cover tightly with plastic wrap pressing against the surface to prevent a skin from forming. Chill thoroughly.

3. **Filling:** In a large mixer bowl, beat whipping cream and liqueur to stiff peaks. Fold half of cream mixture into custard.

4. **Assembly:** Spread half of custard filling in trifle bowl. Put half of cake pieces on top. Sprinkle half of berries over cake. Repeat layers with remaining custard filling, cake and berries. Spread remaining whipped cream on top. Sprinkle almonds on top and drizzle with melted chocolate, if desired. Store leftover dessert in the refrigerator.

Variation: A mixture of berries also works well in this recipe. Strawberries, blackberries and blueberries are always popular.

Little Angels and Berries

Mini angel food cakes are perfect for individual servings of light strawberry shortcake.

SERVES 12		
1	package (16 oz/450 g) white angel food cake mix	1
6 cups	sliced fresh strawberries	1.5 L
CRÈME FRAÎCHE		
2 cups	whipping (35%) cream	500 mL
1 cup	sour cream	250 mL

TIPS
- If you don't have the proper pans, you can make the whole cake according to package directions and cut into 12 slices. Finish as for the minis.
- Prepare crème fraîche at least 2 days before using.
- Bake batter in 24 paper-lined muffin cups.

- **Preheat oven to 350°F (180°C)**
- **Twelve 4-inch (10 cm) mini angel food cake pans, ungreased**

1. Prepare angel food cake according to package directions. Using a piping bag (without top) or a spoon, divide batter evenly among mini cake pans. Run a knife through the batter to eliminate any large air pockets and smooth top with a spoon. Bake for 20 to 25 minutes or until golden and tops springs back when lightly touched. Turn upside down and cool completely. Remove from pan.

2. **Crème Fraîche:** In a nonreactive bowl, combine whipping cream and sour cream. Cover with plastic wrap. Let stand at room temperature for 16 to 24 hours, or until thickened. Refrigerate for 24 hours before using.

3. Place cakes on individual plates. Spoon crème fraîche alongside cake. Top with 1/2 cup (125 mL) sliced strawberries.

Variations: Use your favorite berries or a mixture of different berries. Replace crème fraîche with regular whipped cream.

Pineapple Angel Delight

It's embarrassing to admit how easy it is to make this fantastic cake.

SERVES ABOUT 12		
1	package (16 oz/450 g) white angel food cake mix	1
1	can (19 oz/540 mL) crushed pineapple, with juice	1
	Whipped cream (optional)	

TIP
- Garnish plate with fresh pineapple chunks or slices.

- **Preheat oven to 325°F (160°C)**
- **13- by 9-inch (3 L) cake pan, ungreased**

1. In a large mixer bowl, combine cake mix and crushed pineapple with juice. Beat on low speed for 30 seconds to blend, then on medium speed for 1 minute. Pour into pan. Bake for 30 to 35 minutes or until top is brown and firm. Cool completely in pan on a wire rack. Cover top with whipped cream or serve individual pieces with a generous scoop of ice cream.

Variation: Add grated orange zest or coconut extract to the batter.

Cheesecakes are another treat that is easier to make using a mix as a base, and they are always a perfect choice when you have guests.

Plain-and-Simple Cheesecake

Plain cheesecake is very versatile. You can top it with a pie filling, fresh fruit or fruit sauce, or enjoy it plain and simple.

SERVES 12 TO 16

CRUST

1	package (18.25 oz/515 g) white cake mix	1
⅓ cup	butter, melted	75 mL
1	egg	1

FILLING

1 lb	cream cheese, softened	500 g
1	can (14 oz/398 mL) sweetened condensed milk	1
3	eggs	3
½ cup	sour cream	125 mL
½ cup	reserved cake mix (see Step 1)	125 mL
1 tsp	grated lemon zest	5 mL
2 tbsp	lemon juice	25 mL

TOPPING

2 cups	sour cream	500 mL
¼ cup	granulated sugar	50 mL
1 tsp	vanilla	5 mL

TIPS

- Cheesecakes can be refrigerated for 1 week or frozen for up to 2 months. Thaw overnight in the refrigerator before serving.
- Cheesecakes are best prepared a day ahead to let flavor and texture mellow.
- The center of cheesecake should be soft set, not firm, when you remove it from the oven. Overbaking will result in a cracked top. Running a knife around the pan to loosen cake as soon as it is removed from the oven will also prevent cracking.

- **Preheat oven to 325°F (160°C)**
- **13- by 9-inch (3 L) cake pan, greased**

1. **Crust:** Measure out ½ cup (125 mL) of the cake mix. Reserve for filling. In a large mixer bowl, combine remaining cake mix, melted butter and egg. Beat on low speed for 1 minute or until a soft, smooth dough forms. Pat evenly over bottom and 1 inch (2.5 cm) up sides of prepared pan.

2. **Filling:** In a large mixer bowl, beat cream cheese and sweetened condensed milk on medium speed just to blend. Add eggs, one at a time, beating lightly after each addition until smooth. Add sour cream, reserved cake mix, lemon zest and lemon juice. Beat on medium speed for 1 minute. Spread evenly on crust. Bake for 30 to 35 minutes or just until set.

3. **Topping:** Combine sour cream, sugar and vanilla. Spread evenly over hot cheesecake. Return to oven and bake for 5 to 7 minutes longer or until topping is set. Run knife around edge of pan to loosen cake. Cool completely on a wire rack. Refrigerate overnight to let flavors mellow. Store leftover cheesecake in the refrigerator.

Variation: You may prefer a yellow cake mix for a "graham cracker" crust taste.

Chocolate Marble Cheesecake

The marbling of light and dark batters on a dark crust is stunning.

CRUST

1	package (18.25 oz/515 g) devil's food cake mix	1
½ cup	butter, melted	125 mL

FILLING

1½ lbs	cream cheese, softened	750 g
¾ cup	granulated sugar	175 mL
3	eggs	3
1 oz	unsweetened chocolate, melted (see tip, below)	30 g

TIP

- Chop chocolate for even melting. Melt in microwave on Medium for 1 to 1½ minutes, until almost melted, then stir until smooth.

- **Preheat oven to 350°F (180°C)**
- **10-inch (25 cm) springform pan**

1. **Crust:** Combine cake mix and melted butter. Stir together until well blended. Press evenly on bottom of pan. Bake for 10 minutes. Remove from oven. Cool while preparing filling. Increase oven temperature to 450°F (230°C).

2. **Filling:** In a large mixer bowl, beat cream cheese and sugar on medium speed until smooth. Add eggs, one at a time, beating well after each addition. Remove 1 cup (250 mL) filling; stir in melted chocolate. Spread plain filling over crust. Drop spoonfuls of chocolate filling on top. Run knife through batters to create marbling effect. Bake for 7 minutes, then reduce temperature to 250°F (120°C) and bake for 30 minutes longer or just until set. Run knife around edge of pan to loosen cake. Cool completely on a wire rack. Chill until serving. Store leftover cheesecake in the refrigerator.

Chocolate Toffee Crunch Cheesecake

The combination of crunchy caramel on top, a rich creamy chocolate cheesecake filling and decadent chocolate base is a real winner.

CRUST

1	package (18.25 oz/515 g) devil's food cake mix	1
⅓ cup	butter, melted	75 mL
1	egg	1

FILLING

1 lb	cream cheese, softened	500 g
1	can (14 oz/398 mL) sweetened condensed milk	1
2 oz	semi-sweet chocolate, melted and cooled (see tip, above)	60 g
3	eggs	3
½ cup	sour cream	125 mL
½ cup	reserved cake mix (see Step 1)	125 mL
1⅓ cups	crunchy toffee bits	325 mL

- **Preheat oven to 325°F (160°C)**
- **13- by 9-inch (3 L) cake pan, greased**

1. **Crust:** Measure out ½ cup (125 mL) of the cake mix. Reserve for filling. In a large mixer bowl, combine remaining cake mix, melted butter and egg. Beat on low speed for 1 minute or until a soft, smooth dough forms. Pat evenly over bottom and 1 inch (2.5 cm) up sides of prepared pan.

2. **Filling:** In a large mixer bowl, beat cream cheese, sweetened condensed milk and melted chocolate on medium speed just to blend. Add eggs, one at a time, beating lightly after each addition until smooth. Add sour cream and reserved cake mix. Beat on medium speed for 1 minute. Stir in 1 cup (250 mL) of the toffee bits. Spread evenly on crust. Sprinkle remaining ⅓ cup (75 mL) toffee bits on top. Bake for 45 to 50 minutes or just until set. Run knife around edge of pan to loosen cake. Cool completely on a wire rack. Refrigerate overnight to let flavors mellow. Store leftover cheesecake in the refrigerator.

Chocolate Coffee Marble Cheesecake

Pockets of creamy chocolate swirl through the coffee-flavored cheesecake in this stunning dessert.

SERVES 12 TO 16

CRUST

1	package (18.25 oz/515 g) devil's food cake mix	1
⅓ cup	butter, melted	75 mL
1	egg	1

FILLING

1½ lbs	cream cheese, softened	750 g
1 cup	granulated sugar	250 mL
3	eggs	3
2 tbsp	instant coffee powder, dissolved in 1 tbsp (15 mL) hot water	25 mL
¼ cup	butter, melted and cooled	50 mL
6 oz	bittersweet chocolate, chopped	175 g
¼ cup	whipping (35%) cream	50 mL

TIPS

- Use semi-sweet and bittersweet chocolate interchangeably.
- Chill cheesecake overnight or up to 3 days before serving. Let stand at room temperature for 1 hour before cutting.
- When cooked, cheesecake will still be jiggly in the center. It firms up as it cools. Be careful not to overbake, as this can cause cracks on the top.

- **Preheat oven to 350°F (180°C)**
- **10-inch (25 cm) springform pan, greased**

1. **Crust:** In a large mixer bowl, combine cake mix, melted butter and egg. Beat on low speed until dough forms. Press evenly over bottom and 1 inch (2.5 cm) up sides of prepared pan. Chill while preparing filling.

2. **Filling:** In a large mixer bowl, beat cream cheese and sugar on medium speed until smooth. Add eggs, one at a time, beating well after each addition. Add coffee mixture and melted butter. Mix well. In a saucepan, on low heat, melt chocolate with cream. Pour half of cheese filling (about 2½ cups/625 mL) into prepared crust. Drop 5 large spoonfuls of chocolate mixture around the edge, spacing evenly. Run tip of knife, through batters to create a marble effect. Pour remaining cheese filling on top and drop spoonfuls of chocolate mixture into the center 6 inches (15 cm) of filling, spacing evenly. Swirl to create a marble effect. Bake for 55 to 65 minutes or just until the center has a slight jiggle to it. Run knife around edge of pan to loosen cake. Cool completely on a wire rack. Store in the refrigerator.

Variation: Use espresso coffee powder for a stronger coffee flavor.

Dutch Apple Crumble Cheesecake

Replace the pie part of Dutch apple pie with cheesecake, and you've really got a winner.

SERVES 12 TO 16

CRUST

1	package (18.25 oz/515 g) white cake mix, divided	1
½ cup	butter, melted	125 mL

TOPPING

¼ cup	packed brown sugar	50 mL
¾ tsp	ground cinnamon	4 mL
2 tbsp	butter, softened	25 mL

FILLING

1½ lbs	cream cheese, softened	750 g
1 cup	packed brown sugar	250 mL
1 cup	sour cream	250 mL
4	eggs	4
2 tsp	vanilla	10 mL
1 tsp	ground cinnamon	5 mL
½ tsp	ground nutmeg	2 mL
¼ tsp	ground cloves	1 mL
1	large apple, peeled, cored and cut in ¼-inch (1 cm) slices (about 16 slices)	1

TIPS

- Turn bottom of springform pan over before filling so the lip side is down. With no lip to contend with, cutting is easy.
- Cut cheesecakes with a long sharp knife dipped in hot water and wiped off between each slice.

- **Preheat oven to 350°F (180°C)**
- **10-inch (25 cm) springform pan, greased**

1. **Crust:** Reserve ⅓ cup (75 mL) cake mix for topping. Combine remaining cake mix with melted butter. Mix well until a soft dough forms. Press evenly over bottom and 1 inch (2.5 cm) up sides of prepared pan. Bake for 8 to 10 minutes or until starting to set but still soft and not golden. Cool in pan on a wire rack.

2. **Topping:** In a bowl, combine reserved cake mix, brown sugar, cinnamon and butter, mixing until crumbly. Set aside.

3. **Filling:** In a large mixer bowl, combine cream cheese, brown sugar and sour cream. Beat on medium speed for 3 minutes. Add eggs, one at a time, beating well after each addition. Beat in vanilla, cinnamon, nutmeg and cloves. Pour filling into prepared crust. Arrange apple slices on top in a circular pattern, overlapping slightly as necessary. Sprinkle topping evenly over apples. Bake for 50 to 60 minutes or just until edges are set and the center has a slight jiggle to it. Run knife around edge of pan to loosen cake. Cool completely on a wire rack. Cover and refrigerate overnight before cutting. Store in the refrigerator.

Variation: Replace apple with a nectarine or pear or a mixture.

Bumbleberry Cheesecake

This light but creamy cheesecake is bursting with fresh berry flavor.

CRUST

1	package (18.25 oz/515 g) white cake mix	1
⅓ cup	butter, melted	75 mL
1	egg	1

FILLING

1	envelope (¼ oz/7 g) unflavored gelatin	1
¼ cup	cold water	50 mL
1 lb	cream cheese, softened	500 g
1 cup	granulated sugar	250 mL
2 tbsp	lemon juice	25 mL
1½ cups	whipping (35%) cream	375 mL
1½ cups	crushed fresh strawberries	375 mL
1 cup	crushed fresh blueberries	250 mL
1 cup	crushed fresh raspberries	250 mL

GARNISH

1 cup	whipping (35%) cream	250 mL
¼ cup	confectioner's (icing) sugar, sifted	50 mL
1 cup	mixed whole berries	250 mL

- **Preheat oven to 350°F (180°C)**
- **10-inch (25 cm) springform pan, greased**

1. **Crust:** In a large mixer bowl, combine cake mix, melted butter and egg. Beat on low speed for 1 minute or until a soft, moist dough forms. Press firmly in bottom of pan. Bake for 10 to 15 minutes or until golden. Cool in pan on a wire rack.

2. **Filling:** Sprinkle gelatin over water in small saucepan. Let stand for 2 minutes. Heat over low heat, stirring until dissolved. Remove from heat. Set aside to cool slightly. Combine cream cheese and sugar in large mixer bowl. Beat on medium speed for 3 minutes or until light and creamy. Gradually add gelatin mixture and lemon juice, beating until smooth. In a separate mixer bowl, beat cream to soft peaks. Fold into cheese mixture. Fold in crushed berries, gently but thoroughly. Pour over crust. Chill until firm, about 2 hours or overnight.

3. **Garnish:** In a large mixer bowl, beat cream and confectioner's sugar until stiff peaks form. Pipe rosettes around top of cheesecake and garnish with fresh berries. Store in the refrigerator.

Variation: Use your favorite berries as long as the total amount is 3½ cups (875 mL). Blackberries are nice in season.

TIPS
- I prefer regular cream cheese for baked cheesecake, but the light is well suited to unbaked versions and works well with other light ingredients such as fresh berries.
- A set of springform pans is a good investment. With a removable ring, you never have to worry about cakes sticking to the pan.

Caramel Cashew Cheesecake

This dessert is a knockout — it will dazzle your guests.

SERVES 12 TO 16

CRUST

1	package (18.25 oz/515 g) white cake mix	1
¾ cup	finely chopped roasted unsalted cashews	175 mL
⅓ cup	butter, melted	75 mL
1	egg	1

FILLING

1½ lbs	cream cheese, softened	750 g
1 cup	granulated sugar	250 mL
4	eggs	4
¼ cup	whipping (35%) cream	50 mL
2 tsp	vanilla	10 mL

TOPPING

1 cup	granulated sugar	250 mL
3 tbsp	water	45 mL
⅔ cup	whipping (35%) cream	150 mL
1 cup	coarsely chopped roasted unsalted cashews	250 mL

TIPS

- The topping looks amazing, but the taste of this cake is so good that it works as a plain cheesecake, too.
- The filling puffs during baking and settles on cooling.
- Don't overbeat cheesecake fillings. This can cause them to crack during baking.

- **Preheat oven to 325°F (160°C)**
- **10-inch (25 cm) springform pan, greased**

1. **Crust:** In a large mixer bowl, combine cake mix, cashews, melted butter and egg. Beat on low speed for 1 minute or until a soft, moist dough forms. Press evenly over bottom and 1½ inches (3.5 cm) up sides of prepared pan. Chill while preparing filling.

2. **Filling:** In a large mixer bowl, beat cream cheese and sugar on medium speed until smooth. Add eggs, one at a time, beating well after each addition. Add cream and vanilla, beating just until blended. Pour filling into prepared crust. Bake for 70 to 80 minutes or just until edges are set and the center has a slight jiggle to it. Run knife around edge of pan to loosen cake. Cool completely on a wire rack.

3. **Topping:** In a saucepan, over low heat, heat sugar and water, stirring constantly, until sugar dissolves. Increase heat to medium-high and boil, swirling the pan often until the mixture turns amber, about 10 minutes. Carefully add cream (mixture will bubble up). Bring to a simmer, stirring until smooth. Remove from heat. Stir in cashews. Cool to lukewarm. Carefully spoon topping over cheesecake. Chill overnight or up to 3 days before serving. Let stand at room temperature for 1 hour before cutting. Store in the refrigerator.

Variation: Omit topping. Serve with a drizzle of caramel or chocolate sauce.

Raspberry Pear Cheesecake

A creamy filling with fresh raspberries throughout, a layer of pear slices and a crumble topping make this a showstopper.

SERVES 12 TO 16

CRUST

1	package (18.25 oz/515 g) white cake mix	1
¾ cup	ground almonds	175 mL
⅔ cup	butter, melted	150 mL

TOPPING

¼ cup	packed brown sugar	50 mL
1 tsp	ground cinnamon	5 mL
2 tbsp	butter, softened	30 mL

FILLING

1½ lbs	cream cheese, softened	750 g
1 cup	granulated sugar	250 mL
1 cup	sour cream	250 mL
4	eggs	4
2 tsp	vanilla	10 mL
1 cup	fresh raspberries	250 mL
2	large pears, peeled, cored and cut in ¼-inch (1 cm) slices (about 16)	2

TIPS

- Prepare a day ahead for maximum flavor and easy entertaining.
- Run a knife around edge of cheesecake as soon as it comes out of the oven to prevent cracking on top.
- Serve cheesecake at room temperature for the creamiest texture.

- **Preheat oven to 350°F (180°C)**
- **10-inch (25 cm) springform pan, greased**

1. **Crust:** Reserve ⅓ cup (75 mL) of the cake mix for topping. Combine remaining cake mix, almonds and melted butter. Mix well until a soft dough forms. Press evenly over bottom and 1 inch (2.5 cm) up sides of prepared pan. Bake for 8 to 10 minutes or until starting to set but still soft and not golden. Cool in pan on a wire rack.

2. **Topping:** In a small bowl, combine reserved cake mix, brown sugar, cinnamon and butter, mixing until crumbly. Set aside.

3. **Filling:** In large mixer bowl, combine cream cheese, sugar and sour cream. Beat on medium speed for 3 minutes. Add eggs, one at a time, beating well after each addition. Beat in vanilla. Fold in raspberries. Pour filling into partially baked crust. Arrange pear slices on top in a circular pattern, overlapping slightly as necessary. Sprinkle topping evenly over pears. Bake for 50 to 60 minutes or until edges are just set and center has a slight jiggle to it. Run a knife around edge of pan to loosen cake. Cool completely on a wire rack. Cover and refrigerate overnight before cutting. Store in the refrigerator.

Variation: Replace pears with peeled apple or plum slices.

Pumpkin Cheesecake

Tired of traditional pumpkin pie during the holiday season? Even pumpkin-haters will love this dessert.

SERVES 12 TO 16

CRUST

1	package (18.25 oz/515 g) spice cake mix	1
½ cup	butter, melted	125 mL

FILLING

1½ lbs	cream cheese, softened	750 g
1	can (14 oz/398 mL) sweetened condensed milk	1
1	can (14 oz/398 mL) pumpkin purée (not pie filling)	1
4	eggs	4
1 tbsp	pumpkin pie spice	15 mL

TOPPING

1½ cups	whipping (35%) cream	375 mL
¼ cup	confectioner's (icing) sugar, sifted	50 mL
¼ cup	toasted sliced almonds	50 mL

TIPS

- Be sure to use pumpkin purée — not pumpkin pie filling, which has sugar and spices added to it.
- Don't be alarmed if the cake puffs up while baking — it will settle on cooling.
- Replace pumpkin pie spice with 2 tsp (10 mL) ground cinnamon, and ¼ to ½ tsp (1 to 2 mL) each ground nutmeg and ground cloves.

- **Preheat oven to 350°F (180°C)**
- **10-inch (25 cm) springform pan**

1. **Crust:** Combine cake mix and melted butter. Mix well. Press firmly on bottom of pan. Set aside.

2. **Filling:** In a large mixer bowl, beat cream cheese and sweetened condensed milk on high speed for 2 minutes. Add pumpkin, eggs and spice. Beat for 1 minute longer or until smooth. Pour over prepared crust. Bake for 55 to 60 minutes or just until set. Run knife around edge of pan to loosen cake. Cool completely on a wire rack, then chill for 2 hours or overnight.

3. **Topping:** Beat cream and confectioner's sugar to stiff peaks. Spread over cheesecake. Sprinkle with almonds. Chill until serving. Store leftover cheesecake in the refrigerator.

Variation: Bake cheesecake in a 13- by 9-inch (3 L) pan at 350°F (180°C) for 30 to 35 minutes. You can cut this into large dessert pieces or small cookie-tray-size treats.

Fruit-Topped Mini Cheesecakes

A perfect make-ahead dessert for your next party. Top with a variety of fruit pie fillings or fresh fruit for an attractive presentation. A fresh mint leaf is a pretty finishing touch.

SERVES 24

CRUST

1	package (18.25 oz/515 g) white cake mix	1
1/3 cup	butter, melted	75 mL

FILLING

1 lb	cream cheese, softened	500 g
3/4 cup	granulated sugar	175 mL
3	eggs	3
1 tsp	vanilla	5 mL

TOPPING

2 cups	sour cream	500 mL
1/3 cup	granulated sugar	75 mL
	Fruit pie filling or fresh fruit	

TIPS

- Buy deep paper cup liners if possible. While paper liners make storage and transportation easy, you can also bake these cheesecakes in greased muffin cups with no liners if using within a day.
- For another attractive presentation, omit sour cream layer. Place cheesecakes upside down on plate and serve with fresh fruit sauce.

- **Preheat oven to 350°F (180°C)**
- **Two 12-cup muffin tins, greased or paper-lined**

1. **Crust:** In a large mixer bowl, combine cake mix and melted butter. Beat on low speed for 2 minutes or until crumble mixture is thoroughly blended. Divide mixture evenly in muffin cups. Press down firmly with back of a spoon.

2. **Filling:** Beat cream cheese and sugar together on low speed until blended. Add eggs, one at a time, then vanilla, beating until smooth. Spoon into prepared cups, dividing evenly. Bake for 20 to 25 minutes or until set.

3. **Topping:** Combine sour cream and sugar. Spoon over hot baked cheesecakes, spreading to cover tops. Return to oven and bake for 5 minutes longer. Cool completely in pan on a wire rack.

4. To serve, carefully remove paper cups and top cheesecakes with a spoonful of pie filling or a small piece of fruit such as a mandarin, raspberry, strawberry or kiwi. Store leftover cheesecakes in the refrigerator.

Fruit-Topped Mini Cheesecakes ▶

Strawberry Cheesecake Squares

Cut these into large squares for a dessert or bite-size for a cookie tray.

MAKES ABOUT 3 DOZEN SQUARES

CRUST

1	package (18.25 oz/515 g) white cake mix	1
¾ cup	finely chopped almonds	175 mL
¾ cup	butter	175 mL

FILLING

1 lb	cream cheese, softened	500 g
⅔ cup	granulated sugar	150 mL
2	eggs, at room temperature	2
½ tsp	almond extract	2 mL
1 cup	strawberry jam	250 mL
¾ cup	sliced almonds	175 mL

TIPS

- Refrigerate for at least 3 hours or overnight before serving.
- Cooking spray is very easy for greasing baking pans. Don't overdo it, though; a light spray is all that you need.

- Preheat oven to 350°F (180°C)
- 13- by 9-inch (3 L) cake pan, greased

1. **Crust:** In a large bowl, combine cake mix and chopped almonds. With a pastry blender or two knives, cut in butter until crumbly. Reserve 1 cup (250 mL) for topping. Press remainder into prepared pan. Bake for 15 minutes or until light golden.

2. **Filling:** In a large mixer bowl, beat cream cheese, sugar, eggs and extract together on medium speed until smooth and creamy. Spread evenly over hot crust. Bake for 15 minutes longer. Cool for 10 minutes on a wire rack. Stir jam until smooth. Spread evenly over filling. Stir sliced almonds into reserved crumble mixture. Sprinkle over jam. Bake for 15 minutes longer. Cool completely in pan on a wire rack. Chill for 3 hours or overnight before cutting into squares. Store leftover squares in the refrigerator.

Variations: Replace strawberry jam with raspberry, apricot or cherry. Replace almond extract with vanilla.

Blueberry Cheesecake Squares

A double hit of blueberry not only tastes great but looks terrific too.

MAKES ABOUT 3 DOZEN SQUARES

CRUST

1	package (18.25 oz/515 g) white cake mix	1
1 cup	graham wafer crumbs	250 mL
¾ cup	butter, melted	175 mL

FILLING

1 lb	cream cheese, softened	500 g
¾ cup	granulated sugar	175 mL
2	eggs, at room temperature	2
1 tbsp	lemon juice	15 mL
1 cup	blueberry jam	250 mL
1 cup	fresh blueberries	250 mL

- Preheat oven to 350°F (180°C)
- 13- by 9-inch (3 L) cake pan, greased

1. **Crust:** In a large bowl, combine cake mix, graham wafer crumbs and melted butter, mixing until crumbly. Press firmly into prepared pan. Bake for 15 to 20 minutes or until light golden. Cool for 10 minutes.

2. **Filling:** In a large mixer bowl, beat cream cheese, sugar, eggs and lemon juice on medium speed until smooth and creamy. Spread jam over crust. Sprinkle with blueberries. Pour cheese mixture evenly over berries. Bake for 25 to 30 minutes or until set. Cool completely in pan on a wire rack. Chill for 3 hours or overnight before cutting into squares. Store leftover squares in the refrigerator.

Variation: Replace blueberry jam and blueberries with raspberry jam and raspberries.

Lemon-Glazed Cheesecake Squares

If you like lemon, you'll love this dessert — light and creamy with a great lemon taste. Cut into bite-size pieces for a cookie tray or into larger pieces for a dessert.

SERVES 12 TO 16

CRUST

1	package (18.25 oz/515 g) white cake mix	1
½ cup	butter, melted	125 mL

FILLING

1½ lbs	cream cheese, softened	750 g
¾ cup	granulated sugar	175 mL
3	eggs	3
⅓ cup	lemon juice	75 mL

TOPPING

2 cups	sour cream	500 mL
3 tbsp	granulated sugar	45 mL

GLAZE

½ cup	granulated sugar	125 mL
2 tbsp	cornstarch	25 mL
¾ cup	water	175 mL
⅓ cup	lemon juice	75 mL
1	egg yolk, beaten	1
1 tbsp	butter	15 mL

TIP

- For best flavor (and convenience), prepare a day ahead. Line pan completely with aluminum foil or parchment paper. You can then remove the cooled cake for easy slicing.

- **Preheat oven to 350°F (180°C)**
- **13- by 9-inch (3 L) cake pan, greased**

1. **Crust:** Combine cake mix and melted butter; stir together until well blended. Press firmly into prepared pan. Bake for 15 to 20 minutes or until light golden.

2. **Filling:** In a large mixer bowl, beat cream cheese and sugar on high speed until smooth. Add eggs, one at a time, and lemon juice, beating until smooth. Spread over crust. Bake for 35 to 40 minutes or just until set in center.

3. **Topping:** Combine sour cream and sugar. Spread over hot cheesecake. Return to oven and bake for 5 minutes longer. Cool for 1 hour on a wire rack.

4. **Glaze:** Prepare glaze while cheesecake is cooling. In a small saucepan, combine sugar and cornstarch. Stir in water, lemon juice and egg yolk. Cook over medium heat, stirring constantly, until mixture comes to a boil and thickens. Add butter, stirring until melted. Cool slightly. Spread evenly over cheesecake. Chill until serving. Store leftover cheesecake in the refrigerator.

Variations: Add ½ cup (125 mL) ground nuts to the crust. For a stronger lemon taste, try making the crust with a lemon cake mix.

Cherry Cheesecake Bars

Enjoy these bite-size cheesecakes for dessert or a snack. Vary the flavor to suit your family.

MAKES ABOUT 3 DOZEN BARS

CRUST

1	package (18.25 oz/515 g) white cake mix, divided	1
½ cup	crushed corn flakes cereal	125 mL
1	egg	1
½ cup	butter, melted	125 mL

FILLING

1 lb	cream cheese, softened	500 g
⅓ cup	granulated sugar	75 mL
2	eggs	2
1 tsp	grated lemon zest	5 mL
1 tbsp	lemon juice	15 mL
1	can (19 oz/540 mL) cherry pie filling	1

TOPPING

½ cup	chopped pecans	125 mL
½ tsp	ground cinnamon	2 mL
¼ cup	butter, melted	50 mL

TIP

- Melt butter in a measuring cup in the microwave for easy drizzling.

- **Preheat oven to 350°F (180°C)**
- **13- by 9-inch (3 L) cake pan, greased**

1. **Crust:** Reserve ½ cup (125 mL) cake mix for topping. In a large bowl, combine remaining mix, crushed corn flakes, egg and melted butter. Using a wooden spoon, mix until a soft dough forms. Press firmly into bottom and slightly up sides of prepared pan. Chill while preparing filling.

2. **Filling:** In a large mixer bowl, beat cream cheese and sugar until blended. Add eggs, one at a time, beating thoroughly after each addition. Stir in lemon zest and juice. Spread over crust. Dollop tablespoonfuls of pie filling over cheese mixture.

3. **Topping:** In a bowl, combine reserved cake mix, pecans and cinnamon. Sprinkle over filling. Drizzle with melted butter. Bake for 40 to 50 minutes or just until set. Cool completely in pan on a wire rack. Refrigerate until serving. Cut into bars. Store leftover bars in the refrigerator.

Variation: Use any flavor of pie filling. Peach and blueberry are both delicious.

As the name implies, coffee cakes are a perfect match for a cup of steaming coffee, cappuccino or tea at any time of day. These cakes tend to be less sweet than most, and they often contain fresh fruit. They are always wonderful served warm. One taste of the Raspberry Streusel Cake, a personal favorite, will sell you on their special charms.

Sour Cream Coffee Cake

The sour cream keeps this cake moist, making it ideal to prepare for a brunch.

SERVES 12 TO 16		
CAKE		
1	package (18.25 oz/515 g) white cake mix	1
1	package (4-serving size) vanilla instant pudding mix	1
4	eggs	4
1 cup	sour cream	250 mL
½ cup	vegetable oil	125 mL
TOPPING		
⅓ cup	granulated sugar	75 mL
1½ tsp	ground cinnamon	7 mL
¾ cup	chopped nuts	175 mL

TIP
- Prepare topping first and set aside while mixing the cake.

- **Preheat oven to 350°F (180°C)**
- **10-inch (4 L) tube pan, greased and floured**

1. **Cake:** In a large mixer bowl, combine cake mix, pudding mix, eggs, sour cream and oil. Beat on medium speed for 4 minutes.

2. **Topping:** Combine sugar and cinnamon until blended. Stir in nuts.

3. **Assembly:** Spread half of batter in prepared pan. Sprinkle half of topping mixture evenly over batter. Repeat with remaining batter and topping. Bake for 50 to 55 minutes or until a tester inserted in center comes out clean. Cool for 25 minutes in pan on a wire rack, then remove coffee cake from pan. Serve warm or cool.

Variation: Use any type of nut you like. I prefer pecans, but walnuts, almonds and hazelnuts are all great.

Sour Cream Poppy Seed Coffee Cake

Poppy seeds add a nice crunch to this tender, moist cake.

SERVES 12 TO 16		
FILLING		
⅓ cup	packed brown sugar	75 mL
2 tsp	ground cinnamon	10 mL
½ tsp	instant coffee powder	2 mL
CAKE		
1	package (18.25 oz/515 g) white cake mix	1
1	package (4-serving size) vanilla instant pudding mix	1
4	eggs	4
1 cup	sour cream	250 mL
½ cup	vegetable oil	125 mL
¼ cup	poppy seeds	50 mL

- **Preheat oven to 350°F (180°C)**
- **10-inch (4 L) tube pan, greased and floured**

1. **Filling:** In a small bowl, combine brown sugar, cinnamon and coffee powder. Set aside.

2. **Cake:** In a large mixer bowl, combine cake mix, pudding mix, eggs, sour cream, oil and poppy seeds. Beat on medium speed for 4 minutes. Spread half of batter in prepared pan. Sprinkle filling mixture evenly over batter. Cover with remaining batter. Bake for 50 to 55 minutes or until a tester inserted in center comes out clean. Cool for 25 minutes in pan on a wire rack, then remove from pan and place on rack. Serve warm or cool.

Variation: Add ⅓ cup (75 mL) chopped nuts to the filling.

TIPS
- If you prefer a stronger coffee flavor, use instant espresso coffee powder.
- For an attractive finish, dust the top of this cake with confectioner's (icing) sugar. A small sieve, salt shaker or spice bottle with holes in the top work well for dusting.

Chocolate Banana Coffee Cake

This moist cake is easy to make and keeps well. It is perfect for a lunchbox treat or after-school snack.

SERVES 12 TO 16		
TOPPING		
½ cup	packed brown sugar	125 mL
1 tsp	ground cinnamon	5 mL
1½ cups	miniature semi-sweet chocolate chips	375 mL
CAKE		
1	package (18.25 oz/515 g) devil's food cake mix	1
1	package (4-serving size) vanilla instant pudding mix	1
4	eggs	4
1½ cups	mashed ripe bananas (3 to 4 large)	375 mL
⅓ cup	vegetable oil	75 mL

- **Preheat oven to 350°F (180°C)**
- **13- by 9-inch (3 L) cake pan, greased**

1. **Topping:** In a small bowl, combine brown sugar and cinnamon. Set aside.

2. **Cake:** In a large mixer bowl, combine cake mix, pudding mix, eggs, bananas and oil. Beat on medium speed for 2 minutes. Spread half of batter in prepared pan. Sprinkle half of topping over batter in pan. Sprinkle with half of the chocolate chips. Repeat layers with remaining cake batter, topping and chips. Bake for 45 to 50 minutes or until a tester inserted in center comes out clean. Cool for 30 minutes in pan on a wire rack. Serve warm or cool.

Variations: Try using regular chocolate chips in place of the miniature version for a chunkier top. For a stronger banana flavor, use a banana cream instant pudding mix instead of the vanilla.

Crunchy White Chocolate Banana Coffee Cake

This cake is very simple, yet very good.

SERVES 12 TO 16		
CAKE		
1	package (18.25 oz/515 g) white cake mix	1
1	package (4-serving size) vanilla instant pudding mix	1
4	eggs	4
1¼ cups	mashed ripe bananas (3 large)	300 mL
⅓ cup	vegetable oil	75 mL
1 cup	white chocolate chips	250 mL
TOPPING		
¾ cup	chopped almonds	175 mL
½ cup	packed brown sugar	125 mL
2 tbsp	butter, melted	25 mL

- **Preheat oven to 350°F (180°C)**
- **13- by 9-inch (3 L) cake pan, greased**

1. **Cake:** In a large mixer bowl, combine cake mix, pudding mix, eggs, bananas and oil. Beat on medium speed for 2 minutes. Stir in white chocolate chips. Spread batter evenly in prepared pan.

2. **Topping:** In a bowl, combine almonds, brown sugar and melted butter. Mix well. Sprinkle evenly over batter. Bake for 35 to 40 minutes or until a tester inserted in center comes out clean. Cool for 30 minutes in pan on a wire rack. Serve warm or cool.

Variations: Try substituting a butterscotch or chocolate pudding for the vanilla. They make an interesting combination with banana. Omit topping and spread Banana Butter Frosting (see recipe, page 264) over cooled cake.

Banana Toffee Crumb Cake

A few simple changes to an all-time favorite can make it company fare.

CRUMB TOPPING

¼ cup	all-purpose flour	50 mL
¼ cup	confectioner's (icing) sugar	50 mL
1 tsp	ground cinnamon	5 mL
2 tbsp	butter, softened	25 mL
⅓ cup	crunchy toffee bits	75 mL

CAKE

1	package (18.25 oz/515 g) white cake mix	1
1	package (4-serving size) vanilla instant pudding mix	1
4	eggs	4
1¼ cups	mashed ripe bananas (3 large)	300 mL
⅓ cup	vegetable oil	75 mL
⅔ cup	crunchy toffee bits	150 mL

- **Preheat oven to 350°F (180°C)**
- **10-inch (25 cm) springform pan, greased**

1. **Crumb Topping:** In a small bowl, combine flour, confectioner's sugar, cinnamon and butter, mixing with a fork or your fingers until crumbly. Stir in toffee bits. Set aside.

2. **Cake:** In a large mixer bowl, combine cake mix, pudding mix, eggs, bananas and oil. Beat on low speed for 1 minute to blend, then on medium speed for 2 minutes. Stir in toffee bits. Spread batter evenly in prepared pan. Sprinkle topping evenly over batter. Bake for 55 to 60 minutes or until a tester inserted in center comes out clean. Cool completely in pan on a wire rack.

Variation: Use butterscotch pudding for another great taste.

TIP
- Coffee cakes don't usually require a frosting, so all the work is done in one step.

Chocolate Chip Coffee Cake

A perfect coffee-time treat that freezes well.

CAKE

1	package (18.25 oz/515 g) white cake mix	1
1	package (4-serving size) vanilla instant pudding mix	1
4	eggs	4
1⅓ cups	sour cream	325 mL
⅓ cup	vegetable oil	75 mL
1 cup	miniature semi-sweet chocolate chips	250 mL

TOPPING

½ cup	packed brown sugar	125 mL
½ cup	Grape-Nuts-type cereal	125 mL
½ tsp	ground cinnamon	2 mL

CHOCOLATE DRIZZLE (OPTIONAL)

2 oz	semi-sweet chocolate	60 g

- **Preheat oven to 350°F (180°C)**
- **13- by 9-inch (3 L) cake pan, greased**

1. **Cake:** In a large mixer bowl, combine cake mix, pudding mix, eggs, sour cream and oil. Beat on medium speed for 2 minutes or until smooth. Stir in chocolate chips. Spread batter evenly in prepared pan.

2. **Topping:** Combine brown sugar, cereal and cinnamon. Sprinkle evenly over batter. Bake for 40 to 50 minutes or until a tester inserted in center comes out clean. Cool completely in pan on a wire rack.

3. **Drizzle:** If desired, melt chocolate in a saucepan over low heat, or in microwave on Medium for about 1½ minutes. Stir until smooth. Drizzle over cooled cake.

Variations: A white chocolate drizzle is attractive. Replace cereal with chopped nuts in the topping.

Apple Pinwheel Cake

This versatile cake is sure to impress your guests.

SERVES 12 TO 16

TOPPING

4 to 5	apples	4 to 5
1 tbsp	lemon juice	15 mL
1½ tbsp	granulated sugar	22 mL
1½ tsp	ground cinnamon	7 mL

CAKE

1	package (18.25 oz/515 g) white cake mix	1
¼ cup	granulated sugar	50 mL
8 oz	cream cheese, softened	250 g
3	eggs	3
⅓ cup	vegetable oil	75 mL
¼ cup	water	50 mL
1 tsp	ground cinnamon	5 mL

TIP

- Although this cake is very attractive plain, you can dress it up with a white drizzle and some toasted pecan halves on top. It's also delicious served with a drizzle of caramel sauce and whipped cream.

- **Preheat oven to 350°F (180°C)**
- **10½-inch (26 cm) springform pan, greased**

1. **Topping:** Peel, core and thinly slice apples to make 4 cups (1 L). Toss with lemon juice. Set aside. In a separate bowl, combine sugar and cinnamon. Set aside.

2. **Cake:** In a large mixer bowl, combine cake mix, sugar, cream cheese, eggs, oil, water and cinnamon. Beat on low speed for 1 minute to blend, then on medium speed for 2 minutes. Spread batter evenly in prepared pan. Arrange apple slices attractively on top of batter, overlapping slightly as necessary. Sprinkle with cinnamon-sugar mixture. Bake for 60 to 70 minutes or until a tester inserted in center of cake portion comes out clean. Cool for 30 minutes in pan on a wire rack. Serve warm or cool.

Variation: Try other fruits such as pears, plums or nectarines, instead of apples.

Apple Coffee Cake

Which is better, this coffee cake or fresh apple pie? It's a close call.

SERVES 12 TO 16

FILLING

4 cups	peeled, thinly sliced apples (4 large)	1 L
⅓ cup	granulated sugar	75 mL
2 tsp	ground cinnamon	10 mL

CAKE

1	package (18.25 oz/515 g) white cake mix	1
¼ cup	granulated sugar	50 mL
3	eggs	3
8 oz	cream cheese, softened	250 g
½ cup	vegetable oil	125 mL
¼ cup	water	50 mL

- **Preheat oven to 350°F (180°C)**
- **10-inch (4 L) tube pan, greased and floured**

1. **Filling:** In a large bowl, combine apples, sugar and cinnamon, tossing to coat apples thoroughly. Set aside.

2. **Cake:** In a large mixer bowl, combine cake mix, sugar, eggs, cream cheese, oil and water. Beat on low speed for 1 minute to blend, then on medium speed for 2 minutes or until smooth. Spread one third of the batter in prepared pan. Scatter half of the apples on top. Repeat layers once and spread remaining batter on top. Bake for 60 to 65 minutes or until a tester inserted in center comes out clean. Cool for 25 minutes in pan on a rack, then remove and cool completely on rack.

Variation: Replace apples with fresh blueberries.

Raspberry Coffee Cake

A wonderful way to enjoy fresh raspberries while they are in season.

SERVES 12 TO 16		
STREUSEL		
⅔ cup	all-purpose flour	150 mL
½ cup	packed brown sugar	125 mL
⅓ cup	butter, softened	75 mL
½ tsp	ground cinnamon	2 mL
CAKE		
1	package (18.25 oz/515 g) white cake mix	1
⅓ cup	granulated sugar	75 mL
8 oz	cream cheese, softened	250 g
3	eggs	3
½ cup	vegetable oil	125 mL
¼ cup	water	50 mL
3 cups	fresh raspberries	750 mL

- **Preheat oven to 375°F (190°C)**
- **13- by 9-inch (3 L) cake pan, greased**

1. **Streusel:** Combine flour, brown sugar, butter and cinnamon, mixing until crumbly. Set aside.

2. **Cake:** In a large mixer bowl, combine cake mix, sugar, cream cheese, eggs, oil and water. Beat on low speed for 1 minute to blend, then on medium speed for 2 minutes or until smooth. Spread half of batter in prepared pan. Scatter raspberries over batter. Spread remaining batter over berries. Sprinkle streusel evenly over batter. Bake for 40 to 45 minutes or until top springs back when lightly touched. Cool for at least 30 minutes in pan on a wire rack. Serve warm or cool.

Variation: A mixture of blueberries and raspberries, or all blueberries, also tastes great.

TIP
- If raspberries seem very juicy, toss with a little flour before putting in cake.

Blueberry Pecan Coffee Cake

Enjoy fresh berries at their best — especially with a tender cake underneath and a crunchy nut streusel on top.

SERVES 12 TO 16		
TOPPING		
1 cup	chopped pecans	250 mL
½ cup	packed brown sugar	125 mL
2 tbsp	all-purpose flour	25 mL
½ tsp	ground cinnamon	2 mL
3 tbsp	butter, melted	45 mL
CAKE		
1	package (18.25 oz/515 g) white cake mix	1
⅓ cup	granulated sugar	75 mL
8 oz	cream cheese, softened	250 g
3	eggs	3
½ cup	vegetable oil	125 mL
¼ cup	water	50 mL
2 cups	fresh blueberries	500 mL

- **Preheat oven to 350°F (180°C)**
- **13- by 9-inch (3 L) cake pan, greased**

1. **Topping:** In a small bowl, combine pecans, brown sugar, flour, cinnamon and melted butter. Mix well and set aside.

2. **Cake:** In a large mixer bowl, combine cake mix, sugar, cream cheese, eggs, oil and water. Beat on low speed for 1 minute to blend, then on medium speed for 2 minutes or until smooth. Spread batter evenly in prepared pan. Scatter blueberries evenly over batter. Sprinkle topping over berries. Bake for 45 to 50 minutes or until a tester inserted in center comes out clean. Cool for at least 30 minutes in pan on a wire rack. Serve warm or cool.

TIP
- Small wild blueberries are wonderful in this cake. The next best choice is regular fresh berries or, failing these, use frozen berries, thawed and patted dry.

Cinnamon Brunch Cake

This is one of my mother's favorite cakes. I'm not sure if it's because she likes the taste or because I can make it ahead to leave in her freezer!

SERVES 12 TO 16

CAKE

½ cup	packed brown sugar	125 mL
2 tsp	ground cinnamon	10 mL
¾ cup	finely chopped almonds	175 mL
1	package (18.25 oz/515 g) white cake mix	1
1	package (4-serving size) vanilla instant pudding mix	1
4	eggs	4
¾ cup	vegetable oil	175 mL
¾ cup	water	175 mL
1 tsp	almond extract	5 mL

GLAZE (OPTIONAL)

1 cup	confectioner's (icing) sugar, sifted	250 mL
½ tsp	vanilla	2 mL
1 to 2 tbsp	milk	15 to 25 mL

- **Preheat oven to 350°F (180°C)**
- **10-inch (3 L) Bundt pan, greased**

1. **Cake:** Combine brown sugar and cinnamon. Set aside for filling. Sprinkle almonds evenly in bottom of prepared pan. In a large mixer bowl, combine cake mix, pudding mix, eggs, oil, water and almond extract. Beat on medium speed for 2 minutes. Spread one-third of batter over nuts in pan. Sprinkle half of cinnamon-sugar filling over batter. Spread another third of batter on top, remaining filling, then remaining batter. Bake for 45 to 55 minutes or until a tester inserted in center comes out clean. Cool for 25 minutes in pan on a wire rack, then remove cake.

2. **Glaze:** If desired, in a small bowl, combine confectioner's sugar and vanilla. Add enough milk to make a smooth drizzling consistency. Drizzle over cake. Serve warm or cool.

Variation: Use your favorite kind of nuts. If using pecans or walnuts, replace almond extract with vanilla.

TIPS

- If freezing the cake, leave off the drizzle. Serve plain, sprinkle with confectioner's sugar or glaze thawed cake just before serving.
- Use a skewer or cake tester to test doneness of tube cakes. Toothpicks are not usually long enough

Apricot-Glazed Apple Torte

A not-too-sweet treat that's very impressive to serve.

SERVES 12 TO 16		
CAKE		
1	package (18.25 oz/515 g) white cake mix	1
1	package (4-serving size) vanilla instant pudding mix	1
4	eggs	4
½ cup	sour cream	125 mL
¼ cup	vegetable oil	50 mL
TOPPING		
3	large apples, peeled and cored	3
1 tbsp	granulated sugar	15 mL
1 tbsp	ground cinnamon	15 mL
⅓ cup	strained apricot jam	75 mL

- **Preheat oven to 350°F (180°C)**
- **11-inch (27 cm) springform pan, greased**

1. Cake: In a large mixer bowl, combine cake mix, pudding mix, eggs, sour cream and oil. Beat on medium speed for 2 minutes or until smooth. Spread evenly in prepared pan.

2. Topping: Slice peeled and cored apples into eighths. Press apple slices round-side up into batter in a circular pattern. Mix sugar and cinnamon. Sprinkle evenly over apples. Bake for 60 to 70 minutes or until cake is firm in the center. Remove pan to a wire rack and cool slightly. Warm jam if necessary to soften to a spreading consistency. Brush over top of apples and cake. Serve warm or cool.

Variation: Replace apricot jam with strained marmalade.

TIPS
- This cake is best prepared and enjoyed the same day.
- Golden Delicious apples are a good choice, since they're a nice size and keep their shape during baking.

Apple Nut Coffee Cake

This easy one-step cake has a delicious baked-on topping.

SERVES 12 TO 16		
CAKE		
1	package (18.25 oz/515 g) white cake mix	1
3	eggs	3
½ cup	water	125 mL
⅓ cup	vegetable oil	75 mL
2 cups	grated peeled apples (3 large)	500 mL
TOPPING		
½ cup	packed brown sugar	125 mL
½ cup	chopped nuts	125 mL
1 tsp	ground cinnamon	5 mL
1 tbsp	butter, melted	15 mL

- **Preheat oven to 350°F (180°C)**
- **13- by 9-inch (3 L) cake pan, greased**

1. Cake: In a large mixer bowl, combine cake mix, eggs, water and oil. Beat on medium speed for 2 minutes. Stir in apples, mixing until thoroughly blended. Spread batter evenly in prepared pan.

2. Topping: In a bowl, combine brown sugar, nuts, cinnamon and melted butter. Mix well. Sprinkle evenly over batter. Bake for 35 to 45 minutes or until a tester inserted in center comes out clean. Cool for 30 minutes in pan on a wire rack. Serve warm or cool.

Variations: Substitute firm pears for the apples. Try adding 1 tbsp (15 mL) grated orange zest to the batter.

TIP
- Use the medium coarse grater size for the apples. The cake will be too moist if the apples are too finely grated.

Lemon Streusel Cake

The glaze adds a very attractive finish, but it's not necessary if preparation time is tight.

SERVES 12 TO 16

STREUSEL

½ cup	all-purpose flour	125 mL
½ cup	confectioner's (icing) sugar, sifted	125 mL
2 tbsp	butter, melted	25 mL
1 tsp	lemon extract	5 mL
3	drops yellow food coloring	3

CAKE

1	package (18.25 oz/515 g) lemon cake mix	1
3	eggs	3
1 cup	water	250 mL
⅓ cup	butter, softened	75 mL

GLAZE

1 cup	confectioner's (icing) sugar, sifted	250 mL
1 to 2 tbsp	water	15 to 25 mL
¼ tsp	lemon extract	1 mL
3	drops yellow food coloring	3

- **Preheat oven to 375°F (190°C)**
- **10-inch (4 L) tube pan, greased and floured**

1. **Streusel:** Combine all ingredients for streusel. Mix well and set aside.

2. **Cake:** In a large mixer bowl, combine cake mix, eggs, water and butter. Beat on medium speed for 2 minutes. Spread one-third of batter in prepared pan. Sprinkle with one-third of streusel. Repeat layering two more times, ending with streusel. Bake for 40 to 50 minutes or until a tester inserted in center comes out clean. Cool for 25 minutes in pan on a wire rack, then remove cake and cool completely.

3. **Glaze:** Combine all ingredients, adding enough water to make a smooth drizzling consistency. Drizzle over cake.

Variation: Replace lemon extract with orange extract for a mixed citrus flavor.

TIP

- Another quick drizzle can be made by mixing ¾ cup (175 mL) ready-to-serve vanilla frosting with 1 tsp (5 mL) lemon juice and 3 drops food coloring. Simply heat in microwave or stove-top just to soften to drizzling consistency.

Lemon Cranberry Coffee Cake

Serve this delicious cake warm with eggnog ice cream for a holiday treat. But don't limit it to the holiday season!

SERVES 12 TO 16

STREUSEL

¾ cup	chopped walnuts	175 mL
½ cup	packed brown sugar	125 mL
2 tbsp	all-purpose flour	25 mL
½ tsp	ground cinnamon	2 mL
2 tbsp	butter, melted	25 mL

CAKE

1	package (18.25 oz/515 g) white cake mix	1
¼ cup	granulated sugar	50 mL
3	eggs	3
8 oz	cream cheese, softened	250 g
½ cup	vegetable oil	125 mL
¼ cup	water	50 mL
1 tbsp	grated lemon zest	15 mL
2 to 3 cups	fresh or frozen, thawed cranberries	500 to 750 mL

- **Preheat oven to 375°F (190°C)**
- **13- by 9-inch (3 L) cake pan, greased**

1. **Streusel:** In a small bowl, combine walnuts, brown sugar, flour, cinnamon and melted butter, mixing until crumbly. Set aside.

2. **Cake:** In a large mixer bowl, combine cake mix, sugar, eggs, cream cheese, oil and water. Beat on low speed for 1 minute to blend, then on medium speed for 2 minutes or until smooth. Stir in lemon zest. Spread half of the batter in prepared pan. Scatter cranberries over batter. Spread remaining batter over berries. Sprinkle streusel evenly over batter. Bake for 40 to 45 minutes or until top springs back when lightly touched. Cool for 30 minutes in pan on a wire rack. Serve warm or cool.

Variation: A lemon drizzle over the streusel adds a nice touch.

TIP
- Stir in zest after beating so it doesn't stick to the beaters.

Plum Sour Cream Coffee Cake

A great way to enjoy fresh plums while they are in season.

SERVES 12 TO 16

CAKE

1	package (18.25 oz/515 g) white cake mix	1
1	egg	1
1 cup	sour cream	250 mL
¼ cup	butter, melted	50 mL
½ tsp	almond extract	2 mL

TOPPING

3½ cups	thinly sliced (¼-inch/ 3 cm thick) fresh plums (6 large)	875 mL
½ cup	packed brown sugar	125 mL
½ cup	sliced hazelnuts	125 mL
1 tsp	ground cinnamon	5 mL
½ cup	butter, melted	50 mL

- **Preheat oven to 350°F (180°C)**
- **13- by 9-inch (3 L) cake pan, greased and floured**

1. **Cake:** In a large mixer bowl, combine cake mix, egg, sour cream, butter and almond extract. Beat on low speed for 1 minute or until a soft dough forms. Spread evenly in prepared pan. Bake for 12 minutes.

2. **Topping:** Arrange plum slices over cake base. In a small bowl, combine brown sugar, hazelnuts and cinnamon. Sprinkle evenly over plums. Drizzle melted butter on top. Bake for 30 to 35 minutes or until golden brown. Cool for at least 30 minutes in pan on a wire rack. Serve warm or cool.

Variation: Replace plums with nectarines or apples. Replace almond extract with 2 tsp (10 mL) grated orange or lemon zest.

Cranberry Almond Coffee Cake

Don't limit this cake to the holiday season. The tart cranberry taste and crunchy almond top are a hit year-round.

SERVES 12 TO 16		
CAKE		
2 cups	fresh cranberries	500 mL
¼ cup	all-purpose flour	50 mL
1	package (18.25 oz/515 g) white cake mix	1
3	eggs	3
1¼ cups	water	300 mL
⅓ cup	vegetable oil	75 mL
½ tsp	almond extract	2 mL
TOPPING		
¾ cup	sliced almonds	175 mL
⅓ cup	packed brown sugar	75 mL
½ tsp	ground cinnamon	2 mL

- **Preheat oven to 350°F (180°C)**
- **13- by 9-inch (3 L) cake pan, greased**

1. **Cake:** In a small bowl, toss cranberries in flour to coat well. In a large mixer bowl, combine cake mix, eggs, water, oil and almond extract. Beat for 2 minutes on medium speed. Stir in floured cranberries. Spread batter evenly in prepared pan.

2. **Topping:** In a small bowl, combine almonds, brown sugar and cinnamon. Mix well. Sprinkle evenly over batter. Bake for 30 to 40 minutes or until a tester inserted in center comes out clean. Cool for 30 minutes in pan on a wire rack. Serve warm or cool.

Variation: Replace cranberries with fresh blueberries or raspberries.

TIP
- When cranberries are in season, buy a few bags for your freezer. Thaw slightly and pat dry before using.

Apple Sour Cream Coffee Cake

A delicious fall cake with fresh tart apples. It's also nice with pears, plums or peaches.

SERVES 12 TO 16		
CAKE		
1	package (18.25 oz/515 g) white cake mix	1
1	egg	1
1 cup	sour cream	250 mL
¼ cup	butter, melted	50 mL
TOPPING		
3½ cups	thinly sliced (¼ inch/ 3 cm thick) apples (4 to 5 large)	875 mL
½ cup	packed brown sugar	125 mL
1 tsp	ground cinnamon	5 mL
⅓ cup	sliced almonds	75 mL
¼ cup	butter, melted	50 mL

- **Preheat oven to 350°F (180°C)**
- **13- by 9-inch (3 L) cake pan, greased and floured**

1. **Cake:** In a large mixer bowl, combine cake mix, egg, sour cream and melted butter. Beat on low speed for 1 minute or until a soft dough forms. Spread evenly in prepared pan. Bake for 12 minutes.

2. **Topping:** Arrange apple slices over cake base. Combine brown sugar, cinnamon and almonds. Sprinkle evenly over apples. Drizzle melted butter on top. Bake for 30 to 35 minutes longer or until golden brown and apples are tender-crisp. Cool for at least 30 minutes in pan on a wire rack. Serve warm or cool.

Variation: A mixture of other fall fruits gives a different taste and appearance to this versatile batter.

TIP
- Slice apples thinly for quick, even baking. You want them to be tender-crisp.

Raspberry Streusel Coffee Cake

Here's a great way to enjoy this delicious fruit when it is in season and at its peak of perfection.

STREUSEL

½ cup	packed brown sugar	125 mL
2 tbsp	all-purpose flour	25 mL
2 tbsp	butter, melted	25 mL
½ tsp	ground cinnamon	2 mL
¾ cup	sliced hazelnuts	175 mL

CAKE

1	package (18.25 oz/515 g) white cake mix	1
⅓ cup	granulated sugar	75 mL
8 oz	cream cheese, softened	250 g
3	eggs	3
½ cup	vegetable oil	125 mL
¼ cup	water	50 mL
2 to 3 cups	fresh raspberries	500 to 750 mL

- **Preheat oven to 375°F (190°C)**
- **13- by 9-inch (3 L) cake pan, greased**

1. **Streusel:** In a bowl, combine sugar, flour, melted butter, cinnamon and hazelnuts, mixing until crumbly. Set aside.

2. **Cake:** In a large mixer bowl, combine cake mix, sugar, cream cheese, eggs, oil and water. Beat on low speed for 1 minute to blend, then on medium speed for 2 minutes or until smooth. Spread half of batter in prepared pan. Scatter raspberries over batter. Spread remaining batter over berries. Sprinkle streusel evenly over batter. Bake for 40 to 45 minutes or until top springs back when lightly touched. Cool for 30 minutes in pan on a wire rack. Serve warm or cool.

Variation: A mixture of blueberries and raspberries or blueberries alone also taste great.

TIP
- If the raspberries seem overly juicy, toss them with a little flour before adding to the batter.

Loaves and muffins are another favorite accompaniment for coffee. They don't require a lot of preparation time, and they offer many of the same satisfactions as freshly baked yeast breads. These recipes usually freeze well. You can't go wrong with an extra Cranberry Banana Loaf in the freezer.

Spicy Apple 'n' Oats Loaf

Here's a great way to enjoy fruit and cereal for breakfast.

MAKES ABOUT 30 SLICES		
1	package (18.25 oz/515 g) spice cake mix	1
½ cup	quick-cooking rolled oats	125 mL
3	eggs	3
1½ cups	applesauce	375 mL
⅓ cup	vegetable oil	75 mL
1 cup	raisins, dried cranberries or dried cherries	250 mL

- **Preheat oven to 350°F (180°C)**
- **Two 8½- by 4½-inch (1.5 L) loaf pans, greased and floured**

1. In a large mixer bowl, combine cake mix, oats, eggs, applesauce and oil. Beat on low speed for 1 minute to blend, then on medium speed for 2 minutes. Stir in raisins. Spread batter in prepared pans, dividing evenly. Bake for 50 to 60 minutes or until a tester inserted in center comes out clean. Cool for 20 minutes in pans on a wire rack, then remove from pan and cool completely on rack.

Variation: Sprinkle 2 tbsp (25 mL) of toasted oats over top before baking.

TIPS

- Lightly toasting oats until they are golden gives them a nutty flavor.
- If using homemade applesauce that is chunky, press out most of the lumps with a potato masher. Use sweetened or unsweetened, depending on your preference.
- For a delicious snack, toast a slice of this bread and sprinkle it with cinnamon-sugar.

Applesauce Loaf

A hint of spice is always nice with apples. The addition of dried cranberries or raisins makes it even better in this tender, moist loaf.

MAKES ABOUT 30 SLICES		
1	package (18.25 oz/515 g) yellow cake mix	1
1	package (4-serving size) vanilla instant pudding mix	1
4	eggs	4
1 cup	applesauce	250 mL
½ cup	water	125 mL
¼ cup	vegetable oil	50 mL
1½ tsp	ground cinnamon	7 mL
½ tsp	ground nutmeg	2 mL
1 cup	dried cranberries or raisins	250 mL

- **Preheat oven to 350°F (180°C)**
- **Two 8½- by 4½-inch (1.5 L) loaf pans, greased and floured**

1. In a large mixer bowl, combine cake mix, pudding mix, eggs, applesauce, water, oil and spices. Beat on low speed for 1 minute to blend, then on medium speed for 3 minutes. Fold in cranberries. Spread batter in prepared pans, dividing evenly. Bake for 50 to 60 minutes or until a tester inserted in center comes out clean. Cool for 20 minutes in pans on a wire rack, then remove loaves and cool completely.

Variation: Use 1½ tsp (7 mL) pumpkin pie spice in place of cinnamon and nutmeg.

TIP

- For best texture and flavor, loaves are best left overnight before slicing.

Banana Berry Loaf

Banana adds an enticing flavor to traditional plain cranberry bread.

MAKES ABOUT 30 SLICES		
1	package (18.25 oz/515 g) white cake mix	1
1	package (4-serving size) banana cream instant pudding mix	1
4	eggs	4
1½ cups	mashed ripe bananas (3 to 4 large)	375 mL
¼ cup	vegetable oil	50 mL
1½ cups	fresh cranberries	375 mL
2 tbsp	all-purpose flour	25 mL

TIP

- Try a thick slice of this bread, warm, with vanilla sauce for dessert.

- **Preheat oven to 350°F (180°C)**
- **Two 8½- by 4½-inch (1.5 L) loaf pans, greased and floured**

1. In a large mixer bowl, combine cake mix, pudding mix, eggs, bananas and oil. Beat on low speed for 1 minute to blend, then on medium speed for 2 minutes. Toss cranberries in flour to coat. Fold into batter. Spread batter in prepared pans, dividing evenly. Bake for 50 to 60 minutes or until a tester inserted in center comes out clean. Cool for 20 minutes in pans on a wire rack, then remove from pan and cool completely on rack.

Variations: Add 1 tbsp (15 mL) grated orange zest to batter. For a milder, vanilla flavor, use a vanilla pudding mix.

Triple Berry Loaf

A mixture of berries is colorful and flavorful.

MAKES ABOUT 30 SLICES		
LOAF		
1	package (18.25 oz/515 g) white cake mix	1
¾ cup	all-purpose flour, divided	175 mL
3	eggs	3
1¼ cups	water	300 mL
⅓ cup	vegetable oil	75 mL
1 tbsp	grated lemon zest	15 mL
¾ cup	fresh cranberries	175 mL
¾ cup	fresh blueberries	175 mL
¾ cup	fresh raspberries	175 mL
GLAZE		
½ cup	granulated sugar	125 mL
¼ cup	lemon juice	50 mL

TIP

- This loaf is nicest with fresh blueberries and raspberries. The frozen ones bleed too much and you end up with a pink loaf.

- **Preheat oven to 350°F (180°C)**
- **Two 8½- by 4½-inch (1.5 L) loaf pans, greased and floured**

1. **Loaf:** In a large mixer bowl, combine cake mix, ½ cup (125 mL) of the flour, eggs, water, oil and lemon zest. Beat on low speed for 1 minute to blend, then on medium speed for 2 minutes. Toss berries in remaining flour to coat thoroughly. Stir into batter gently but thoroughly. Spread batter in prepared pans, dividing evenly. Bake for 50 to 60 minutes or until a tester inserted in center comes out clean. Cool for 10 minutes in pans on a wire rack.

2. **Glaze:** In a small saucepan, over low heat, heat sugar and lemon juice together to dissolve sugar. Poke holes in top of warm loaves with a fork or toothpick. Brush glaze on tops, letting it soak in. Cool loaves completely, then remove from pans.

Variation: Vary the fruits, keeping the total amount to 2¼ cups (550 mL).

Cranberry Banana Loaf

Bananas combine well with other ingredients such as nuts and chocolate chips, but cranberries always seem to be a favorite.

MAKES ABOUT 30 SLICES		
1	package (18.25 oz/515 g) white cake mix	1
4 oz	cream cheese, softened	125 g
1	egg	1
1½ cups	mashed ripe bananas (3 to 4 large)	375 mL
1½ cups	fresh cranberries	375 mL

TIPS
- Use very ripe bananas for the best flavor and texture in baked goods.
- Most loaves freeze beautifully. Wrap completely in plastic wrap or airtight freezer bags or wrap individual slices in plastic and freeze for up to 3 months.

- **Preheat oven to 350°F (180°C)**
- **Two 8½- by 4½-inch (1.5 L) loaf pans, greased and floured**

1. In a large mixer bowl, combine cake mix, cream cheese, egg and bananas. Beat on low speed until smoothly blended, about 2 minutes. Batter will be stiff. Fold in cranberries. Spread batter in prepared pans, dividing evenly. Bake for 45 to 50 minutes or until a tester inserted in center comes out clean. Cool for 20 minutes in pans on a wire rack, then remove loaves and cool completely.

Variation: Replace cranberries with ¾ cup (175 mL) chopped nuts or miniature chocolate chips.

White Chocolate Cranberry Loaf

This recipe makes two loaves. Enjoy one fresh and freeze the other to serve if company drops in unexpectedly.

MAKES ABOUT 30 SLICES		
1	package (18.25 oz/515 g) white cake mix	1
¾ cup	all-purpose flour, divided	175 mL
3	eggs	3
¾ cup	water	175 mL
1 tbsp	grated orange zest	15 mL
½ cup	orange juice	125 mL
⅓ cup	vegetable oil	75 mL
1 cup	fresh cranberries	250 mL
1 cup	chopped white chocolate	250 mL

TIPS
- Keep a few bags of cranberries in the freezer for year-round use.
- Use 1 cup (250 mL) of white chocolate chips instead of a chopped bar of chocolate.

- **Preheat oven to 350°F (180°C)**
- **Two 8½- by 4½-inch (1.5 L) loaf pans, greased and floured**

1. In a large mixer bowl, combine cake mix, ½ cup (125 mL) of the flour, eggs, water, orange zest, orange juice and oil. Beat on low speed for 1 minute to blend, then on medium speed for 2 minutes. Toss cranberries in remaining flour to coat thoroughly. Stir into batter with chocolate. Spread batter in prepared pans, dividing evenly. Bake for 50 to 60 minutes or until a tester inserted in center comes out clean. Cool for 20 minutes in pans on a wire rack, then remove from pans and cool completely on rack.

Variation: Replace cranberries with blueberries or raspberries.

Glazed Lemon Loaf

Lemon loaf is an old-fashioned favorite for an anytime treat with coffee or tea.

LOAF

1	package (18.25 oz/515 g) lemon cake mix	1
3	eggs	3
1 cup + 3 tbsp	water	295 mL
1/3 cup	vegetable oil	75 mL

GLAZE

1/2 cup	granulated sugar	125 mL
1/4 cup	lemon juice	50 mL

TIPS

- Use freshly squeezed lemon juice whenever possible for the best lemon flavor.
- You can make a dessert by topping a thick slice of lemon loaf with fresh berries and whipped cream.

- **Preheat oven to 350°F (180°C)**
- **Two 8½- by 4½-inch (1.5 L) loaf pans, greased and lined with aluminum foil**

1. **Loaf:** In a large mixer bowl, combine cake mix, eggs, water and oil. Beat on medium speed for 2 minutes. Spread batter in prepared pans, dividing evenly. Bake for 35 to 45 minutes or until a tester inserted in center comes out clean. Cool for 10 minutes in pans on a wire rack.

2. **Glaze:** Heat sugar and lemon juice together to dissolve sugar. Poke holes in top of loaves with a fork or toothpick. Brush glaze on tops, letting it soak in. Cool loaves completely, then remove from pans.

Variation: Add ½ cup (125 mL) finely chopped hazelnuts to batter.

Lemon Blueberry Loaf

When fresh blueberries are in season, prepare a few extra loaves of this tasty treat for the freezer.

1¼ cups	fresh blueberries	300 mL
¾ cup	sliced hazelnuts	175 mL
1 tbsp	all-purpose flour	15 mL
1	package (18.25 oz/515 g) lemon cake mix	1
4	eggs	4
4 oz	cream cheese, softened	125 g
⅔ cup	milk	150 mL

TIPS

- When using cream cheese in baking, make sure it is at room temperature for easy blending.
- To serve this as a dessert cake, frost with Lemon Buttercream Frosting (see recipe, page 264) or Very Creamy Butter Frosting, flavored with lemon (see recipe, page 259).

- **Preheat oven to 350°F (180°C)**
- **Two 8½- by 4½-inch (1.5 L) loaf pans, greased and floured**

1. Toss blueberries and nuts with flour to coat. Set aside.

2. In a large mixer bowl, combine cake mix, eggs, cream cheese and milk. Beat on low speed for 1 minute to blend, then on medium speed for 2 minutes. Fold in blueberry mixture. Spread batter in prepared pans, dividing evenly. Bake for 45 to 50 minutes or until a tester inserted in center comes out clean. Cool for 20 minutes in pans on a wire rack, then remove from pan and cool completely on rack.

Variation: Replace blueberries with cranberries and hazelnuts with almonds or pecans.

Apple Oatmeal Muffins

A quick and easy way to prepare tender, moist muffins for breakfast on the run.

MAKES 18 MUFFINS		
1	package (18.25 oz/515 g) white cake mix	1
1 cup	quick-cooking rolled oats	250 mL
2 tsp	ground cinnamon	10 mL
½ tsp	baking powder	2 mL
3	eggs	3
1¾ cups	chopped peeled apples (2 large)	425 mL
1⅓ cups	milk	325 mL
½ cup	butter, melted	125 mL

TIPS

- Keep a bag of baked muffins in the freezer and remove them as you need them. Thaw overnight at room temperature or in the microwave.
- If you have only 12-cup muffin tins, fill unused cups three-quarters full of water before baking.

- **Preheat oven to 375°F (190°C)**
- **One 12-cup and one 6-cup muffin tin, greased or paper-lined**

1. In a large bowl, combine cake mix, oats, cinnamon and baking powder. Stir to blend. In another large bowl, whisk together eggs, apples, milk and melted butter. Add dry ingredients, stirring with a wooden spoon just until blended. Spoon batter into prepared muffins tins. Bake for 20 to 25 minutes or until set and golden.

Variation: For a different flavor, add raisins or dried cranberries to batter.

Apple Carrot Oatmeal Muffins

Here's a delicious way to enjoy your vegetables.

MAKES 18 MUFFINS		
1	package (18.25 oz/515 g) white cake mix	1
1½ cups	quick-cooking rolled oats	375 mL
2 tsp	ground cinnamon	10 mL
½ tsp	baking powder	2 mL
3	eggs	3
1¼ cups	grated peeled apples (2 large)	300 mL
1¼ cups	grated peeled carrots	300 mL
1¼ cups	milk	300 mL
½ cup	butter, melted	125 mL
¾ cup	raisins	175 mL
¾ cup	chopped nuts	175 mL

TIP
- Be sure to peel the carrots before grating them for use in this recipe. The reaction of the peel with the leavening in the batter can form green specks.

- **Preheat oven to 375°F (190°C)**
- **One 12-cup and one 6-cup muffin tin, greased or paper-lined**

1. In a large bowl, combine cake mix, oats, cinnamon and baking powder. Stir to blend. In another large bowl, whisk together eggs, apples, carrots, milk and melted butter. Add dry ingredients, stirring with a wooden spoon just until blended. Stir in raisins and nuts. Spoon batter into prepared muffin tins. Bake for 20 to 25 minutes or until tops spring back when lightly touched. Cool for 15 minutes in pans on a wire rack, then remove from pan and cool completely on rack.

Variation: For a different flavor, replace raisins with dried cranberries or dried cherries.

Chocolate Banana Muffins

This combination of banana and chocolate is one of my favorites.

MAKES 24 MUFFINS		
1	package (18.25 oz/515 g) devil's food cake mix	1
1	package (4-serving size) banana cream instant pudding mix	1
3	eggs	3
1½ cups	mashed ripe bananas (3 to 4 large)	375 mL
¼ cup	vegetable oil	50 mL
1⅓ cups	miniature semi-sweet chocolate chips	325 mL

- **Preheat oven to 375°F (190°C)**
- **Two 12-cup muffin tins, greased or paper-lined**

1. In a large bowl, combine cake mix, pudding mix, eggs, bananas and oil. Stir with wooden spoon just until blended. Fold in chocolate chips. Spoon batter into prepared muffin tins. Bake for 15 to 20 minutes or until set and golden. Cool for 15 minutes in pans on a wire rack, then remove from pans and cool completely on rack.

Variation: Replace miniature chips with regular size, or try peanut butter chips for a different flavor.

TIP
- These muffins are so tender and moist that you don't need paper liners. Cool them completely in the pans, then loosen with the tip of a knife, and they'll come out in one piece.

Apple Carrot Oatmeal Muffins and Chocolate Banana Muffins ▶

Chocolate Chocolate Chunk Muffins

Definitely not your "healthy" breakfast muffin — but definitely a favorite treat.

MAKES 24 MUFFINS

1	package (18.25 oz/515 g) deep chocolate cake mix	1
1	package (4-serving size) chocolate instant pudding mix	1
4	eggs	4
1 cup	sour cream	250 mL
½ cup	water	125 mL
⅓ cup	vegetable oil	75 mL
1⅔ cups	jumbo chocolate chips	400 mL

- **Preheat oven to 350°F (180°C)**
- **Two 12-cup muffin tins, greased or paper-lined**

1. In a large mixer bowl, combine cake mix, pudding mix, eggs, sour cream, water and oil. Beat on low speed for 1 minute to blend, then on medium speed for 1 minute. Stir in chocolate chips. Spoon batter into prepared muffin tins. Bake for 20 to 25 minutes or until top springs back when lightly touched.

Variation: Use chocolate chunks, jumbo chips or regular-size chips.

> **TIP**
> - Paper muffin-cup liners make for easy pan cleanup. They are also excellent to use if you're transporting or freezing the muffins.

Chocolate Cheesecake Muffins

These decadent muffins make a great dessert.

MAKES 24 MUFFINS

FILLING

8 oz	cream cheese, softened	250 g
1	egg	1
⅓ cup	granulated sugar	75 mL
⅔ cup	miniature semi-sweet chocolate chips	150 mL

MUFFIN BATTER

1	package (18.25 oz/515 g) devil's food cake mix	1
1	package (4-serving size) chocolate instant pudding mix	1
4	eggs	4
1 cup	sour cream	250 mL
½ cup	water	125 mL
⅓ cup	vegetable oil	75 mL

- **Preheat oven to 350°F (180°C)**
- **Two 12-cup muffin tins, greased or paper-lined**

1. Filling: In a small bowl, beat cream cheese, egg and sugar until smooth. Stir in chocolate chips. Set aside.

2. Muffin Batter: In a large mixer bowl, combine cake mix, pudding mix, eggs, sour cream, water and oil. Beat on low speed for 1 minute to blend, then on medium speed for 1 minute. Spoon half of batter into prepared muffin tins. Put about 1 tbsp (15 mL) cheese filling mixture on top. Spoon remaining batter over filling. Bake for 20 to 25 minutes or until top springs back when lightly touched. Cool for 15 minutes in pans on a wire rack, then remove from pans and cool completely on rack.

Variation: For the flavor of Black Forest cake, replace half the water with cherry liqueur.

Cranberry Double Banana Muffins

The combination of banana and cranberries is outstanding.

MAKES 24 MUFFINS		
1	package (18.25 oz/515 g) white cake mix	1
1	package (4-serving size) banana cream instant pudding mix	1
3	eggs	3
1½ cups	mashed ripe bananas (3 to 4 large)	375 mL
¼ cup	vegetable oil	50 mL
2 cups	fresh cranberries	500 mL

- **Preheat oven to 375°F (190°C)**
- **Two 12-cup muffin tins, greased or paper-lined**

1. In a large bowl, combine cake mix, pudding mix, eggs, bananas and oil. Stir with a wooden spoon just until blended. Fold in cranberries. Spoon batter into prepared muffins pans. Bake for 15 to 20 minutes or until set and golden.

Variation: Replace cranberries with blueberries, raisins or nuts.

TIPS

- Muffins containing fresh fruit like cranberries and blueberries are usually quite fragile to remove from pan without paper liners. Cool them completely, then loosen with the tip of a knife, and they'll come out in one piece.
- For nicely shaped, uniform-size muffins, use an ice cream scoop to fill muffin cups.
- Don't overmix the batter or the muffins will be tough.
- Store overly ripe bananas in the freezer, skin and all, until you have enough to use in a recipe.

Blueberry Muffins

When available, wild blueberries are wonderful in muffins.

MAKES 18 MUFFINS		
1	package (18.25 oz/515 g) lemon cake mix	1
¼ cup	all-purpose flour	50 mL
1 tsp	baking powder	5 mL
3	eggs	3
⅔ cup	milk	150 mL
⅓ cup	vegetable oil	75 mL
1½ cups	fresh blueberries	375 mL

- Preheat oven to 375°F (190°C)
- One 12-cup and one 6-cup muffin tin, greased or paper-lined

1. In a medium bowl, combine cake mix, flour and baking powder. Stir to blend. In a large bowl, whisk eggs, milk and oil. Add dry ingredients, stirring just until blended. Fold in blueberries. Spoon batter into prepared muffin pans. Bake for 17 to 23 minutes or until set and golden.

Variations: Replace blueberries with cranberries. If lemon isn't a favorite, try a white cake mix for another great taste.

TIPS

- Frozen blueberries, thawed and patted dry, can be used if fresh are not available. If blueberries are wet, toss with a spoonful of flour before mixing into batter.
- Keep a bag of baked muffins in the freezer and remove them as you need them. Thaw overnight at room temperature or in the microwave.

Lemon Poppy Seed Muffins

Ricotta cheese in the batter keeps these muffins tender and moist. The poppy seeds add a pleasant crunch.

MAKES 18 MUFFINS		
1	package (18.25 oz/515 g) lemon cake mix	1
1	package (4-serving size) vanilla instant pudding mix	1
4	eggs	4
1 cup	ricotta cheese	250 mL
⅓ cup	vegetable oil	75 mL
¼ cup	poppy seeds	50 mL
2 tsp	grated lemon zest	10 mL
¼ cup	granulated sugar	50 ml

- Preheat oven to 350°F (180°C)
- One 12-cup and one 6-cup muffin tin, greased or paper-lined

1. In a large mixer bowl, combine cake mix, pudding mix, eggs, ricotta cheese, oil, poppy seeds and lemon zest. Beat on medium speed for 2 minutes. Spoon batter evenly into prepared muffin cups. Bake for 20 to 25 minutes or until tops spring back when lightly touched. Sprinkle tops lightly with sugar.

Variations: Omit poppy seeds. Add 1 cup (250 mL) chopped almonds, if desired. Replace ricotta cheese with yogurt.

TIPS

- Make sure you buy instant pudding, not the kind that requires cooking.
- Store poppy seeds in the freezer to maintain their freshness.

Paradise Island Muffins

Loaded with dried tropical ingredients, these muffins will help you through the winter blahs.

½ cup	diced dried mango or papaya	125 mL
⅓ cup	diced dried pineapple	75 mL
¼ cup	rum, divided	50 mL
1 tsp	coconut extract	5 mL
1	package (18.25 oz/515 g) white cake mix	1
¼ cup	all-purpose flour	50 mL
1 tsp	baking powder	5 mL
3	eggs	3
½ cup	milk	125 mL
⅓ cup	vegetable oil	75 mL
½ cup	chopped macadamia nuts	125 mL
¼ cup	flaked coconut	50 mL

TIPS

- Muffins freeze very well. Wrap them individually so you can take out the required number at any time. Pack frozen in lunchboxes to keep other items cold.
- Fill empty muffin cups with water before baking to protect your pans and for even baking.

- **Preheat oven to 375°F (190°C)**
- **Two 12-cup muffin tins, greased or paper-lined**

1. In a small microwave-safe bowl, combine dried fruits, 2 tbsp (25 mL) of the rum and coconut extract. Heat on High for 30 seconds. Set aside to cool.

2. In a medium bowl, combine cake mix, flour and baking powder. Stir to blend. In a large bowl, whisk eggs, milk, the remaining rum and oil. Add dry ingredients, stirring just until blended. Fold in soaked dried fruits, nuts and coconut. Spoon batter into prepared muffin pans. Bake for 17 to 23 minutes or until set and golden.

Variation: Try various fruits and nuts to suit your own personal tastes and budget. Keep the total amount the same as in the original recipe.

These recipes will convince you that cake mixes are versatile. The cookies taste better than those made from most cookie mixes. I find it very hard to pick a favorite. But that's not a problem, since a selection of cookies makes up a wonderful cookie tray.

Chunky Chocolate Pecan Cookies

A good choice for the cookie jar.

MAKES ABOUT 4½ DOZEN COOKIES

1	package (18.25 oz/515 g) white cake mix	1
½ cup	butter, melted	125 mL
2	eggs	2
1 tsp	vanilla	5 mL
1½ cups	semi-sweet chocolate chunks or chips	375 mL
1¼ cups	coarsely chopped pecans	300 mL

TIP

- Make smaller cookies for cookie boxes or cookie trays where there are a variety of items. That way, people can try several different kinds. For lunchboxes, you may prefer larger cookies.

- **Preheat oven to 375°F (190°C)**
- **Baking sheets, greased**

1. In a large mixer bowl, combine cake mix, melted butter, eggs and vanilla. Beat on low speed for 1 minute or just until smooth. Stir in chocolate chips and nuts.

2. Drop dough by rounded tablespoonfuls (15 mL) onto prepared baking sheets, 2 inches (5 cm) apart. Bake for 10 to 15 minutes or until light golden. Cool on baking sheets for 1 minute or until firm, then remove to wire racks and cool completely.

Variation: Vary the type of nuts and chocolate to suit your personal taste. Try macadamia nuts and white chocolate chunks.

Chocolate Peanut Butter Cookies

These cookies are just like peanuts — you can't stop at just one.

MAKES ABOUT 3½ DOZEN COOKIES

1	package (18.25 oz/515 g) devil's food cake mix	1
1 cup	creamy peanut butter	250 mL
2	eggs	2
¼ cup	milk	50 mL
1 cup	peanut butter chips	250 mL
¾ cup	chopped peanuts	175 mL

TIPS

- Use creamy peanut butter for easy blending. You can always add chopped peanuts for the crunch.
- The best baking sheets for cookies have low or no sides. This allows the heat to circulate during baking, resulting in even browning.
- Whether you use salted or unsalted nuts is a personal preference.

- **Preheat oven to 350°F (180°C)**
- **Baking sheets, greased**

1. In a large mixer bowl, combine cake mix, peanut butter, eggs and milk. Mix with wooden spoon or on low speed of mixer for 1 minute or until blended. Stir in chips and peanuts. Mix well.

2. Drop dough by rounded tablespoonfuls (15 mL) onto prepared baking sheets, 2 inches (5 cm) apart. Bake, one sheet at a time, for 10 to 12 minutes or until lightly browned. Cool on baking sheets for 1 minute or until firm, then remove to wire racks and cool completely.

Variation: For chocolate lovers, use chocolate chips or chocolate-covered peanuts.

Chunky Chocolate Pecan Cookies ▶

Peanut Butter Cookies

An old-fashioned favorite made easier to prepare.

MAKES ABOUT 4 DOZEN COOKIES		
1 cup	peanut butter	250 mL
2	eggs	2
1 tbsp	milk	15 mL
1	package (18.25 oz/515 g) white cake mix	1
	Granulated sugar	

TIPS

- Be sure to use fresh peanut butter. Because of its high oil content, peanut butter can go rancid quite quickly.
- A potato masher works well for pressing a pattern on top of cookies.
- For extra-crunchy cookies, use crunchy peanut butter. You may need a bit more to make a soft dough.

- **Preheat oven to 375°F (190°C)**
- **Baking sheets, greased**

1. In a large bowl, combine peanut butter, eggs, milk and half of cake mix. Stir thoroughly to blend. Add remaining cake mix. Blend thoroughly, using hands to form a smooth dough.

2. Shape dough into 1-inch (2.5 cm) balls. Place on prepared baking sheets. Press flat with a fork dipped in sugar. Bake for 10 to 12 minutes or until set. Cool on baking sheet for 5 minutes or until firm, then remove to wire racks and cool completely.

Variation: Press a chocolate kiss candy or whole peanut on top of cookie for decoration.

Chocolate Cherry Oat Drops

A festive cookie to enjoy year-round.

MAKES ABOUT 3½ DOZEN COOKIES		
1	package (18.25 oz/515 g) white cake mix	1
1 cup	quick-cooking rolled oats	250 mL
2	eggs	2
½ cup	butter, melted	125 mL
1 tsp	vanilla	5 mL
¾ cup	chopped red candied cherries	175 mL
¾ cup	white chocolate chips	175 mL
¾ cup	semi-sweet chocolate chips	175 mL
½ cup	slivered almonds	125 mL

TIPS

- Check cookies halfway through baking. If they're browning more at the back, turn tray around.
- Cookies will bake more evenly if you bake one tray at a time on the middle oven rack.

- **Preheat oven to 375°F (190°C)**
- **Baking sheets, greased**

1. In a large mixer bowl, combine cake mix, oats, eggs, melted butter and vanilla. Beat on low speed for 1 minute or just until smooth. Stir in cherries, white and semi-sweet chocolate chips and almonds. Mix well.

2. Drop dough by rounded tablespoonfuls (15 mL) onto prepared baking sheets, 2 inches (5 cm) apart. Flatten slightly with fingers. Bake for 10 to 12 minutes or until lightly browned. Cool for 1 minute on baking sheets or until firm, then transfer cookies to wire racks and cool completely.

Variation: Use your favorite nut or replace with more chocolate chips if nut allergy is a problem.

Chocolate Macadamia Nut Oatmeal Cookies

You can't go wrong with a blend of chocolate and macadamia nuts.

MAKES ABOUT 5 DOZEN COOKIES		
1	package (18.25 oz/515 g) white cake mix	1
½ cup	quick-cooking rolled oats	125 mL
½ cup	butter, melted	125 mL
2	eggs	2
1 tsp	vanilla	5 mL
1½ cups	coarsely chopped macadamia nuts	375 mL
1½ cups	semi-sweet chocolate chunks or chips	375 mL

TIP

• Use large-flake oats for a more "oaty" taste. Be sure not to use instant oatmeal.

• **Preheat oven to 375°F (190°C)**
• **Baking sheets, greased**

1. In a large mixer bowl, combine cake mix, oats, melted butter, eggs and vanilla. Beat on low speed for 1 minute or just until smooth. Stir in nuts and chocolate chunks.

2. Drop dough by rounded tablespoonfuls (15 mL) onto prepared sheets, 2 inches (5 cm) apart. Bake for 10 to 15 minutes or until light golden. Cool on baking sheets on wire racks for 1 minute or until firm, then remove to racks and cool completely.

Variation: Try substituting pecans for macadamia nuts and white chocolate chunks for semi-sweet.

Toffee Almond Chocolate Chip Cookies

Crunchy toffee bits, almonds and chocolate chips make these cookies a certain favorite.

MAKES ABOUT 3½ DOZEN COOKIES		
1	package (18.25 oz/515 g) white cake mix	1
2	eggs	2
½ cup	butter, melted	125 mL
1 tsp	vanilla	5 mL
1 cup	chopped almonds	250 mL
¾ cup	crunchy toffee bits	175 mL
¾ cup	milk chocolate chips	175 mL

TIPS

• Bake cookies, one tray at a time, on middle oven rack.
• For even browning, turn cookie sheet back to front halfway through baking.
• To easily remove cookies, line sheets with parchment paper.
• Bake less time for chewy cookies and more time for crisp cookies.

• **Preheat oven to 375°F (190°C)**
• **Baking sheets, greased**

1. In a large mixer bowl, combine cake mix, eggs, melted butter and vanilla. Beat on low speed for 1 minute or just until smooth. Stir in almonds, toffee bits and chocolate chips. Mix well.

2. Drop dough by rounded tablespoonfuls (15 mL) onto prepared baking sheets, 2 inches (5 cm) apart. Flatten slightly with fingers. Bake, one sheet at a time, for 10 to 12 minutes or until lightly browned. Cool on baking sheets for 1 minute or until firm, then remove to wire racks and cool completely.

Variation: Replace almonds with pecans and milk chocolate chips with semi-sweet or white chocolate chips.

Chocolate Caramel Pecan Cookies

Pecans and chocolate chips always go well together in cookies.

MAKES ABOUT 4 DOZEN COOKIES		
1	package (18.25 oz/515 g) white cake mix	1
2	eggs	2
½ cup	butter, melted	125 mL
6 oz	semi-sweet chocolate, chopped	175 g
25	individual soft caramels, quartered	25
¾ cup	chopped pecans	175 mL

TIPS

- Place cookies 2 inches (5 cm) apart to allow for spreading during baking.
- Bake cookies, one tray at a time, on middle oven rack.
- If baking sheets are warm, let them cool before putting dough on them.

- **Preheat oven to 375°F (190°C)**
- **Baking sheets, greased**

1. In a large mixer bowl, combine cake mix, eggs and melted butter. Beat on low speed for 1 minute or just until smooth. Stir in chocolate, caramels and pecans. Mix well.

2. Drop dough by rounded tablespoonfuls (15 mL) onto prepared baking sheets, 2 inches (5 cm) apart. Flatten slightly with fingers. Bake, one sheet at a time, for 8 to 12 minutes or until lightly browned. Cool on baking sheets for 1 minute or until firm, then remove to wire racks and cool completely.

Variation: Replace white cake mix with yellow.

Crispy Chocolate Chunk Cookies

The addition of crispy rice cereal gives these cookies a pleasingly chewy texture that complements the chocolate.

MAKES ABOUT 4 DOZEN COOKIES		
1	package (18.25 oz/515 g) devil's food cake mix	1
2	eggs	2
½ cup	butter, melted	125 mL
6 oz	semi-sweet chocolate, coarsely chopped	175 g
1½ cups	crisp rice cereal	375 mL

TIPS

- Shiny aluminum baking sheets produce cookies that are evenly browned and crisp on the bottom, which also improves the flavor. Insulated pans prevent browning, producing a softer cookie.
- To ensure even browning, turn sheet back to front halfway through baking.

- **Preheat oven to 375°F (190°C)**
- **Baking sheets, greased**

1. In a large mixer bowl, combine cake mix, eggs and melted butter. Beat on low speed for 1 minute or just until smooth. Stir in chocolate and cereal. Mix well.

2. Drop dough by rounded tablespoonfuls (15 mL) onto prepared baking sheets, 2 inches (5 cm) apart. Flatten slightly with fingers. Bake, one sheet at a time, for 8 to 12 minutes or until set. Cool on baking sheets for 1 minute or until firm, then remove to wire racks and cool completely.

Variation: Replace chocolate cake mix with white.

Crunchy Chocolate Toffee Cookies

The taste of these rich, dark cookies resembles a chocolate bar.

MAKES ABOUT 4 DOZEN COOKIES		
1	package (18.25 oz/515 g) devil's food cake mix	1
2	eggs	2
½ cup	vegetable oil	125 mL
1 cup	semi-sweet chocolate chips	250 mL
¾ cup	chopped nuts	175 mL
¾ cup	crunchy toffee bits	175 mL

TIP

- Line baking sheets with parchment paper or special baking liners for easy removal and cleanup. This is especially handy for cookies that tend to stick.

- **Preheat oven to 375°F (190°C)**
- **Baking sheets, greased**

1. In a large mixer bowl, combine cake mix, eggs and oil. With a wooden spoon or on low speed of mixer, mix for 1 minute or until well blended. Dough will be stiff. Stir in chocolate, nuts and toffee bits.

2. Drop dough by rounded tablespoonfuls (15 mL) onto prepared baking sheets, 2 inches (5 cm) apart. Bake, one sheet at a time, for 8 to 12 minutes or until firm around the edges. Cool for 1 minute on baking sheets, then remove to wire racks and cool completely.

Variations: Use yellow cake mix for a traditional chocolate chip cookie look. Replace nuts with 1 cup (250 mL) flaked coconut or dried fruit.

Double Chocolate Chewies

A versatile chocolate cookie that lends itself to a variety of additions such as chips, nuts and dried fruit.

MAKES ABOUT 4 DOZEN COOKIES		
1	package (18.25 oz/515 g) devil's cake mix	1
1	egg	1
⅓ cup	water	75 mL
¼ cup	butter, melted	50 mL
1½ cups	white chocolate chips	375 mL
½ cup	dried cranberries	125 mL
½ cup	slivered almonds or pecans	125 mL

TIPS

- Don't store crisp cookies and soft cookies together. The crisp ones won't stay that way for long!
- Use sheets of waxed paper between layers to prevent cookies from sticking together.
- Cookies freeze very well for up to 6 months. They thaw in about 15 minutes.

- **Preheat oven to 375°F (190°C)**
- **Baking sheets, greased**

1. In a large mixer bowl, combine cake mix, egg, water and melted butter. Beat on low speed for 1 minute or just until smooth. Stir in chocolate chips, cranberries and nuts. Mix well.

2. Drop dough by rounded tablespoonfuls (15 mL) onto prepared baking sheets, 2 inches (5 cm) apart. Bake for 8 to 10 minutes or just until softly set. Cool on baking sheets for 1 minute or until firm, then remove to wire racks and cool completely.

Variation: Substitute cold strong coffee for the water.

Double Chocolate Dreams

A chocoholic's dream. Try them warm from the oven, but be prepared to make a second batch.

MAKES ABOUT 4 DOZEN COOKIES		
1	package (18.25 oz/515 g) devil's food cake mix	1
2	eggs	2
½ cup	vegetable oil	125 mL
2 cups	semi-sweet chocolate chips	500 mL
¾ cup	chopped nuts	175 mL

TIP

- A small ice cream scoop with wire release is ideal for spooning out the dough. You get nicely shaped cookies of uniform size.

- **Preheat oven to 375°F (190°C)**
- **Baking sheets, greased**

1. In a large mixer bowl, combine cake mix, eggs and oil. With a wooden spoon or on low speed of mixer, mix for 1 minute or until well blended. Dough will be stiff. Stir in chocolate chips and nuts.

2. Drop dough by rounded tablespoonfuls (15 mL) onto prepared baking sheets, 2 inches (5 cm) apart. Bake for 8 to 12 minutes or just until set. Cool for 1 minute on baking sheets on wire racks, then remove to racks and cool completely.

Variations: Use yellow cake mix for a regular chocolate chip cookie. Replace nuts with more chocolate chips.

Trail Mix Cookies

Loaded with seeds and dried fruits, these are especially good for lunchboxes and backpacks.

MAKES ABOUT 4 DOZEN COOKIES		
1	package (18.25 oz/515 g) white cake mix	1
1 cup	quick-cooking oats	250 mL
1 tbsp	ground cinnamon	15 mL
2	eggs	2
½ cup	vegetable oil	125 mL
¼ cup	water	50 mL
¾ cup	slivered almonds	175 mL
¾ cup	dried cranberries	175 mL
⅔ cup	chopped dried apricots	150 mL
⅔ cup	pumpkin seeds	150 mL
¼ cup	sesame seeds	50 mL
¼ cup	flaxseeds	50 ml

Preheat oven to 375°F (190°C)
Baking sheets, greased

1. In a large mixer bowl, combine cake mix, oats, cinnamon, eggs, oil and water. Beat on low speed for 1 minute or just until blended. Stir in almonds, cranberries, apricots, pumpkin seeds, sesame seeds and flaxseeds. Mix well.

2. Drop dough by rounded tablespoonfuls (15 mL) onto prepared baking sheets, 2 inches (5 cm) apart. Flatten slightly with fingers. Bake for 10 to 12 minutes or until lightly browned. Cool for 1 minute on baking sheets or until firm, then transfer cookies to wire racks and cool completely.

Variations: Substitute sunflower seeds for the pumpkin seeds. Substitute more sesame seeds for the flaxseeds.

TIPS

- Store seeds, nuts and grains in the freezer to keep them fresh.
- Cool cookies completely before storing or they will soften.
- Bake cookies slightly longer for a crisper texture.
- Mix dough with your hands to blend thoroughly.

Hazelnut Biscotti

A double baking makes biscotti extra crunchy so they are ideal to dunk into your favorite drink. They are also a good choice if you want to ship or mail a homemade gift.

MAKES ABOUT 3 1/2 DOZEN COOKIES

1	package (18.25 oz/515 g) white cake mix	1
2/3 cup	all-purpose flour	150 mL
1/3 cup	ground hazelnuts	75 mL
2	eggs	2
1/2 cup	vegetable oil	125 mL
1 tbsp	grated lemon zest	15 mL
2/3 cup	coarsely chopped hazelnuts	150 mL

TIPS

- When shaping the dough into rectangles, keep in mind that it will expand during baking, so start slightly smaller than you prefer.
- Parchment paper makes it easy to remove the baked rectangle.
- Store biscotti in airtight containers for up to 3 weeks.

- **Preheat oven to 350°F (180°C)**
- **Baking sheets, lined with parchment paper or greased**

1. In a large mixer bowl, combine cake mix, flour, ground hazelnuts, eggs, oil and lemon zest. Beat on low speed for 1 minute or until blended. Work in chopped hazelnuts with hands to form smooth dough. Divide dough in half.

2. On a prepared baking sheet, shape each half into a 10- by 3-inch (25 by 8 cm) rectangle that is 1/2 inch (1 cm) deep. Bake, one sheet at a time, for 15 minutes. Remove from oven and cool for 10 minutes on baking sheet. Carefully transfer to a cutting board and cut each rectangle into 1/2-inch (1 cm) slices. Place slices on their side on baking sheets. Bake, one tray at a time, for 10 minutes. Turn slices over and bake for 5 to 10 minutes longer or until crisp and golden. Cool for 1 minute on baking sheets, then remove to wire racks and cool completely.

Variations: Use your favorite nut. Pecans and almonds are popular. Omit lemon zest, if desired.

Fruit and Nut Refrigerator Cookies

Keep a roll of refrigerator cookie dough on hand, and you're always ready for a cookie emergency.

MAKES ABOUT 7 DOZEN COOKIES		
1	package (18.25 oz/515 g) white cake mix	1
1	egg	1
½ cup	butter, melted	125 mL
1 tbsp	water	15 mL
1 tsp	rum extract	5 mL
1½ cups	chopped candied cherries	375 mL
½ cup	chopped pecans	125 mL

TIPS

- Wrap dough tightly in plastic wrap for storage. If the wrapping isn't tight, the dough will dry out.
- Freeze rolls for up to 3 months. Thaw in the refrigerator overnight before baking.

- **Preheat oven to 375°F (190°C)**
- **Baking sheets, greased**

1. In a large mixing bowl, combine cake mix, egg, melted butter, water and rum extract. Stir with a wooden spoon to blend. Stir in cherries and pecans.

2. Divide dough in half. Shape each half into a 2-inch (5 cm) thick log. Wrap in plastic wrap or waxed paper and chill overnight in the refrigerator. Cut dough into ⅛-inch (3 mm) thick slices. Place on prepared baking sheets, 2 inches (5 cm) apart. Bake for 7 to 9 minutes or until lightly browned. Cool for 1 minute on baking sheets or until firm, then transfer cookies to racks and cool completely.

Variations: Use your favorite nut. Mix red and green cherries or use all of one color. Replace rum extract with almond extract.

Refrigerator Nut Wafers

With a roll of dough in the refrigerator, fresh baked cookies are only minutes away.

MAKES ABOUT 7 DOZEN COOKIES		
1	package (18.25 oz/515 g) white cake mix	1
1	egg	1
½ cup	butter, melted	125 mL
1 tbsp	water	15 mL
1 tsp	vanilla	5 mL
1½ cups	chopped pecans or hazelnuts	375 mL

TIPS

- You can make square cookies by packing dough into small plastic wrap boxes.
- Roll dough in finely chopped nuts before slicing for an attractive edge around the cookie.

- **Preheat oven to 375°F (190°C)**
- **Baking sheets, greased**

1. In a large bowl, combine cake mix, egg, melted butter, water and vanilla. Stir with wooden spoon to blend. Work in nuts with your hands to form smooth dough.

2. Divide dough in half. Shape each half into a 2-inch (5 cm) thick log. Wrap in plastic wrap or waxed paper and chill overnight in the refrigerator. Cut dough into ⅛-inch (3 mm) thick slices. Place on prepared baking sheets, 2 inches (5 cm) apart. Bake, one sheet at a time, for 7 to 9 minutes or until lightly browned. Cool on baking sheets for 1 minute or until firm, then remove to wire racks and cool completely.

Variation: Try pistachio nuts for an unusual look. The green is especially pretty at Christmas.

Almond Crisps

A plain crisp cookie with a delightful almond flavor.

MAKES ABOUT 4 DOZEN COOKIES		
1	package (18.25 oz/515 g) white cake mix	1
1 cup	very finely chopped or ground almonds	250 mL
1	egg	1
½ cup	butter, melted	125 mL
1 tbsp	water	15 mL
1 tsp	almond extract	5 mL
	Granulated sugar	
	Whole almonds (optional)	

TIPS

- Use unblanched almonds for an attractive appearance. The flecks of brown skin add a nice flavor, too.
- Cooled cookies can be frozen in airtight plastic bags for up to 6 months.

- **Preheat oven to 375°F (190°C)**
- **Baking sheets, greased**

1. In a large bowl, combine cake mix, almonds, egg, melted butter, water and almond extract. Mix with wooden spoon or on low speed of mixer until blended, about 1 minute.

2. Shape dough into 1-inch (2.5 cm) balls. Place on prepared baking sheets, 2 inches (5 cm) apart. Press flat with bottom of glass dipped in sugar. If desired, press an almond on top of each cookie. Bake, one sheet at a time, for 10 to 12 minutes or until lightly browned. Cool on baking sheets for 1 minute or until firm, then remove to wire racks and cool completely.

Variation: Replace almonds with hazelnuts or pecans. Replace almond extract with vanilla.

Cereal Crisps

Cereal never tasted so good. There's a lot of crunch packed into every bite. It won't be hard to convince kids to eat breakfast.

MAKES ABOUT 4 DOZEN COOKIES		
1	package (18.25 oz/515 g) white cake mix	1
1	egg	1
½ cup	water	125 mL
½ cup	vegetable oil	125 mL
1¼ cups	crisp rice cereal	300 mL
¾ cup	corn flakes cereal	175 mL
½ cup	flaked coconut	125 mL
½ cup	chopped walnuts	125 mL

- **Preheat oven to 375°F (190°C)**
- **Baking sheets, greased**

1. In a large mixer bowl, combine cake mix, egg, water and oil. Beat on low speed for 1 minute or until blended. Stir in cereals, coconut and nuts. Mix well.

2. Drop dough by rounded tablespoonfuls (15 mL) onto prepared baking sheets, 2 inches (5 cm) apart. Bake, one sheet at a time, for 9 to 11 minutes or until lightly browned. Cool on baking sheets for 1 minute or until firm, then remove to wire racks and cool completely.

Variation: Omit nuts if allergies are a problem.

TIPS

- Measure cereal, then crush it slightly. If you crush and then measure, you will have too much.
- Cookies bake quickly. Always check them at the minimum time, and then watch carefully. It's always wise to slightly underbake rather than overbake cookies. This means you'll have a slightly chewy cookie, which is preferable to hard rocks!

Lemon Crisps

Crisp and lemony — a wonderful plain cookie to enjoy with a cup of tea.

MAKES ABOUT 4 DOZEN COOKIES

1	package (18.25 oz/515 g) lemon cake mix	1
1	egg	1
½ cup	butter, melted	125 mL
1 tsp	grated lemon zest	5 mL
	Granulated sugar	

TIPS

- When grating the zest from lemons and oranges, use only the colored part. The white underneath has a bitter flavor.
- You can mix the dough easily with an electric mixer on low speed for 1 minute.

- **Preheat oven to 350°F (180°C)**
- **Baking sheets, greased**

1. In a large mixer bowl, combine cake mix, egg, melted butter and lemon zest. Mix with wooden spoon until well blended.

2. Shape dough into 1-inch (2.5 cm) balls. Roll in granulated sugar. Place on prepared baking sheets, 2 inches (5 cm) apart. Press flat with bottom of a glass dipped in sugar. Bake, one tray at a time, for 10 to 12 minutes or until lightly browned around edges. Cool on baking sheets for 1 minute or until firm, then remove to wire racks and cool completely.

Variation: Make these into sandwich cookies by putting 2 cookies together with a lemon frosting or raspberry jam.

Spicy Oatmeal Raisin Cookies

Once a favorite, always a favorite.

MAKES ABOUT 4 DOZEN COOKIES

1	package (18.25 oz/515 g) white cake mix	1
1 cup	quick-cooking rolled oats	250 mL
2 tsp	ground cinnamon	10 mL
1 tsp	ground nutmeg	5 mL
2	eggs	2
½ cup	vegetable oil	125 mL
1 cup	raisins	250 mL

TIPS

- Use quick-cooking oats to make cookies. You can use large-flake for a more "oaty" taste but the texture will change slightly.
- Don't let cookies remain on the baking sheet longer than 1 minute. They will continue to cook and be more difficult to remove.

- **Preheat oven to 375°F (190°C)**
- **Baking sheets, greased**

1. In a large mixer bowl, combine cake mix, oats, cinnamon, nutmeg, eggs and oil. Beat on low speed for 1 minute or just until blended. Stir in raisins. Mix well.

2. Drop dough by rounded tablespoonfuls (15 mL) onto prepared baking sheets, 2 inches (5 cm) apart. Flatten slightly with fingers. Bake, one sheet at a time, for 8 to 12 minutes or until lightly browned. Cool on baking sheets for 1 minute or until firm, then remove to wire racks and cool completely.

Variation: Replace raisins with dried cranberries or a mixture of other dried fruits such as papaya, pineapple, mango and dates. Adjust spice to suit your own tastes.

Rum Balls

There are many recipes for this classic no-bake treat. It's nice to make while another recipe is in the oven — or in the summer, when you don't want to put the oven on.

1	package (18.25 oz/515 g) chocolate cake mix, baked and cooled	1
1 cup	finely chopped walnuts or almonds	250 mL
4 tsp	rum	20 mL
2 cups	confectioner's (icing) sugar, sifted	500 mL
¼ cup	unsweetened cocoa powder, sifted	50 mL
	Finely chopped nuts or chocolate sprinkles	

1. Crumble cake into a large bowl. Stir with fork until crumbs are fine and uniform in size. Add nuts, rum, confectioner's sugar and cocoa. Stir until thoroughly blended. Shape heaping tablespoonfuls of cake mixture into balls. Roll in nuts or chocolate sprinkles, pressing firmly to adhere coating to balls. Place on waxed paper and let set for 1 hour. Store in an airtight container in the refrigerator.

Variation: Rum can be replaced with 1 tbsp (15 mL) rum extract.

TIPS

- An excellent way to use leftover cake, if that ever happens.
- Keep this recipe in mind if you have the opportunity to bake an extra cake when preparing another cake recipe.
- Prepare several days ahead to let flavors develop.
- Place in small paper cups to serve or for gift-giving.

These bars taste as though they were made from scratch. Use the recipes from this section to easily prepare lunchbox treats and decadent desserts for your family and for special occasions.

Butterscotch Nut Bars

A versatile bar that is also great cut into larger squares and served warm with ice cream for dessert.

MAKES ABOUT 3 DOZEN BARS

CRUST

1	package (18.25 oz/515 g) white cake mix	1
2/3 cup	butter, melted	150 mL

TOPPING

4	eggs	4
1 cup	granulated sugar	250 mL
1 cup	corn syrup	250 mL
1/4 cup	butter, melted	50 mL
1	package (10 oz/300 g) butterscotch chips	1
1½ cups	coarsely chopped pecans	375 mL

TIP
- Store nuts in the freezer to keep them fresh.

- **Preheat oven to 350°F (180°C)**
- **13- by 9-inch (3 L) cake pan, greased**

1. **Crust:** In a large bowl, combine cake mix and melted butter, mixing until well blended. Press firmly into prepared pan. Bake for 15 minutes or until light golden.

2. **Topping:** In a medium bowl, whisk eggs just to blend. Add sugar, syrup and melted butter, whisking until smooth. Stir in chips and nuts. Pour over warm crust. Bake for 30 to 35 minutes longer or until set and golden. Cool completely in pan on a wire rack. Cut into bars.

Variation: Semi-sweet chocolate chips and walnuts are another good combination.

Chocolate Cherry Bars

These bars have an unusual taste and texture. They're moist and cake-like with an attractive shiny top. Serve with whipped cream for dessert.

MAKES ABOUT 5 DOZEN BARS

1	package (6-serving size) chocolate pudding and pie filling (not instant)	1
1	package (18.25 oz/515 g) chocolate cake mix	1
1 cup	chopped maraschino cherries	250 mL
1 cup	semi-sweet chocolate chips	250 mL
3/4 cup	chopped nuts	175 mL

TIP
- Be sure to prepare the pudding just when you're going to make these bars, not ahead of time. It should be warm.

- **Preheat oven to 350°F (180°C)**
- **17- by 11-inch (43 by 28 cm) jellyroll pan, greased**

1. Cook pudding according to package directions. Remove 1 cup (250 mL) for another use — or simply enjoy eating it now! In a large mixer bowl, combine remaining warm pudding and cake mix. Beat on low speed or by hand for 1 minute or until smooth. Stir in cherries. Spread evenly in prepared pan. Sprinkle with chocolate chips and nuts. Bake for 20 to 25 minutes or until set. Cool completely on a wire rack. Cut into bars.

Variations: Vary the topping. It's great with a combination of white, milk and semi-sweet chocolate chips. Omit nuts and increase chips to 2 cups (500 mL).

Caramel-Filled Brownies

There are many varieties of bars that taste like chocolate caramel candies, but this is one of my favorites (based on many taste comparisons!).

MAKES ABOUT 4 DOZEN SQUARES

FILLING

14 oz	caramels (about 50)	425 g
½ cup	evaporated milk	125 mL

BASE AND TOPPING

1	package (18.25 oz/515 g) devil's food cake mix	1
1 cup	chopped pecans	250 mL
½ cup	butter, softened	125 mL
½ cup	evaporated milk	125 mL
1 cup	semi-sweet chocolate chips	250 mL

TIP

- Chill caramels for easier unwrapping. It's still a fussy job, but easily forgotten when you taste the squares.

- **Preheat oven to 350°F (180°C)**
- **13- by 9-inch (3 L) cake pan, greased**

1. **Filling:** In a saucepan, combine caramels and evaporated milk. Cook over low heat, stirring often, until smoothly melted. Keep warm while preparing brownie batter.

2. **Base and Topping:** In a large bowl, combine cake mix and pecans. Cut in butter with a pastry blender or a fork until crumbly. Add evaporated milk. Mix well. Batter will be thick. Spread half of batter in prepared pan. Bake for 12 to 15 minutes or until set. Remove from oven. Sprinkle chocolate chips on top. Drizzle caramel sauce over chips. Spread carefully to cover base. Drop remaining batter by spoonfuls over caramel. Bake for 15 to 20 minutes longer or just until set. Brownies will firm up on cooling. Cool completely in pan on a wire rack. Cut into squares.

Variation: Try using chocolate caramels. It doesn't look as attractive, but real chocoholics won't care!

Caramel Pecan Bars

These look fabulous and taste even better. Bet your tasters they can't eat just one!

CRUST

1	package (18.25 oz/515 g) white cake mix	1
¾ cup	butter, melted	175 mL

TOPPING

3½ cups	pecan halves	875 mL
¾ cup	butter	175 mL
½ cup	liquid honey	125 mL
¾ cup	packed brown sugar	175 mL
¼ cup	whipping (35%) cream	50 mL

TIPS

- To ensure crust is evenly distributed, put blobs of dough evenly over pan, then press out with heel of hand to cover pan.
- Do not substitute margarine for butter.

- Preheat oven to 350°F (180°C)
- 17- by 11-inch (43 by 28 cm) jellyroll pan, greased

1. **Crust:** Combine cake mix and melted butter, mixing until well blended. Press firmly into prepared pan. Bake for 15 minutes or until light golden. Cool for 5 minutes on a wire rack.

2. **Topping:** Scatter pecans evenly over crust. For the most attractive appearance, turn rounded-side up. In a large, heavy saucepan, melt butter and honey. Add brown sugar. Boil for 5 to 7 minutes, stirring constantly, until mixture is thickened and a rich caramel color. Remove from heat. Carefully stir in cream. Mix well and pour evenly over pecans. Bake for 15 minutes longer or just until topping is bubbling around sides of pan. Cool completely in pan on a wire rack. Cut into bars.

Variation: Replace white cake mix with yellow.

Peanut Butter Chocolate Squares

Just like salted peanuts, these squares can quickly become addictive.

FILLING

1⅔ cups	peanut butter chips (1 package/10 oz/300 g)	400 mL
1	can (14 oz/398 mL) sweetened condensed milk	1
2 tbsp	butter	25 mL

TOP AND BOTTOM LAYER

1	package (18.25 oz/515 g) Swiss chocolate cake mix	1
⅔ cup	butter, softened	150 mL
½ cup	milk	125 mL
¾ cup	chopped peanuts	175 mL
⅔ cup	quick-cooking rolled oats	150 mL

TIP

- Squares will puff during baking, then settle on cooling.

- Preheat oven to 350°F (180°C)
- 13- by 9-inch (3 L) cake pan, greased

1. **Filling:** In a saucepan, combine chips, sweetened condensed milk and butter. Heat, stirring occasionally, over low heat until smoothly melted. Set aside while preparing chocolate mixture.

2. **Top and Bottom Layer:** In a large mixer bowl, combine cake mix, butter and milk. Beat on low speed for 2 minutes or until smooth. Batter will be thick. Stir in peanuts and oats. Spread half the batter in prepared pan. Spread filling over top. Drop remaining chocolate batter by small spoonfuls over filling. Spread carefully to cover filling as much as possible. Bake for 30 to 35 minutes or until softly set. Squares will firm up on cooling. Cool completely in pan on a wire rack. Cut into squares.

Variations: Butterscotch chips and walnuts make a different-tasting square. A good choice when peanut allergies are a problem. Any chocolate cake mix will be great.

Toffee Chocolate Bars

Layers of crunchy toffee bits, creamy caramel and chocolate cover a crisp cookie-like base, making every bite a sensation.

CRUST

1	package (18.25 oz/515 g) white cake mix	1
2 tbsp	packed brown sugar	25 mL
½ cup	butter, melted	125 mL

FILLING

1	can (10 oz/300 mL) sweetened condensed milk	1
2 tbsp	butter	25 mL

TOPPING

1⅔ cups	semi-sweet chocolate chips	400 mL
1 cup	crunchy toffee bits	250 mL

TIPS

- The toffee bits get softer if you freeze these bars.
- We love them both ways, frozen and soft or unfrozen and crunchy. Take your pick.
- Don't leave the filling unattended on the stove — even for a minute. It burns very quickly.
- If you line the pan with foil and grease the foil, once the squares have cooled completely you can remove the whole thing from the pan and peel off the foil. This makes cutting easy.

- **Preheat oven to 350°F (180°C)**
- **13- by 9-inch (3 L) cake pan, greased**

1. **Crust:** In a large bowl, combine cake mix, brown sugar and melted butter. Using a wooden spoon, mix until a soft dough forms. Press firmly into prepared pan. Bake for 15 minutes or until light golden. Cool slightly in pan on a wire rack.

2. **Filling:** Meanwhile, heat sweetened condensed milk and butter in a heavy saucepan, stirring constantly over low heat for 5 to 10 minutes or until thickened. Spread over crust. Bake for 10 to 15 minutes or until golden. Cool for 1 hour in pan on a wire rack.

3. **Topping:** In a saucepan, over low heat (or in microwave on Medium for 2 minutes), melt chocolate chips, stirring until smooth. Spread evenly over filling. Sprinkle toffee bits on top, pressing lightly into chocolate. Cool completely. If necessary, chill briefly to set chocolate. Cut into bars.

Variation: Use milk chocolate chips in place of semi-sweet, if you prefer.

Toffee Crunch Bars

Here's a different way to enjoy your favorite chocolate bar.

MAKES ABOUT 3 DOZEN BARS		
1	package (18.25 oz/515 g) white cake mix	1
⅓ cup	packed brown sugar	75 mL
2	eggs	2
½ cup	butter, melted	125 mL
1 cup	crushed toffee-crunch chocolate bars	250 mL
⅔ cup	chopped almonds	150 mL

- **Preheat oven to 350°F (180°C)**
- **13- by 9-inch (3 L) cake pan, greased**

1. In a large mixer bowl, combine cake mix, brown sugar, eggs and melted butter. Beat on low speed for 2 minutes or until smooth. Stir in crushed chocolate bar and almonds. Spread batter evenly in prepared pan. Bake for 25 to 30 minutes or until golden. Cool completely in pan on a wire rack. Cut into bars.

Variations: Almost any chocolate bar will work. The softer chewy ones will have to be cold to chop. Or replace chocolate bars with toffee bits and chocolate chips.

TIPS

- Freeze chocolate bars so they become brittle and break up easily without melting.
- Buy "misshaped" chocolate bars on sale and keep a supply in the freezer for this recipe.
- If the chocolate bar you choose has lots of nuts, decrease the quantity of nuts in the recipe.

Pecan Toffee Bars

This easy-to-make treat is quite sweet and very popular.

MAKES ABOUT 3 DOZEN BARS		
CRUST		
1	package (18.25 oz/515 g) white cake mix	1
½ cup	butter, melted	125 mL
1	egg	1
TOPPING		
1	can (10 oz/300 mL) sweetened condensed milk	1
1	egg	1
1¼ cups	chopped pecans	300 mL
1⅓ cups	crunchy toffee bits	325 mL

- **Preheat oven to 350°F (180°C)**
- **13- by 9-inch (3 L) cake pan, greased**

1. **Crust:** In a large mixer bowl, combine cake mix, melted butter and egg. Beat on low speed for about 1 minute, until crumbly. Press firmly in prepared pan. Bake for 15 to 20 minutes or until light golden.

2. **Topping:** In a bowl, combine sweetened condensed milk and egg. Mix well. Stir in pecans and toffee bits. Pour evenly over crust. Bake for 25 to 30 minutes or until set. Cool completely in pan on a wire rack. Cut into bars.

Variation: Replace toffee bits with chopped toffee-crunch chocolate bars.

TIPS

- Cut cooled bars and pack them in a single layer to freeze. If the bars are cut when they are frozen, you can thaw at any time just the number you want to serve.
- A drizzle of melted chocolate makes these bars special.
- If they have been frozen, add the drizzle just before serving.

Chocolate Caramel Pecan Crumble Bars

Easy to make and delicious to eat! These bars are an excellent choice to keep on hand in the freezer.

MAKES ABOUT 3 DOZEN BARS

CRUST

1	package (18.25 oz/515 g) devil's food cake mix	1
1 cup	chopped pecans	250 mL
¾ cup	quick-cooking rolled oats	175 mL
¾ cup	butter, melted	175 mL

TOPPING

1	can (10 oz/300 mL) sweetened condensed milk	1
7 oz	soft caramels (about 25)	210 g
¼ cup	butter	50 mL

TIPS

- Chill caramels to make unwrapping a little easier. Slit wrapper with a small sharp knife to start.
- Break up any large lumps in crumble mixture with your fingers.

- **Preheat oven to 350°F (180°C)**
- **13- by 9-inch (3 L) cake pan, greased**

1. **Crust:** In a large bowl, combine cake mix, pecans, oats and melted butter. Using a wooden spoon, mix until a soft dough forms. Reserve 1⅓ cups (325 mL) for topping. Press remainder in prepared pan. Bake for 15 minutes or until light golden.

2. **Topping:** In a heavy saucepan, over low heat, heat sweetened condensed milk, caramels and butter, stirring constantly until melted and smooth. Pour over warm crust. Sprinkle reserved crumble mixture evenly on top. Bake for 20 to 25 minutes longer or until golden and bubbly. Cool completely in pan on a wire rack. Cut into bars.

Variation: Use your favorite nut in place of the pecans. Walnuts, hazelnuts, cashews and almonds all work well.

Chocolate Nut Bars

The large pan goes a long way. Think of this easy-to-make treat when you've got a crowd coming or for your next family reunion.

MAKES ABOUT 5 DOZEN BARS

1	package (18.25 oz/515 g) dark chocolate cake mix	1
¼ cup	packed brown sugar	50 mL
2	eggs	2
¼ cup	water	50 mL
¼ cup	butter, softened	50 mL
1 cup	chopped pecans or walnuts	250 mL
1	container (15 oz/450 g) ready-to-serve chocolate frosting	1

- **Preheat oven to 350°F (180°C)**
- **15- by 10-inch (38 by 25 cm) jellyroll pan, greased**

1. In a large mixer bowl, combine cake mix, brown sugar, eggs, water and butter. Beat on low speed for 1 minute or just until blended. Stir in nuts. Spread evenly in prepared pan. Bake for 15 to 20 minutes or just until set. Cool completely in pan on a wire rack. Spread evenly with chocolate frosting. Cut into bars.

Variation: For a mocha taste, dissolve 1 tbsp (15 mL) instant coffee in the water of the batter. Frost with a mocha butter frosting.

TIP

- Line the pan with greased parchment or aluminum foil for easy removal and cleanup.

Chocolate Pecan Bars

One pan goes a long way, so this recipe is a good choice for gift-giving.

CRUST

1	package (18.25 oz/515 g) white cake mix	1
⅔ cup	butter, melted	150 mL

TOPPING

5 oz	semi-sweet chocolate, chopped	150 g
1 cup	corn syrup	250 mL
1 cup	granulated sugar	250 mL
3	eggs	3
1 tsp	vanilla	5 mL
2½ cups	chopped pecans	625 mL

DRIZZLE (OPTIONAL)

2 oz	semi-sweet chocolate, melted (see page 13)	60 g

- **Preheat oven to 350°F (180°C)**
- **17- by 11-inch (43 by 28 cm) jellyroll pan, greased**

1. **Crust:** In a large bowl, combine cake mix and melted butter. Using a wooden spoon, mix until a soft dough forms. Press firmly into prepared pan. Bake for 10 to 12 minutes or until light golden.

2. **Topping:** In a saucepan, over low heat, heat chocolate and corn syrup, stirring until chocolate is melted and smooth. Remove from heat. Stir in sugar, eggs and vanilla until blended. Stir in pecans. Pour filling over warm crust; spread evenly. Bake for 30 to 35 minutes or until filling is set around edges and slightly soft in center. Cool completely in pan on a wire rack.

3. **Drizzle:** If desired, drizzle randomly with melted chocolate. Chill just to set chocolate. Cut into bars.

Variation: For better storage, omit the drizzle.

TIPS

- If you don't do much baking, shop at bulk stores for specialty items and smaller quantities. Remember to store nuts in the freezer.
- Purchase good-quality shiny metal pans for baking. They bake evenly and don't rust. If using glass pans or dark metal, decrease your oven temperature by 25°F (10°C).

Chewy Coconut Nut Bars

These are quick to make and a treat to eat.

MAKES ABOUT 4 DOZEN BARS

CRUST

1	package (18.25 oz/515 g) white cake mix	1
½ cup	butter, melted	125 mL

TOPPING

4	eggs	4
1¾ cups	packed brown sugar	425 mL
¼ cup	all-purpose flour	50 mL
2 tsp	baking powder	10 mL
1 tsp	vanilla	5 mL
1½ cups	chopped nuts	375 mL
1 cup	flaked coconut	250 mL

- **Preheat oven to 350°F (180°C)**
- **13- by 9-inch (3 L) cake pan, greased**

1. **Crust:** In a large bowl, combine cake mix and melted butter. Using a wooden spoon, mix until a soft dough forms. Press firmly into prepared pan. Bake for 15 minutes or until light golden.

2. **Topping:** In a bowl, beat eggs and brown sugar until blended. Stir in flour, baking powder and vanilla. Stir in nuts and coconut. Spread over warm crust. Bake for 25 to 30 minutes or until set and golden. Cool completely in pan on a wire rack. Cut into bars.

Variation: Pecans or walnuts work well in this recipe.

TIPS

- I prefer flaked or shredded coconut. Desiccated coconut is very fine and results in drier baked products.
- If you like a topping that is less sweet, add 1 tbsp (15 mL) lemon juice.

Candy Bar Bars

The name says it all. These tasty bars are just like a candy bar.

MAKES ABOUT 4 DOZEN BARS

CRUST

1	package (18.25 oz/515 g) white cake mix	1
¾ cup	butter, melted	175 mL

FILLING

14 oz	soft caramels (about 50)	425 g
⅓ cup	evaporated milk	75 mL
⅓ cup	butter	75 mL
1⅔ cups	confectioner's (icing) sugar, sifted	400 mL
1 cup	chopped pecans	250 mL

GLAZE

1 cup	semi-sweet chocolate chips, melted	250 mL

- **Preheat oven to 350°F (180°C)**
- **13- by 9-inch (3 L) cake pan, greased**

1. **Crust:** In a large bowl, combine cake mix and melted butter. Using a wooden spoon, mix until a soft dough forms. Press firmly into prepared pan. Bake for 15 to 20 minutes or until light golden.

2. **Filling:** In a saucepan, over low heat, heat caramels and evaporated milk, stirring often until smooth. Add butter, then stir until melted. Remove from heat. Stir in confectioner's sugar and pecans. Mix well. Spread over crust. Let cool until set.

3. **Glaze:** Spread melted chocolate over filling. Chill just to set chocolate. Cut into bars.

Variation: Peanuts or a combination of peanuts and pecans also work well in this bar.

TIP

- There are several brands of soft caramels. Choose ones that are easy to unwrap, unless you have kids to do that for you.

Chewy Cherry Bars

A colorful addition to your Christmas cookie tray. You'll never go wrong with extras in the freezer.

CRUST

1	package (18.25 oz/515 g) white cake mix	1
¾ cup	butter, softened	175 mL

FILLING

2	eggs	2
1 cup	packed brown sugar	250 mL
½ tsp	almond extract	2 mL
2 tbsp	all-purpose flour	25 mL
1 tsp	baking powder	5 mL
1 cup	flaked coconut	250 mL
1 cup	chopped drained maraschino cherries	250 mL
½ cup	chopped pecans or walnuts	125 mL

FROSTING

¼ cup	butter, softened	50 mL
½ tsp	almond extract	2 mL
2 cups	confectioner's (icing) sugar, sifted	500 mL
3 to 4 tbsp	half-and-half (10%) cream	45 to 60 mL

- **Preheat oven to 350°F (180°C)**
- **13- by 9-inch (3 L) cake pan, greased**

1. **Crust:** In a large mixer bowl, combine cake mix and butter. Beat on low speed until well blended. Press firmly into prepared pan. Bake for 10 to 12 minutes or until light golden.

2. **Filling:** In a large mixer bowl, beat eggs, brown sugar and extract together until smoothly blended. Stir in flour and baking powder. Mix well. Stir in coconut, cherries and nuts. Spread evenly over warm crust. Bake for 25 to 30 minutes longer or until set and golden. Cool completely in pan on a wire rack.

3. **Frosting:** In a small mixer bowl, beat butter and almond extract until smooth. Gradually add confectioner's sugar and cream, beating on medium speed until smooth and creamy. Spread over cooled bars. Chill until frosting is firm. Cut into bars.

Variation: Replace each ½ tsp (2 mL) almond extract with 1 tbsp (15 mL) lemon juice in the filling and frosting.

TIPS

- If you're counting calories during the holiday season, omit the frosting.
- Chill bars for easy cutting and storing.

Cranberry Chip Bars

Creamy white chocolate, crunchy nuts and tart cranberries combine in this colorful, festive bar.

MAKES ABOUT 4 DOZEN BARS		
1	package (18.25 oz/515 g) white cake mix	1
¼ cup	packed brown sugar	50 mL
2	eggs	2
¼ cup	butter, softened	50 mL
¼ cup	water	50 mL
1 cup	dried cranberries	250 mL
1 cup	white chocolate chips	250 mL
1 cup	chopped almonds	250 mL

- **Preheat oven to 350°F (180°C)**
- **13- by 9-inch (3 L) cake pan, greased**

1. In a large mixer bowl, combine cake mix, brown sugar, eggs, butter and water. Beat on low speed for 1 minute or until smooth. Stir in cranberries, chips and nuts. Spread batter evenly in prepared pan. Bake for 25 to 30 minutes or until set and light golden. Cool completely in pan on a wire rack. Cut into bars.

Variation: Replace almonds with pecans or walnuts and cranberries with chopped dried apricots.

TIPS
- For a sweeter bar, top with a lemon glaze or frosting.
- Check for doneness at the minimum time recommended. Ovens are often hot and dark pans bake contents faster. You can always bake it longer rather than being disappointed with an overdone item.
- It's a good idea to keep a reliable oven thermometer in your oven as a check on the temperature.

Cranberry Pecan Bars

A combination of sweet pecan pie and tart cranberries in an easy-to-eat, bite-size bar.

MAKES ABOUT 4 DOZEN BARS		
CRUST		
1	package (18.25 oz/515 g) white cake mix	1
½ cup	butter, melted	125 mL
TOPPING		
4	eggs	4
1 cup	granulated sugar	250 mL
1 cup	corn syrup	250 mL
3 tbsp	butter, melted	45 mL
1½ cups	coarsely chopped pecans	375 mL
¾ cup	dried cranberries	175 mL

- **Preheat oven to 350°F (180°C)**
- **13-by 9-inch (3 L) cake pan, greased**

1. **Crust:** In a large bowl, combine cake mix and melted butter, mixing until well blended. Press firmly into prepared pan. Bake for 15 minutes or until light golden. Cool for 5 minutes on a wire rack before topping.

2. **Topping:** In a medium bowl, beat eggs, sugar, syrup and melted butter together until blended. Stir in pecans and cranberries. Pour evenly over crust. Bake for 35 to 40 minutes longer or until set and golden. Cool completely in pan on rack. Cut into bars.

Variation: Replace dried cranberries with chocolate chips.

TIP
- The crust will puff slightly during baking but settles down again on cooling.

Pineapple Coconut Dream Bars

These bars taste like piña colada without the rum.

CRUST

1	package (18.25 oz/515 g) white cake mix	1
½ cup	butter, melted	125 mL

TOPPING

2	cans (each 14 oz/398 mL) crushed pineapple, well drained	2
2	eggs	2
1½ cups	granulated sugar	375 mL
⅓ cup	butter, melted	75 mL
1 tsp	vanilla	5 mL
2 cups	flaked coconut	500 mL

- Preheat oven to 350°F (180°C)
- 13- by 9-inch (3 L) cake pan, greased

1. **Crust:** In a large bowl, combine cake mix and melted butter. Using a wooden spoon, mix until well blended. Press firmly into prepared pan. Bake for 12 to 15 minutes or until light golden. Cool for 10 minutes.

2. **Topping:** Spread well-drained pineapple over crust. In a large mixer bowl, beat eggs and sugar until blended. Add melted butter and vanilla. Mix well. Stir in coconut. Spread over pineapple. Bake for 30 to 40 minutes or until set and golden. Cool completely in pan on a wire rack. Cut into bars.

Variation: Add rum flavoring to taste to the topping mixture.

TIP

- Brands of crushed pineapple vary considerably in texture, as well as in the ratio of solid to liquid. I like the coarser cut pieces with not too much liquid.

Raspberry Raisin Bars

Similar to date squares without the hassle of cooking the dates. The jam adds a unique taste.

1	package (18.25 oz/515 g) yellow cake mix	1
2½ cups	quick-cooking rolled oats	625 mL
1¼ cups	chopped walnuts	300 mL
1 cup	butter, melted	250 mL
2¼ cups	raisins	550 mL
1¼ cups	raspberry jam	300 mL

TIPS

- Raisins should be soft and chewy. If they have dried out too much, pour boiling water over them and let stand 5 minutes, then drain and pat well with paper towels to dry.
- Golden raisins have a light color and milder taste.

- Preheat oven to 375°F (190°C)
- 13- by 9-inch (3 L) cake pan, greased

1. In a large bowl, combine cake mix, oats, walnuts and melted butter, mixing until well blended. Press half of the crumble mixture (2¾ cups/675 mL) firmly into prepared pan. Mix raisins and jam together. Spread evenly over unbaked crust. Sprinkle remaining crumble mixture over raisins. Bake for 35 to 40 minutes or until golden. Cool completely in pan on a wire rack. Cut into bars.

Variation: Try different kinds of jams or preserves for different flavors. For a very different taste, replace the jam with chocolate hazelnut spread.

Raspberry Dream Bars

Raspberry and coconut are a natural flavor combination.

CRUST

1	package (18.25 oz/515 g) white cake mix	1
¾ cup	butter, melted	175 mL

TOPPING

⅔ cup	raspberry jam	150 mL
2¼ cups	packed brown sugar	550 mL
¼ cup	all-purpose flour	50 mL
1½ tsp	baking powder	7 mL
¼ tsp	salt	1 mL
3	eggs	3
1 tbsp	lemon juice	15 mL
¾ cup	chopped walnuts	175 mL
¾ cup	shredded or flaked coconut	175 mL

- **Preheat oven to 350°F (180°C)**
- **13- by 9-inch (3 L) cake pan, greased**

1. **Crust:** In a large bowl, combine cake mix and melted butter, mixing until well blended. Press firmly into prepared pan. Bake for 12 to 15 minutes or until light golden. Cool for 10 minutes on a wire rack.

2. **Topping:** Spread jam carefully over warm crust. In a large bowl, combine brown sugar, flour, baking powder and salt. Add eggs and lemon juice, mixing until smooth. Stir in nuts and coconut. Spread evenly over jam. Bake for 20 to 25 minutes longer or until set and golden. Cool completely in pan on rack. Cut into bars.

TIPS

- Buy good-quality jams. They have the best flavor and a softer consistency that is excellent for spreading.
- I prefer the flavor of golden brown sugar. The dark variety works well in recipes but seems to mask delicate flavors such as raspberry.

Raspberry Meringue Bars

A chewy meringue topping with lots of nuts and coconut covers a layer of jam on a shortbread-like base.

CRUST

1	package (18.25 oz/515 g) white cake mix	1
½ cup	butter, melted	125 mL
2	egg yolks	2

TOPPING

1 cup	raspberry jam	250 mL
½ cup	flaked coconut	125 mL
2	egg whites	2
½ cup	granulated sugar	125 mL
1 cup	chopped walnuts	250 mL

- **Preheat oven to 350°F (180°C)**
- **13- by 9-inch (3 L) cake pan, greased**

1. **Crust:** In a large mixer bowl, combine cake mix, melted butter and egg yolks. Beat on low speed for about 1 minute, until well blended. Press firmly in prepared pan. Bake for 12 to 15 minutes or until very lightly browned.

2. **Topping:** Spread jam over warm crust. Sprinkle coconut on top. In a small mixer bowl, beat egg whites until frothy. Gradually add sugar, beating until stiff peaks form. Fold in walnuts. Carefully spread over coconut. Bake for 20 to 25 minutes or until light golden. Cool completely in pan on a wire rack. Cut into bars.

Variation: Try other flavors of jam and nuts, such as apricot jam with hazelnuts.

TIPS

- Before beating egg whites, wipe the bowl with the cut surface of a lemon to make sure it is free of grease.
- Cut bars with a hot, damp knife.

Chocolate Raspberry Almond Oat Bars

The best of both worlds — healthy oats and decadent chocolate chips.

MAKES ABOUT 3 DOZEN BARS		
1	package (18.25 oz/515 g) white cake mix	1
2½ cups	quick-cooking rolled oats	625 mL
1 cup	butter, melted	250 mL
1 cup	seedless raspberry jam	250 mL
1⅓ cups	semi-sweet chocolate chips	325 mL
¾ cup	chopped almonds or pecans	175 mL
	Confectioner's (icing) sugar (optional)	

- **Preheat oven to 375°F (190°C)**
- **13- by 9-inch (3 L) cake pan, greased**

1. In a large bowl, combine cake mix, oats and melted butter, mixing until well blended. Press half of crumbles (3 cups/750 mL) firmly into prepared pan. Spread jam evenly over unbaked crust. Sprinkle chocolate chips over jam. Stir almonds into remaining crumble mixture. Sprinkle evenly over chips. Bake for 35 to 40 minutes or until golden. Cool completely in pan on a wire rack. Cut into bars.

Variation: Replace raspberry jam with apricot. It's not as pretty but it tastes good.

TIPS
- Stir jam to soften for easy spreading.
- Spread jam over base, leaving a ½-inch (1 cm) border. This prevents jam from sticking to side of pan.
- Regular raspberry jam works fine, although the seedless variety has a more intense flavor.

Lemon Layered Bars

Lots of lemon in the crust, filling and crumble topping.

MAKES ABOUT 4 DOZEN BARS		
CRUST		
1	package (18.25 oz/515 g) lemon cake mix	1
1	egg	1
⅓ cup	butter, melted	75 mL
FILLING		
2	eggs	2
⅔ cup	granulated sugar	150 mL
2 tsp	grated lemon zest	10 mL
⅓ cup	lemon juice	75 mL
½ tsp	baking powder	2 mL
¼ tsp	salt	1 mL
	Confectioner's (icing) sugar (optional)	

- **Preheat oven to 350°F (180°C)**
- **13- by 9-inch (3 L) cake pan, greased**

1. **Crust:** In a large mixer bowl, combine cake mix, egg and melted butter. Beat on low speed until well blended and crumbly. Reserve 1 cup (250 mL) crumbs for topping. Press remaining crumbs firmly in prepared pan. Bake for 12 to 15 minutes or until light golden.

2. **Filling:** In a small mixer bowl, combine eggs, sugar, lemon zest, lemon juice, baking powder and salt. Beat on medium speed until light and foamy. Pour over warm crust. Sprinkle reserved crumble mixture evenly on top. Bake for 15 to 20 minutes longer or until set and golden. Cool completely in pan on a wire rack. Dust with confectioner's sugar before serving, if desired. Cut into bars.

Variation: Replace lemon zest and juice with lime zest and juice.

TIP
- Cool bar completely, then cut into bars and freeze in small packages. Simply remove the number of bars required.

Chunky Butterscotch Nut Squares

Made-to-order for nut fans.

MAKES ABOUT 4 DOZEN SQUARES		
CRUST		
1	package (18.25 oz/515 g) yellow cake mix	1
⅔ cup	butter, melted	150 mL
TOPPING		
1⅔ cups	butterscotch chips (1 package/10 oz/300g)	400 mL
¾ cup	corn syrup	175 mL
3 tbsp	butter	45 mL
2 cups	salted mixed nuts	500 mL

TIP
- You can buy mixed nuts or make up a combination of your own favorite salted nuts.

- **Preheat oven to 350°F (180°C)**
- **13- by 9-inch (3 L) cake pan, greased**

1. **Crust:** In a large bowl, combine cake mix and melted butter, mixing until well blended. Press firmly into prepared pan. Bake for 25 to 30 minutes or until golden. Cool completely in pan on a wire rack.

2. **Topping:** In a saucepan, over low heat, combine butterscotch chips, corn syrup and butter. Cook, stirring often until smoothly melted. Cool slightly. Spread over cooled base. Scatter nuts evenly over top. Press gently into topping. Chill for 1 hour or until firm for easy slicing. Cut into squares.

Variations: For real peanut-lovers, use peanut butter chips and peanuts. Milk chocolate chips also look and taste good with the mixed nuts.

Chewy Peanut Candy Squares

These chewy treats are always a big hit with kids, young and old.

MAKES ABOUT 4 DOZEN BARS		
CRUST		
1	package (18.25 oz/515 g) white cake mix	1
½ cup	butter, softened	125 mL
1	egg	1
TOPPING		
3½ cups	miniature marshmallows	875 mL
¾ cup	corn syrup	175 mL
¾ cup	packed brown sugar	175 mL
¾ cup	creamy peanut butter	175 mL
2 cups	crisp rice cereal	500 mL
1¾ cups	salted peanuts	425 mL
1¼ cups	miniature candy-coated chocolate bits	300 mL

TIP
- Buy peanut butter just as you need it to retain the fresh taste in baked goods.

- **Preheat oven to 350°F (180°C)**
- **15- by 10-inch (38 by 25 cm) jellyroll pan, greased**

1. **Crust:** In a large mixer bowl, combine cake mix, butter and egg. Beat on low speed for 1 minute, until crumbly. Press firmly in prepared pan. Bake for 10 to 15 minutes or until light golden.

2. **Topping:** Sprinkle marshmallows over hot crust. Return to oven for 1 to 2 minutes or just until marshmallows begin to puff. Cool slightly in pan on a wire rack.

3. In a large saucepan, combine syrup, brown sugar and peanut butter. Heat over low heat, stirring constantly, until smooth. Remove from heat. Stir in cereal, peanuts and candy. Spread evenly over marshmallows. Cool completely before cutting into squares.

Variation: Colored marshmallows are a fun choice.

Lots of Lemon Squares

A hazelnut cookie base with tart, lemony topping. These squares make a refreshing complement to decadent chocolate delights.

MAKES ABOUT 4 DOZEN SQUARES

CRUST

1	package (18.25 oz/515 g) lemon cake mix	1
½ cup	finely chopped hazelnuts	125 mL
½ cup	butter, melted	125 mL

TOPPING

4	eggs	4
2 cups	granulated sugar	500 mL
⅓ cup	lemon juice	75 mL
¼ cup	all-purpose flour	50 mL
1 tsp	baking powder	5 mL
1 tsp	grated lemon zest	5 mL
	Confectioner's (icing) sugar (optional)	

- **Preheat oven to 350°F (180°C)**
- **13- by 9-inch (3 L) cake pan, greased**

1. **Crust:** In a large bowl, combine cake mix, hazelnuts and melted butter, mixing until well blended. Press firmly into prepared pan. Bake for 12 minutes or until light golden.

2. **Topping:** In a small bowl, whisk together eggs, sugar and lemon juice until blended. Add flour, baking powder and lemon zest. Mix well. Pour over hot crust. Bake for 20 to 25 minutes longer or until set and light golden. Cool completely in pan on a wire rack. Dust with confectioner's sugar before serving, if desired. Cut into squares.

Variation: Replace hazelnuts with unblanched almonds.

TIPS

- A sprinkling of confectioner's sugar before serving makes a nice finishing touch.
- Toast hazelnuts (see page 14) for the best flavor. There's no need to remove the skins. They add a wonderfully nutty color and flavor.

Deep and Delicious Marbled Cream Cheese Brownies

A creamy cheesecake filling swirled through a deep, moist and decadent brownie makes these sensational.

MAKES ABOUT 4 DOZEN SQUARES

FILLING

8 oz	cream cheese, softened	250 g
¼ cup	butter, softened	50 mL
½ cup	granulated sugar	125 mL
2 tbsp	all-purpose flour	25 mL
2	eggs	2
1 tsp	vanilla	5 mL

BROWNIES

1	package (18.25 oz/515 g) dark chocolate cake mix	1
¼ cup	packed brown sugar	50 mL
2	eggs	2
¼ cup	water	50 mL
¼ cup	butter, softened	50 mL
1 cup	chopped pecans or walnuts	250 mL

TIPS

- The top layer of brownie batter won't completely cover the filling. Don't worry — after marbling and baking, it looks beautiful.
- These are very tall; cut into thin slices to serve. You can always come back for seconds.
- For even more decadence, add a thin chocolate frosting or glaze.

- **Preheat oven to 350°F (180°C)**
- **13- by 9-inch (3 L) cake pan, greased**

1. **Filling:** In a small mixer bowl, beat cream cheese, butter and sugar on low speed until blended. Add flour, eggs and vanilla, beating until smooth. Set aside.

2. **Brownies:** In a large mixer bowl, combine cake mix, brown sugar, eggs, water and butter. Beat on low speed for 1 minute or just until blended. Stir in nuts. Spread half of the batter evenly in prepared pan. Spread filling on top. Cover evenly with spoonfuls of remaining batter. Swirl mixtures with the tip of a knife just enough to marble. Bake for 35 to 45 minutes or just until set. Cool completely in pan on a wire rack. Cut into squares.

Variations: Add 1 tbsp (15 mL) coffee powder to the cheese mixture. Or add 1 tsp (5 mL) mint extract and green food coloring to the cheese mixture.

In this chapter, I've included recipes that start with a mix but aren't really cakes. Comfort food cobblers, crumbles and crisps are made easy. You'll also find chilled desserts, such as trifle and mousse cakes, and many make-ahead dishes here.

Peach Cobbler

Canned peach slices also work in this recipe, although the flavor can't compare to fresh.

SERVES 10

CRUST

1	package (18.25 oz/515 g) spice cake mix	1
1 cup	quick-cooking rolled oats	250 mL
1 cup	chopped walnuts	250 mL
¾ cup	butter, melted	175 mL

FILLING

6 cups	sliced peeled peaches (7 large)	1.5 L
½ cup	water	125 mL
¼ cup	packed brown sugar	50 mL
2 tbsp	cornstarch	25 mL
4 tsp	lemon juice	20 mL

- **Preheat oven to 350°F (180°C)**
- **13- by 9-inch (3 L) cake pan, greased**

1. **Crust:** Combine dry cake mix, oats, walnuts and melted butter. Mix well. Press 2½ cups (625 mL) of crumble mixture firmly into bottom of prepared pan. Set aside remaining crumbs for topping.

2. **Filling:** In a saucepan, combine peaches, water and brown sugar. Simmer over low heat for 5 minutes, stirring occasionally. Mix cornstarch and lemon juice until smooth. Add to peaches. Cook, stirring, until thickened. Pour over crust. Sprinkle reserved crumbs over fruit. Bake for 25 to 30 minutes or until topping is lightly browned. Serve warm.

Variations: Other fruits also work well in cobblers. Try apples, plums or nectarines. Or add 1 cup (250 mL) cranberries to peaches.

TIP

- If spice cake mix is hard to find — or too spicy for your taste — you can use a white cake mix and add 2 tsp (10 mL) ground cinnamon and 1 tsp (5 mL) ground nutmeg.

Cheery Cherry Cobbler

In this fascinating dessert, the cake and fruit layers reverse during baking.

SERVES 12 TO 16

CRUST

1	package (18.25 oz/515 g) white cake mix	1
3	eggs	3
1¼ cups	water	300 mL
⅓ cup	vegetable oil	75 mL

FRUIT FILLING

1 cup	granulated sugar	250 mL
2 tbsp	cornstarch	25 mL
1	jar (28 oz/796 mL) pitted red sour cherries, with juice	1
2 tbsp	butter, melted	25 mL
½ tsp	almond extract (optional)	2 mL
	Whipped cream or ice cream (optional)	

- **Preheat oven to 350°F (180°C)**
- **13- by 9-inch (3 L) cake pan, greased**

1. **Crust:** In a large mixer bowl, combine cake mix, eggs, water and oil. Beat on medium speed for 2 minutes. Spread evenly in prepared pan.

2. **Fruit Filling:** In a medium bowl, combine sugar and cornstarch. Stir in cherries (with juice), melted butter and extract. Mix well. Spoon evenly over batter. Bake for 50 to 60 minutes or until cake is set and golden. Serve warm or cool with whipped cream or ice cream, if desired.

Variation: Omit almond extract if desired.

TIPS

- Either cornstarch or flour can be used for thickening. To replace cornstarch, you'll need about twice as much flour.
- A few drops of red food coloring in the fruit mixture gives it a brighter color.

Butterscotch Fudge Torte

No matter how it's presented, the combination of butterscotch, chocolate and nuts is a favorite.

SERVES 12 TO 16

²⁄₃ cup	butterscotch chips	150 mL
½ cup	sweetened condensed milk	125 mL
1	package (18.25 oz/515 g) devil's food cake mix	1
½ cup	butter, melted, divided	125 mL
2	eggs	2
1 cup	unsweetened applesauce	250 mL
²⁄₃ cup	coarsely chopped cashews	150 mL

TIPS

- Prepare this a day ahead and leave more time for last-minute dinner preparations.
- Heat the butterscotch mixture in a microwave on Medium power for about 1 minute.
- The applesauce should be unsweetened because there's enough sugar in the cake.

- **Preheat oven to 350°F (180°C)**
- **10-inch (25 cm) springform pan**

1. In a small saucepan, over low heat, heat butterscotch chips and sweetened condensed milk, stirring often until melted and smooth. Set aside.

2. In a large mixer bowl, combine cake mix and ⅓ cup (75 mL) of the melted butter. Beat on low speed until crumbly. Reserve 1 cup (250 mL) of mixture for topping. Add eggs and applesauce to remaining cake mixture. Beat on low speed for 1 minute to blend, then on medium speed for 3 minutes. Spread batter evenly in prepared pan. Drizzle butterscotch mixture over batter. Stir cashews and remaining melted butter into reserved cake mixture. Mix well. Sprinkle over cake. Bake for 45 to 50 minutes or until set. Cool for 20 minutes on a wire rack, then remove from pan and cool completely on rack.

Variation: Replace butterscotch with semi-sweet chocolate chips.

Hot Fudge Pudding Cake

Cake and sauce together in one pan! Chocolate lovers will really enjoy this, especially with a dollop of whipped cream or ice cream.

SERVES 12 TO 16

1	package (18.25 oz/515 g) devil's food cake mix	1
2	eggs	2
1 cup	water	250 mL
1 cup	chopped pecans	250 mL
¾ cup	packed brown sugar	175 mL
½ cup	granulated sugar	125 mL
¼ cup	unsweetened cocoa powder, sifted	50 mL
2½ cups	boiling water	625 mL

- **Preheat oven to 400°F (200°C)**
- **13- by 9-inch (3 L) cake pan, greased**

1. In a large mixer bowl, combine cake mix, eggs and water. Beat on medium speed for 2 minutes. Stir in pecans. Spread evenly in prepared pan.

2. In a small bowl, combine brown sugar, granulated sugar and cocoa. Sprinkle over batter. Pour boiling water gently over top. Do not stir. Bake for 40 to 45 minutes or until set. Serve warm.

Variation: For a more chocolaty taste, use a dark chocolate cake mix.

TIP

- To bring out their flavor, toast pecans on a baking sheet at 350°F (180°C) for 10 minutes, stirring occasionally.

Chocolate Refrigerator Dessert

Lots of chocolate keeps everyone content. This creamy chocolate dessert doesn't resemble cake at all. It's a nice change for a special occasion.

SERVES 12 TO 16		
1	package (18.25 oz/515 g) devil's food cake mix	1
1½ cups	semi-sweet chocolate chips, melted and cooled	375 mL
3	eggs, separated	3
2 tbsp	granulated sugar	25 mL
4 cups	prepared whipped topping	1 L
	Whipped topping or cream to decorate	

TIPS

- This dessert must be made at least a day in advance.
- Prepare an extra cake when you have some spare time. With a few standard ingredients on hand, you can put this dessert together easily.
- Springform pans come in many sizes. If yours is smaller than 10 inches (25 cm), wrap a foil collar around it to extend the height.
- You can bake the cake in any size pan recommended on the package.

- **Preheat oven to 350°F (180°C)**
- **10-inch (4 L) tube pan or 13- by 9-inch (3 L) cake pan, greased and floured**
- **10-inch (25 cm) springform pan, greased**

1. Prepare and bake cake in tube pan or rectangular pan according to package directions. Cool and remove from pan as directed. With a long sharp knife, cut cake into 1-inch (2.5 cm) pieces. Set aside.

2. Combine melted chocolate chips, egg yolks and sugar (mixture will be stiff). Beat egg whites to stiff (but not dry) peaks. Stir one-quarter of egg whites into chocolate mixture thoroughly to soften, then fold remaining egg whites and whipped topping into chocolate mixture.

3. Layer cake pieces and chocolate cream mixture in springform pan, pressing down lightly to cover cake with cream. Cover and chill for 24 hours. Unmold onto a serving plate and decorate with additional whipped topping or cream as desired.

Variations: Use any flavor of chocolate cake. Swiss chocolate is good. Replace whipped topping with 2 cups (500 mL) whipping (35%) cream, beaten to stiff peaks.

Chocolate Coffee Pinwheel Cake

Wow your guests with this stunning dessert. Don't tell them it was easy to make.

CAKE

1	package (18.25 oz/515 g) dark chocolate cake mix	1
4	eggs	4
1 cup	sour cream	250 mL
½ cup	vegetable oil	125 mL
	Confectioner's (icing) sugar	

FILLING AND FROSTING

3 cups	whipping (35%) cream	750 mL
⅓ cup	confectioner's (icing) sugar, sifted	75 mL
3 tbsp	instant coffee powder	45 mL
3 tbsp	cold extra-strong coffee	45 mL
3 tbsp	coffee liqueur	45 mL
	Chocolate curls (see tip, page 20) or shaved chocolate	

TIPS

- This is simply a chocolate jellyroll, but instead of being rolled like a traditional jellyroll it is cut into strips, which are covered with a coffee cream filling and rolled in concentric circles to form a round cake. It's then frosted and decorated. Each slice looks stunning.
- Don't worry if the cake cracks. It's all held together with the cream filling.

- **Preheat oven to 350°F (180°C)**
- **17- by 11-inch (43 by 28 cm) jellyroll pan, greased and lined with parchment paper, leaving an overhang at the sides; grease bottom of parchment paper**

1. **Cake:** In a large mixer bowl, combine cake mix, eggs, sour cream and oil. Beat on medium speed for 2 minutes. Spread batter evenly in prepared pan. Bake for 15 to 20 minutes or until cake springs back when lightly touched. Cool for 10 minutes in pan on a wire rack. Dust with confectioner's sugar. Loosen edges of cake with a knife and turn out onto a tea towel. Trim any crisp edges of cake.

2. **Filling and Frosting:** In a large mixing bowl, beat whipping cream, confectioner's sugar, coffee powder, coffee and liqueur to stiff peaks.

3. **Assembly:** Spread half of the cream mixture over cake. Smooth evenly. Cut cake into 1-inch (2.5 cm) strips across the width. Roll up one strip and place in center of a large round serving platter. Roll second strip around first and continue until all strips are used. Cover top and sides of cake with remaining cream mixture. Decorate with chocolate curls or shaved chocolate. Chill until serving. Store leftover cake in the refrigerator.

Variation: Omit all the coffee in the cream mixture. Decorate with plain whipped cream, fresh raspberries and shaved chocolate.

Chocolate Caramel Cream Dessert

Definite indulgence. Don't even think about the calories — you can diet tomorrow (and the next day!).

SERVES 12 TO 16		
1	package (18.25 oz/515 g) devil's food cake mix	1
1	can (14 oz/398 mL) sweetened condensed milk	1
1½ cups	toffee bits	375 mL
1¼ cups	caramel sundae sauce	300 mL
2 cups	whipping (35%) cream	500 mL
1 cup	milk chocolate chips	250 mL

TIP

- Toffee bits (such as Skor Bits or Heath Bits) can be found where chocolate chips are sold.

- **Preheat oven to 350°F (180°C)**
- **13- by 9-inch (3 L) cake pan, greased**

1. Prepare and bake cake in prepared cake pan according to package directions. Cool completely in pan on a wire rack. Poke holes with end of wooden spoon, about 1 inch (2.5 cm) deep and 1 inch (2.5 cm) apart, over entire surface of cake. Pour sweetened condensed milk on top. Sprinkle half the toffee bits on top. Pour caramel sauce on top. Beat whipping cream to stiff peaks. Spread evenly over cake. Sprinkle chocolate chips and remaining toffee bits over cream. Chill until serving. Store leftover dessert in the refrigerator.

Variation: Replace milk chocolate chips and toffee bits on top of the cake with crushed toffee-crunch chocolate bars.

Death by Chocolate

This is definitely the dessert to die for. It is a chocoholic's dream come true.

SERVES 12 TO 16		
1	package (18.25 oz/515 g) dark chocolate cake mix	1
1	package (4-serving size) chocolate mousse dessert mix, prepared	1
2 cups	whipping (35%) cream	500 mL
2 tbsp	liqueur (such as amaretto or Kahlúa)	25 mL
4	crisp toffee-crunch chocolate bars (each 1.4 oz/40 g), crushed	4

TIPS

- Prepare the cake ahead and freeze. Cut into cubes while still semi-frozen.
- To crush chocolate bars, chill them first then pound them right in the package using an unbreakable utensil such as the back of a wooden spoon, a rolling pin or a hammer.
- Use any liqueur that you like and goes well with chocolate, such as amaretto, Kahlúa, Tia Maria or crème de cacao.

- **Preheat oven to 350°F (180°C)**
- **Two 8-inch (20 cm) or 9-inch (23 cm) round cake pans, greased and floured**
- **Trifle bowl or large glass serving bowl**

1. Prepare and bake cake according to package directions to make two round layers. Cool for 10 minutes in pans on a wire rack, then remove and cool completely on rack. Reserve one layer for another use and cut other layer with a long sharp knife into 1-inch (2.5 cm) cubes.

2. Prepare mousse mix according to package directions. Beat cream to stiff peaks.

3. Put half the cake cubes in trifle bowl. Drizzle half the liqueur on top. Spread half the mousse, then half the whipped cream on top. Sprinkle half the chocolate bars over cream. Repeat layering with remaining ingredients. Cover bowl with plastic wrap and chill for at least 4 hours before serving. Store leftover dessert in the refrigerator.

Variation: If you can't find Skor bars, try any crisp toffee chocolate bar.

Mango Mousse Cake

Refreshingly light but creamy, this is a memorable dessert to complete a special dinner.

CAKE

1	package (18.25 oz/515 g) white cake mix	1
3	eggs	3
1 tbsp	grated orange zest	15 mL
1²⁄₃ cups	orange juice	400 mL
⅓ cup	vegetable oil	75 mL

MANGO MOUSSE

1	envelope (¼ oz/7 g) unflavored gelatin	1
¼ cup	orange liqueur	50 mL
2½ lbs	ripe mangos, peeled, pitted and chopped	1.25 kg
½ cup	granulated sugar	125 mL
1 cup	whipping (35%) cream	250 mL

FROSTING

1 cup	whipping (35%) cream	250 mL
1 tbsp	confectioner's (icing) sugar	15 mL
2 tsp	orange liqueur	10 mL
1½ cups	toasted sliced almonds	375 mL
1	mango, peeled, pitted and sliced	1

TIPS

- Use ripe mangos for the mousse but slightly firmer ones to garnish.
- Brush mango slices lightly with lemon juice to keep them fresh.
- Prepare the day before to let mousse set.
- Two to 3 oranges (1 lb/500 g) will yield 3 tbsp (45 mL) grated zest and 1 cup (250 mL) juice.

- **Preheat oven to 350°F (180°C)**
- **Two 9-inch (23 cm) round cake pans, greased and floured**
- **9-inch (23 cm) springform pan**

1. **Cake:** In a large mixer bowl, combine cake mix, eggs, orange zest, orange juice and oil. Beat on medium speed for 2 minutes. Spread batter in prepared round cake pans, dividing evenly. Bake for 30 to 35 minutes or until a tester inserted in center comes out clean. Cool for 10 minutes in pans on a wire rack, then remove from pans and cool completely on rack. Freeze one cake layer for later use. With a long sharp knife, cut remaining cake horizontally in half.

2. **Mousse:** In a small bowl, sprinkle gelatin over orange liqueur. Let soften for 10 minutes. Purée mangos in food processor until smooth. You should have 2½ cups (625 mL). Set aside any extra for garnish. In a large bowl, stir sugar into purée. Warm gelatin mixture in microwave or over simmering water until dissolved. Stir into mango purée. In a large mixer bowl, beat cream to stiff peaks. Fold into mango purée, gently but thoroughly.

3. **Assembly:** Place bottom cake layer cut-side up in springform pan. Spread mango mousse on top. Place top cake layer cut-side down over mousse. Press down lightly. Cover with plastic wrap and chill for 4 hours or overnight.

4. **Frosting:** In a large mixer bowl, beat cream, confectioner's sugar and liqueur to stiff peaks. Release pan sides. Transfer cake to serving plate. Frost top and sides of cake with cream mixture. Press almonds onto sides. Decorate top with mango slices. Brush slices lightly with any reserved mango purée. Refrigerate until serving. Store leftover dessert in the refrigerator.

Variation: This dessert is also outstanding using a chocolate cake mix.

Apple Coconut Crumble

This simple dessert is always a favorite.

SERVES ABOUT 12		
1	package (18.25 oz/515 g) white or yellow cake mix	1
1 cup	flaked coconut	250 mL
½ cup	butter	125 mL
8	large apples, peeled, cored and cut in eighths (about 8 cups/2 L)	8
1 cup	water	250 mL
⅓ cup	lemon juice	75 mL
	Ice cream or whipped cream (optional)	

- **Preheat oven to 350°F (180°C)**
- **13- by 9-inch (3 L) cake pan, greased**

1. In a large bowl, combine cake mix and coconut. Cut in butter with pastry blender or two knives until crumbly. Place apple slices in prepared pan. Sprinkle cake mixture over apples. Combine water and lemon juice. Pour evenly over crumble, moistening as much as possible. Bake for 45 to 55 minutes or until top is light golden and apples are tender. Serve warm or cool with ice cream or a dollop of whipped cream, if desired.

Variation: Add 1 cup (250 mL) fresh or frozen cranberries to the apples.

TIPS
- Keep apple slices quite chunky, especially when apples are older, to ensure that they don't become mushy in baking.
- Freeze dollops of whipped cream for an easy garnish. Drop sweetened whipped cream in mounds onto waxed paper. Freeze uncovered until firm, about 2 hours. To use, simply lift onto your dessert and let thaw for 15 minutes.

Apple Cherry Almond Dessert

With this recipe and a few convenience products on hand, dessert is never a problem.

SERVES 12 TO 16		
1	can (19 oz/540 mL) cherry pie filling	1
1	can (19 oz/540 mL) apple pie filling	1
1	package (18.25 oz/515 g) white cake mix	1
1 cup	quick-cooking rolled oats	250 mL
½ cup	packed brown sugar	125 mL
1 cup	coarsely chopped almonds	250 mL
¾ cup	butter, melted	175 mL

- **Preheat oven to 350°F (180°C)**
- **13- by 9-inch (3 L) cake pan, greased**

1. In prepared pan, mix cherry and apple pie fillings. Combine dry cake mix, oats, brown sugar and almonds. Sprinkle evenly over fruit. Pour melted butter evenly over crumble mixture, moistening crumbs as much as possible. Bake for 50 to 60 minutes or until golden. Serve warm.

Variation: Try this recipe using all cherry or all apple filling. Or use two cans of any fruit pie filling that suits your family's taste.

TIPS
- Fruit desserts like crisps and cobblers should be served the same day they are baked. In fact, they are best when eaten warm from the oven.
- Prepare the crumble mixture ahead for easy assembly.

Apple Cranberry Crisp

This favorite old-fashioned dessert never goes out of style.

SERVES ABOUT 12

TOPPING

1	package (18.25 oz/515 g) white cake mix	1
1 cup	large-flake oats	250 mL
½ cup	packed brown sugar	125 mL
2 tsp	ground cinnamon	10 mL
⅔ cup	butter, melted	150 mL

FRUIT MIXTURE

9	large apples, peeled, cored and cut in eighths (about 9 cups/2.25 L)	9
2 cups	fresh or frozen cranberries	500 mL
¾ cup	water	175 mL
¼ cup	lemon juice	50 mL

- **Preheat oven to 350°F (180°C)**
- **13- by 9-inch (3 L) cake pan, greased**

1. Topping: In a large mixing bowl, combine cake mix, oats, brown sugar, cinnamon and melted butter. Stir with a wooden spoon until crumbly. Set aside.

2. Fruit Mixture: Combine apples and cranberries in prepared pan. Combine water and lemon juice and pour over fruit. Crumble topping with finger tips evenly over fruit. Bake for 45 to 55 minutes or until top is golden and apples are tender. Serve warm or cool.

Variations: Replace cranberries with raspberries or blueberries. For plain apple crisp, omit cranberries and increase apples by 1 cup (250 mL). Or use half pears and half apples.

TIPS
- Use a firm, tart apple such as Granny Smith, Cortland or Spy for the best texture and flavor.
- Large-flake oats have a more "oaty" flavor and chunky appearance, but quick-cooking oats taste great, too.
- Serve warm with ice cream or whipped cream.

Super Simple Rhubarb Dessert

Welcome spring by enjoying the refreshing flavor of fresh rhubarb in this delicious dessert.

SERVES 12 TO 16

1	package (18.25 oz/515 g) white cake mix	1
3	eggs	3
1⅓ cups	water	325 mL
⅓ cup	vegetable oil	75 mL
1 tsp	ground cinnamon	5 mL
6 cups	fresh or frozen rhubarb	1.5 L
1 cup	granulated sugar	250 mL
1 cup	whipping (35%) cream	250 mL

TIPS
- If using frozen rhubarb, thaw and pat well to dry before using.
- The rhubarb sinks, forming a tart, creamy fruit mixture under a tender, light layer of cake.

- **Preheat oven to 350°F (180°C)**
- **13- by 9-inch (3 L) cake pan, greased**

1. In a large mixer bowl, combine cake mix, eggs, water, oil and cinnamon. Beat on medium speed for 2 minutes. Spread batter evenly in prepared pan. Sprinkle rhubarb evenly over batter. Sprinkle sugar over rhubarb and drizzle cream on top. Do not mix. Bake for 35 to 40 minutes or until set. Cool in pan on a wire rack. Serve warm or cold. Store in the refrigerator.

Variations: Replace 2 cups (500 mL) of the rhubarb with fresh strawberries or raspberries. Replace cinnamon with ground ginger or grated orange zest.

Plum Kuchen

This not-too-sweet German dessert is wonderful when fresh plums are in season.
It's particularly enjoyable with a cup of steaming coffee.

SERVES 12 TO 16

CAKE

1	package (18.25 oz/515 g) white cake mix	1
¾ cup	butter	175 mL
2	eggs	2
⅓ cup	milk	75 mL
6	large plums, pitted and cut into eighths	6
1 cup	green or red seedless grapes	250 mL

TOPPING

¼ cup	butter, melted	50 mL
¼ cup	granulated sugar	50 mL
1 tsp	ground cinnamon	5 mL

- **Preheat oven to 400°F (200°C)**
- **13- by 9-inch (3 L) cake pan, greased**

1. **Cake:** In a large bowl, cut butter into cake mix with pastry blender or two knives until mixture resembles coarse crumbs. Add eggs and milk, stirring until smooth, about 1 minute. Spread evenly in prepared pan. Arrange plum slices in three lengthwise rows over batter. Place grapes between rows.

2. **Topping:** In a small bowl, combine melted butter, sugar and cinnamon. Mix until well blended. Spoon evenly over fruit. Bake for 30 to 40 minutes or until set and fruit is tender. Cool for 30 minutes in pan on a wire rack. Enjoy warm with ice cream or whipped cream.

Variations: Replace plums with nectarines. Use a yellow cake mix in place of the white.

Strawberry Lime Cream Squares

This refreshingly light fruit dessert will remind you of summer any time of the year.

SERVES 12 TO 16

CRUST

1	package (18.25 oz/515 g) white cake mix	1
½ cup	finely chopped pecans	125 mL
½ cup	butter, melted	125 mL

FILLING

1	can (10 oz/300 mL) sweetened condensed milk	1
3	egg yolks	3
1 tbsp	grated lime zest	15 mL
⅔ cup	fresh lime juice	150 mL
1	drop green food coloring (optional)	1

TOPPING

3 cups	sliced fresh strawberries	750 mL
4 cups	frozen whipped topping, thawed	1 L

- **Preheat oven to 350°F (180°C)**
- **13- by 9-inch (3 L) cake pan, greased**

1. **Crust:** In a large bowl, combine cake mix, pecans and melted butter. Using a wooden spoon, mix until a soft dough forms. Press firmly into prepared pan. Bake for 10 minutes or until golden.

2. **Filling:** In a small bowl, combine sweetened condensed milk, egg yolks, lime zest, lime juice and food coloring, stirring until smooth. Pour evenly over crust. Bake for about 15 minutes or until set. Cool for 15 minutes in pan on a wire rack, then refrigerate until cold, about 30 minutes.

3. **Topping:** Scatter berries over filling. Spread whipped topping over fruit. Chill until serving. Store leftover dessert in the refrigerator.

Variation: Use any of your favorite berries in this recipe. Raspberries, blueberries or a combination are all good.

Apricot Upside-Down Cake

A tart apricot topping is a delightful change from the traditional brown-sugar glaze on pineapple upside-down cake.

SERVES 12 TO 16		
¼ cup	butter	50 mL
2	cans (14 oz/398 mL) apricot halves, drained, syrup reserved	2
1½ cups	apricot jam	375 mL
1	package (18.25 oz/515 g) white cake mix	1
3	eggs	3
⅔ cup	water	150 mL
⅓ cup	vegetable oil	75 mL

TIP

• If you're feeling conservative, serve with whipped cream, ice cream or custard sauce with a sprinkle of toasted almonds. For a more adventurous combination, try orange sherbet. It sounds strange, but it's delicious.

• **Preheat oven to 350°F (180°C)**
• **13- by 9-inch (3 L) cake pan, ungreased**

1. Melt butter in cake pan. Arrange apricots, rounded side up, evenly on top. Combine jam and ¼ cup (50 mL) of the reserved apricot syrup. Spread over fruit.

2. In a large mixer bowl, combine cake mix, eggs, ⅔ cup (150 mL) of the reserved apricot syrup, water and oil. Beat on medium speed for 2 minutes. Pour batter over jam mixture. Bake for 45 to 50 minutes or until a tester inserted in center comes out clean. Cool in pan for 30 minutes, then turn upside-down onto a large serving plate.

Variation: Replace jam with orange marmalade.

Apricot Crunch

Here's a great dessert that can easily be made with a few simple ingredients that you likely have on hand.

SERVES ABOUT 8		
3	cans (each 14 oz/398 mL) apricot halves, drained	3
3 tbsp	packed brown sugar	45 mL
1	package (18.25 oz/515 g) white cake mix	1
1 cup	packed brown sugar	250 mL
⅔ cup	chopped nuts	150 mL
½ tsp	ground ginger	2 mL
½ cup	butter, melted	125 mL
	Sour cream, whipped cream or ice cream	

TIP

• Melt butter in a clear liquid measuring cup in the microwave. The handle stays cool, making it easier to pour.

• **Preheat oven to 350°F (180°C)**
• **9-inch (2.5 L) square baking dish, greased**

1. Arrange drained apricots in prepared pan. Sprinkle the 3 tbsp (45 mL) brown sugar on top. In a large bowl, combine cake mix, the 1 cup (250 mL) brown sugar, nuts, ginger and melted butter. Using a wooden spoon, mix until crumbly. Sprinkle crumble mixture evenly over apricots. Bake for 40 to 50 minutes or until topping is crisp and golden. Serve warm with sour cream, whipped cream or ice cream.

Variations: Replace 1 cup (250 mL) or the entire quantity of apricots with peaches or pears. Fresh berries are a nice addition. Mix 1 cup (250 mL) into the apricots.

Raspberry Angel Dome

This spectacular dessert is prepared a day ahead, making it ideal for entertaining.

SERVES 12 TO 16

CAKE

1	package (16 oz/450 g) white angel food cake mix	1

FILLING AND TOPPING

2	envelopes (each ¼ oz/7 g) unflavored gelatin	2
½ cup	granulated sugar	125 mL
1	can (12 oz/341 mL) frozen raspberry juice concentrate, thawed	1
2 cups	water	500 mL
2 cups	whipping (35%) cream, divided	500 mL
1 cup	fresh raspberries (optional)	250 mL
¾ cup	toasted flaked coconut (optional)	175 mL

TIPS

- Be sure to use a clean, ungreased pan or the cake will not rise properly.
- Fresh fruit is nice but not essential to the recipe.
- You can use canned fruit with other flavored juices or leave out the fruit altogether.

- **Preheat oven to 325°F (160°C)**
- **10-inch (4 L) tube pan, ungreased**
- **Large bowl, lined with plastic wrap**

1. **Cake:** Prepare, bake and cool angel food cake according to package directions. With an electric knife or a long sharp serrated knife, cut cake into 1-inch (2.5 cm) cubes. Set aside.

2. **Filling and Topping:** In a small saucepan, combine gelatin and sugar. Stir in juice and water. Bring to a boil, stirring constantly until dissolved. Chill until mixture is starting to set. In a large mixer bowl, on high speed, beat 1 cup (250 mL) cream to stiff peaks. Beat gelatin mixture until light and fluffy, about 5 minutes. Fold in whipped cream and raspberries. Put one-third of cake cubes in large bowl lined with plastic wrap. Cover with one-third of gelatin mixture, pressing down lightly to moisten cake cubes. Repeat layering. Cover with plastic wrap. Chill overnight.

3. **Assembly:** Turn out dessert rounded side up onto a serving plate. Remove plastic wrap. Beat remaining 1 cup (250 mL) cream to stiff peaks. Spread evenly over dessert dome. Sprinkle with coconut, if desired. Chill until serving. Store leftover dessert in the refrigerator.

Variation: Replace raspberry juice concentrate with other frozen juice concentrates such as cranberry, pineapple-orange or fruit punch. Cans vary in size, so keep the amount to about 1½ cups (375 mL).

Lemon Pineapple Cake Dessert

This dessert may not take a prize for appearance, but with its great taste and ease of preparation, who cares?

SERVES 12 TO 16

1	can (14 oz/398 mL) crushed pineapple, with juice	1
1	package (18.25 oz/515 g) lemon cake mix	1
1	egg	1
¼ cup	granulated sugar	50 mL
1⅓ cups	water	325 mL
⅓ cup	vegetable oil	75 mL
1 tsp	vanilla	5 mL

- **Preheat oven to 350°F (180°C)**
- **13- by 9-inch (3 L) cake pan**

1. Spread pineapple and juice evenly in pan. Sprinkle dry cake mix on top. In a small mixer bowl, combine egg, sugar, water, oil and vanilla. Beat on medium speed for 1 minute or until smoothly blended. Pour evenly over cake mix; do not stir. Bake for 30 to 35 minutes or until golden brown. Serve warm or cool.

Variation: Add some maraschino cherry halves for a nice color and flavor.

Lemon Berries 'n' Cream Cake

Here's a stunning summertime dessert that is perfect for special occasions.

LEMON CURD FILLING

1	envelope (¼ oz/7 g) or 1 tbsp (15 mL) unflavored gelatin	1
1 tbsp	water	15 mL
½ cup	granulated sugar	125 mL
2 tsp	grated lemon zest	10 mL
¼ cup	freshly squeezed lemon juice	50 mL
3	egg yolks	3
¼ cup	butter, diced	50 mL

CAKE

1	package (18.25 oz/515 g) white cake mix	1
1 tbsp	grated lemon zest	15 mL

FROSTING AND FILLING

3 cups	whipping (35%) cream	750 mL
⅓ cup	confectioner's (icing) sugar, sifted	75 mL
3 cups	fresh strawberries	750 mL
1 cup	fresh blueberries	250 mL

TIPS

- Prepare lemon curd up to 1 week in advance. Double the recipe to have some on hand. It's nice as a filling for mini tart shells, garnished with fresh berries. With whipped cream folded in, it also makes a delicious topping for fresh fruit.
- Be careful not to boil lemon curd because it will curdle and thin out.

- **Preheat oven to 350°F (180°C)**
- **Two 9-inch (23 cm) round cake pans, greased and floured**

1. **Lemon Curd:** In a small bowl, sprinkle gelatin over water. Let soften for 10 minutes. In a small saucepan, combine sugar, lemon zest, lemon juice and egg yolks. Whisk to blend. Add butter. Cook over medium heat, stirring constantly until mixture thickens and leaves a path on back of spoon when finger is drawn across, about 7 minutes. Do not boil. Remove from heat. Add gelatin mixture. Stir to dissolve. Cover tightly with plastic wrap pressing against the surface to prevent a skin from forming. Chill thoroughly.

2. **Cake:** Add lemon zest to cake mix and prepare, bake and cool according to package directions. Freeze 1 cake for later use. With a long sharp knife, cut remaining cake horizontally in half.

3. **Frosting and Filling:** In a large mixer bowl, beat cream and confectioner's sugar to stiff peaks. Slice 1¾ cups (425 mL) of the strawberries. Set aside.

4. **Assembly:** Place bottom cake layer cut-side up on serving plate. Spread ½ cup (125 mL) lemon curd on top, leaving a 1-inch (2.5 cm) border. Scatter sliced berries on top. Spread 1 cup (250 mL) of the cream over berries. Place top cake layer cut-side down on cream. Spread remaining cream over top and sides of cake. Pipe cream rosettes around top edge. Place ring of strawberries around edge and pile blueberries in center. Refrigerate until serving. Store leftover cake in the refrigerator.

Variations: Replace blueberries with blackberries or raspberries. Although a combination of light and dark berries is most attractive-looking, almost any mixture will taste great. For an extra hit of lemon, use a lemon cake mix.

Triple Orange Delight

A perfect make-ahead dessert for potluck dinners.

CAKE

1	package (16 oz/450 g) white angel food cake mix	1

FILLING

2	cans (each 10 oz/284 mL) mandarin orange segments, drained, juice reserved	2
1 cup	reserved mandarin orange juice	250 mL
2	packages (each 3 oz/85 g) orange-flavored gelatin dessert mix	2
4 cups	orange sherbet, softened	1 L
4 cups	frozen whipped topping, thawed	1 L

TIP

- Line rectangular pan with plastic wrap, then turn out dessert easily onto a serving plate.

- **Preheat oven to 325°F (160°C)**
- **10-inch (4 L) tube pan, ungreased**
- **13- by 9-inch (3 L) cake pan, lined with plastic wrap**

1. **Cake:** Prepare, bake and cool angel food cake according to package directions. With an electric knife or a long sharp serrated knife, cut cake into 1-inch (2.5 cm) cubes. Set aside.

2. **Filling:** Set drained mandarins aside. Bring reserved juice to a boil. Add gelatin, stirring until dissolved. Pour into a large bowl. Add sherbet, stirring until melted. Fold in 2 cups (500 mL) whipped topping gently but thoroughly.

3. **Assembly:** Place half of cake cubes in rectangular pan lined with plastic wrap. Use enough cubes to cover bottom of pan completely. Reserve 12 to 16 mandarins for garnish. Coarsely chop remaining mandarins. Scatter half the mandarins over cake in pan. Cover with half the sherbet mixture. Repeat with remaining cake, mandarins and sherbet mixture. Press down lightly to moisten all cake pieces with sherbet mixture. Cover with plastic wrap and chill overnight. Invert dessert onto a serving plate. Decorate with remaining whipped topping and reserved mandarins. Chill until serving. Store leftover dessert in the refrigerator.

Variation: Use any gelatin mix with a flavor-matched sherbet (such as lime, raspberry or lemon).

Orange Soufflé Cake

Light and refreshing, this cake is ideal for summer entertaining or to finish a heavy meal.

SERVES 12 TO 16

CAKE

1	package (18.25 oz/515 g) white cake mix	1
2	eggs	2
1	can (10 oz/284 mL) mandarin oranges, drained, juice reserved	1
½ cup	reserved mandarin orange juice	125 mL

MOUSSE FILLING

2	envelopes (each ¼ oz/7 g) or 1 tbsp (15 mL) unflavored gelatin	2
½ cup	cold water	125 mL
6	eggs	6
¾ cup	granulated sugar	175 mL
1 tbsp	grated orange zest	15 mL
⅔ cup	orange juice	150 mL
2 tbsp	lemon juice	25 mL
1 cup	whipping (35%) cream	250 mL
	Whipped cream rosettes (optional)	
	Mandarin orange segments (optional)	

TIPS

- Keep one of the baked cake layers in the freezer. It's then easy to put together a dessert with a minimum of preparation time and effort.
- Prepare the day before for easy entertaining.
- If using a 9½-inch (24 cm) springform pan, trim edge of cake a little to allow mousse to fill around it.
- If cake top is domed, even it off to give a neater appearance to dessert slices.

- **Preheat oven to 350°F (180°C)**
- **Two 9-inch (23 cm) round cake pans, greased and floured**
- **10-inch (25 cm) or 9½-inch (24 cm) springform pan**

1. **Cake:** In a large mixer bowl, combine cake mix, eggs, drained mandarins and juice. Beat on medium speed for 2 minutes or until smooth. Spread in prepared round cake pans, dividing evenly. Bake for 25 to 30 minutes or until a tester inserted in center comes out clean. Cool for 10 minutes in pans on a wire rack, then remove and cool completely on rack. Freeze one cake layer for later use. With a long sharp knife, cut remaining cake horizontally in half.

2. **Filling:** In a small bowl, sprinkle gelatin over cold water. Let stand for 10 minutes to soften. Heat just to dissolve. Cool slightly. In a large mixer bowl, beat eggs and sugar together on high speed until very thick, about 7 minutes. Stir in orange zest, orange juice, lemon juice and gelatin. Mix well. Chill for 10 minutes. Beat cream to soft peaks. Fold into gelatin mixture.

3. **Assembly:** Center bottom cake layer in springform pan (there will be a little room around the edge). Pour half of mousse filling over cake, letting it fill around the sides. Chill for 10 minutes. Place remaining cake layer on top, and pour rest of mousse over. Chill until set, 4 hours or overnight.

4. **To serve:** Run knife around inside rim of pan. Remove pan ring. If desired, decorate top with rosettes of whipped cream and place a mandarin on each rosette. Chill until serving. Store leftover cake in the refrigerator.

Variation: A chocolate cake mix also works well and is very attractive.

Pineapple Delight

The top of this tasty dessert is very light, almost like a soufflé, with a crisp crust underneath.

SERVES 12 TO 16		
CRUST		
1	package (18.25 oz/515 g) lemon cake mix, divided	1
½ cup	butter, melted	125 mL
TOPPING		
8 oz	cream cheese, softened	250 g
4	eggs	4
2 cups	milk	500 mL
1	can (19 oz/540 mL) crushed pineapple, well drained	1

TIP

- If you can't find crushed pineapple — or buy chunks by mistake! — you can process pieces in a food processor until they are coarsely chopped.

- **Preheat oven to 400°F (200°C)**
- **13- by 9-inch (3 L) cake pan, greased**

1. **Crust:** Reserve 1 cup (250 mL) of the cake mix for topping. In a large bowl, combine remaining cake mix and melted butter. Using a wooden spoon, mix until a soft dough forms. Press firmly in prepared pan.

2. **Topping:** In a large mixer bowl, beat cream cheese on medium speed until smooth. Add eggs, one at a time, beating lightly after each addition. Beat in reserved cake mix. Add milk gradually, beating on low speed until smooth. Set aside.

3. Spread pineapple evenly over crust. Pour cream cheese mixture on top. Bake for 30 to 40 minutes or until set and golden. Cool completely in pan on a wire rack before cutting.

Variation: Replace lemon cake mix with white or pineapple.

Black Forest Trifle

The favorite Black Forest cake with a new look!

SERVES 12 TO 16		
1	package (18.25 oz/515 g) chocolate cake mix	1
1	package (6-serving size) chocolate pudding and pie filling (not instant)	1
4 cups	milk	1 L
1	can (19 oz/540 mL) cherry pie filling	1
6 tbsp	cherry liqueur	90 mL
2 cups	whipping (35%) cream	500 mL
	Maraschino cherries	
	Shaved chocolate	

TIP

- Preparing a cooked pudding and pie filling with extra milk makes a wonderfully easy sauce. Try vanilla pudding for a quick custard sauce.

- **Preheat oven to 350°F (180°C)**
- **13- by 9-inch (3 L) cake pan, greased**
- **Trifle bowl or large glass serving bowl**

1. Prepare and bake cake according to package directions for 13- by 9-inch (3 L) cake. Cool completely. Cut into 1-inch (2.5 cm) cubes.

2. In a large saucepan, combine pudding mix and milk. Cook, stirring constantly, over medium heat until mixture comes to a boil. Cover surface of pudding with plastic wrap and cool completely.

3. Put ¼ cup (50 mL) pie filling on bottom of trifle bowl or large glass serving bowl. Drizzle 2 tbsp (25 mL) of the liqueur on top. Place half of cake cubes on filling. Sprinkle with half of remaining liqueur. Cover with half of pie filling. Pour half of pudding over filling. Repeat layers with remaining ingredients. Beat cream to stiff peaks. Spread over top of pudding layer. Garnish with cherries and shaved chocolate. Chill until serving. Store leftover trifle in the refrigerator.

Strawberry Bavarian Mold

Bright red berries with whipped cream on puffs of angel food cake combine to make a showstopping dessert.

SERVES 12 TO 16

CAKE

1	package (16 oz/450 g) white angel food cake mix	1

FILLING

16 oz	frozen strawberries, thawed and drained, juice reserved	500 g
1¼ cups	reserved strawberry juice, plus water as necessary	300 mL
1	envelope (¼ oz/7 g) unflavored gelatin	1
½ cup	granulated sugar	125 mL
1 tbsp	lemon juice	15 mL
2 cups	whipping (35%) cream, divided	500 mL
2 tbsp	confectioner's (icing) sugar, sifted	25 mL

TIPS

- Prepare the day before to set and let flavors mellow. You can bake the cake a few days ahead or freeze it for up to 3 months.
- Buy a few fresh berries and mint leaves to garnish.

- **Preheat oven to 325°F (160°C)**
- **10-inch (4 L) tube pan, ungreased**

1. **Cake:** Prepare, bake and cool angel food cake according to package directions. Wash pan and grease for dessert assembly. With an electric knife or a long sharp serrated knife, cut cake into 1-inch (2.5 cm) cubes. Set aside.

2. **Filling:** Chop berries coarsely; set aside. In a small saucepan, combine strawberry juice, gelatin, sugar and lemon juice. Bring to a boil, stirring to dissolve gelatin. Chill to consistency of unbeaten egg whites. In a large mixer bowl, beat gelatin mixture on high speed until fluffy, about 5 minutes. Beat 1 cup (250 mL) whipping cream to stiff peaks. Fold whipped cream and reserved strawberries into gelatin mixture.

3. **Assembly:** Place one-third of cake cubes in greased tube pan. Cover with one-third strawberry mixture, pressing down lightly to moisten cake. Repeat layering until all ingredients are used. Cover with plastic wrap; chill overnight. To serve, dip pan quickly in warm water to loosen gelatin. Unmold upside down onto a serving plate. Whip remaining cream and confectioner's sugar to stiff peaks. Frost cake completely. Garnish if desired. Chill until serving. Store leftover dessert in the refrigerator.

Variation: Replace strawberries with raspberries.

Strawberry Custard Dessert Cake

This dessert is a knockout in appearance as well as taste, a good choice to impress guests.

CRUST

1 cup	all-purpose flour	250 mL
2 tbsp	confectioner's (icing) sugar	25 mL
⅓ cup	butter	75 mL
⅓ cup	strawberry jam	75 mL

CAKE

1	package (18.25 oz/515 g) white cake mix	1

FILLING

3 cups	milk	750 mL
¾ cup	granulated sugar	175 mL
⅓ cup	all-purpose flour	75 mL
¼ tsp	salt	1 mL
3	egg yolks, beaten	3
2 tbsp	butter	25 mL
1 tsp	vanilla	5 mL

TOPPING

4 cups	halved hulled fresh strawberries	1 L
1 cup	granulated sugar	250 mL
3 tbsp	cornstarch	45 mL

TIPS

- Custard thickened with flour in addition to egg yolks is more stable and stiffer than an exclusively egg-based version. This makes it better for cake filling.
- Prepare parts well in advance for easy assembly later on.
- For an easy filling, prepare a vanilla pudding-and-pie mix using 2½ cups (625 mL) milk rather than 3 cups (750 mL).
- Use flat-ended tweezers to hull strawberries easily.

- **Preheat oven to 350°F (180°C)**
- **9-inch (23 cm) springform pan, greased**
- **Two 9-inch (23 cm) round cake pans, greased and floured**

1. **Crust:** In a bowl, combine flour, confectioner's sugar and butter, mixing with a wooden spoon until crumbly. Press firmly into springform pan. Bake for 18 to 25 minutes or until golden. Cool completely in pan on a wire rack. Reserve jam until cake is assembled.

2. **Cake:** Prepare cake according to package directions and bake in prepared round cake pans. Cool for 10 minutes in pans on a wire rack, then remove from pans and cool completely on rack. Reserve one layer for another dessert. Cut other layer in half horizontally.

3. **Filling:** In a saucepan, heat milk over medium heat until bubbles form around edge and it is steaming. (You can also do this in a microwave oven.) In another saucepan, combine sugar, flour and salt. Gradually add scalded milk. Cook, stirring constantly, over medium heat until thickened. Cover and cook for 2 minutes longer, stirring occasionally. Stir a small amount (about ½ cup/125 mL) of hot mixture into egg yolks, then add egg mixture to hot milk mixture. Cook for 1 minute longer, stirring constantly. Remove from heat. Add butter and vanilla, stirring until melted. Cover surface with plastic wrap. Cool completely.

4. **Topping:** In a saucepan, mix 2 cups (500 mL) of strawberries with sugar and cornstarch. Heat on high, stirring constantly until mixture bubbles and forms a sauce. Immediately reduce heat to low and cook until berries are softened and sauce is thickened slightly. Stir in remaining berries. Chill thoroughly.

5. **Assembly:** Spread jam over crust. Place one cake layer over jam, cut-side up. Spread filling on top. Cover with top cake layer, cut-side up. Spread topping over top of cake. Chill for at least 2 hours or overnight before serving. To serve, remove sides of springform pan and place cake on a serving plate. Store leftover cake in the refrigerator.

Variation: A mixture of strawberries and raspberries or blueberries is nice.

Special-Occasion Desserts

These desserts require a little more time, but they are worth the effort. Have some fun during the holidays with family projects such as the Gingerbread Carousel and the Frosty the Snowman Cake.

Choo-Choo Train Birthday Cake

Let kids help decorate their own party cake. They love it for birthdays, but it is also a fun rainy-day project. Use picture opposite to give them ideas to start. Leave the rest to their imagination.

SERVES 12 TO 18

1	package (18.25 oz/515 g) cake mix, any flavor	1
2	containers (each 15 oz/ 450 g) ready-to-serve chocolate frosting	2
	Assorted candies to decorate (round mints, cinnamon hearts, marshmallows, candy-coated chocolate bits, ring-shaped hard candies, gum drops, nuts, colored sprinkles, etc.)	
	String licorice (black) for train track	

TIPS

- If foil mini loaf pans aren't available, bake cake in square or rectangular pans as directed on package, then cut into 6 small rectangles.
- Use birthday candles for the smoke stack.
- Cut one of the cakes in half for a caboose.
- Make up the number of mini cakes to match the size of your party.

- **Preheat oven to 350°F (180°C)**
- **Six 4½- by 2¾-inch (250 mL) mini loaf pans, greased and floured**
- **One 8-inch (2 L) square or 9-inch (23 cm) round cake pan**

1. Prepare cake mix as directed on package. Fill each loaf pan half full of batter. Pour remaining batter into square or round cake pan. Bake loaves for 18 to 23 minutes and large cake as directed on package. Cool for 15 minutes on a wire rack, then remove from pans and cool completely. Freeze large cake for future use.

2. Place loaf cakes upside down on a foil-lined board, a baking sheet or on cardboard. Frost top and sides of loaves with chocolate frosting. Decorate train engine with candle smokestack. Put round candy wheels on each car. Fill top of remaining 5 cars with small candies or sprinkles. Place licorice between cars for the railway track.

Variation: Vary the train colors with different colored frostings.

Merry-Go-Round Magic

This carousel cake makes a great centerpiece for a children's birthday party.

CAKE

1	package (18.25 oz/515 g) devil's food cake mix	1
1	package (4-serving size) chocolate instant pudding mix	1
4	eggs	4
1 cup	sour cream	250 mL
½ cup	vegetable oil	125 mL
½ cup	water	125 mL
1 cup	semi-sweet chocolate chips (optional)	250 mL

DECORATION

½ cup	ready-to-serve vanilla frosting	125 mL
	Food coloring (optional)	
	Candy sprinkles (optional)	
	Paper carousel roof (see directions, at right)	
6	5-inch (12.5 cm) candy sticks	6
6	animal cookies	6

TIPS

- A turntable makes a great cake plate for the carousel.
- Use ready-made cookies or prepare your own using a sugar cookie recipe.

- **Preheat oven to 350°F (180°C)**
- **10-inch (3 L) Bundt pan, greased and floured**

1. **Cake:** In a large mixer bowl, combine cake mix, pudding mix, eggs, sour cream, oil and water. Beat on low speed for 1 minute to blend, then on medium speed for 2 minutes. Stir in chocolate chips. Spread batter evenly in prepared pan. Bake for 50 to 60 minutes or until a tester inserted in center comes out clean. Cool for 25 minutes in pan on a wire rack, then remove from pan and cool completely on rack.

2. **Decoration:** Warm frosting for about 5 seconds in microwave. Tint pale green or pink, if desired. Spoon over cake to glaze. Decorate with sprinkles, if desired.

3. For roof, cut a 12-inch (30 cm) circle from colored paper. Scallop edge and decorate with crayons, if desired. Make 1 slit to center of circle. Overlap cut edges to form a peaked roof. Fasten in place with tape. Arrange candy sticks evenly around cake, pressing in to secure. Lean cookie against each stick. Place roof on top.

Variation: I love the chocolate cake, but you can use any of your favorite flavors prepared in a Bundt pan.

Ice Cream Cookies

These yummy cookies are perfect for birthday parties, pool parties and after-school treats. Let children decorate their treat. You may need a few ice cream flavors, but the results will be worth it.

MAKES 15 SANDWICH COOKIES OR 30 SINGLE COOKIES		
1	package (18.25 oz/515 g) white cake mix	1
2	eggs	2
½ cup	butter, melted	125 mL
1¾ cups	candy-coated chocolate bits, divided	425 mL
2 qts	ice cream, any flavors, slightly softened	2 L

TIPS
- The cookies should be crisp for ice cream sandwiches. Bake cookies on middle oven rack. Turn baking sheet halfway through baking to ensure even browning.
- Let children enjoy making their own ice cream sandwich.

- **Preheat oven to 375°F (190°C)**
- **Baking sheets, greased**

1. In a large mixer bowl, combine cake mix, eggs and melted butter. Beat on low speed for 1 minute or just until smooth. Stir in 1¼ cups (300 mL) of the candy-coated chocolate bits. Mix well.

2. Drop dough by heaping spoonfuls onto prepared baking sheet, 2 inches (5 cm) apart. Flatten slightly with floured fingers. Press 7 or 8 of the remaining candies into each cookie. Bake, one sheet at a time, for 10 to 14 minutes or until lightly browned. Cool on baking sheets for 1 minute or until firm, then remove to wire racks and cool completely.

3. Sandwich two cookies with about ½ cup (125 mL) of the ice cream between them. Press together lightly. Wrap well in plastic wrap. Freeze until firm, about 1 hour, or for up to 3 months.

Decadent Chocolate Cupcakes

Omit topping for a decadent muffin or frost for a dessert.

MAKES 24 CUPCAKES		
CUPCAKES		
1	package (18.25 oz/515 g) devil's food cake mix	1
1	package (4-serving size) chocolate instant pudding mix	1
4	eggs	4
1⅓ cups	chocolate milk	325 mL
⅓ cup	vegetable oil	75 mL
½ tsp	ground cinnamon	2 mL
1⅔ cups	chopped milk chocolate	400 mL
TOPPING		
1½ cups	semi-sweet chocolate chips	375 mL
½ cup	whipping (35%) cream	125 mL
	Milk chocolate curls (see tip, page 20) or shaved chocolate	

- **Preheat oven to 350°F (180°C)**
- **Two 12-cup muffin tins, greased or paper-lined**

1. **Cupcakes:** In a large mixer bowl, combine cake mix, pudding mix, eggs, chocolate milk, oil and cinnamon. Beat on low speed for 1 minute to blend, then on medium speed for 1 minute. Stir in chopped chocolate. Spoon batter into prepared muffin tins. Bake for 20 to 25 minutes or until tops spring back when lightly touched. Cool completely in tins on a wire rack. Remove from tins before frosting.

2. **Topping:** In a medium saucepan, over low heat, melt chocolate and whipping cream, stirring constantly until smooth. Spread over cooled cupcakes. Decorate with chocolate curls or shaved chocolate.

Variations: For an even more chocolaty taste, use semi-sweet or bittersweet chocolate. Add ½ cup (125 mL) coconut to the batter and decorate tops with toasted coconut.

Cupcakes Galore

A great way to entertain kids at a birthday party. Let them decorate their own dessert.

MAKES 24 CUPCAKES		
1	package (18.25 oz/515 g) cake mix, any flavor	1
1 or 2	containers (each 15 oz/ 450 g) ready-to-serve vanilla frosting	1 or 2
1 or 2	containers (each 15 oz/ 450 g) ready-to-serve chocolate frosting	1 or 2

- **Preheat oven to 350°F (180°C)**
- **Line 24 muffin cups with large paper liners**

1. Prepare, bake and cool cupcakes as directed on package. Frost and decorate as desired, using the ideas below to get you started.

Butterfly Cupcakes: With a paring knife, remove cone-shaped piece from top center of each cupcake. Fill hollow with lemon curd, whipped cream or whipped dessert topping. Cut reserved cake cone in half. Press into filling for butterfly wings. Dust with confectioner's (icing) sugar.

Animal Faces: Frost top of cupcake with vanilla or chocolate frosting. Create funny faces using round candies, licorice, nuts, jujubes, sprinkles, etc.

Half-and-Half Cupcakes: Prepare cupcakes using a white cake mix and a chocolate cake mix. Remove paper liners. Cut white and chocolate cupcakes in half vertically. Spread cut surfaces with frosting. Press a white and a chocolate half together and frost tops. Decorate as desired.

Christmas Picture Cupcakes: Cut a small cardboard pattern of a star, tree, etc. Then either (a) for each light-colored cupcake, place pattern on cupcake and sift sweetened cocoa mix over top. Carefully lift off pattern. For dark-colored cupcakes, sift confectioner's sugar on the pattern. Or (b) frost cupcake and place pattern on top. Sprinkle red- or green-colored sugar or cake sprinkles on top, pressing lightly into frosting. Lift off pattern.

Snowball Cupcakes: Spread top and sides of cupcakes with white frosting. Sprinkle or roll in flaked coconut.

Alphabet or Number Cupcakes: Spread top of cupcakes with white frosting. Use string licorice cut into short pieces to make numbers or letters on top. It's a fun way to help children learn numbers and their ABCs.

Variation: Vary the kind of cake and icing to suit the items being made.

TIP
- Set up bowls containing a variety of icings and colorful candies for decorating. Have a few made up to get the ideas flowing, then leave the rest to the creator's imagination.

Pumpkin Cupcakes

An ideal treat for Halloween and Thanksgiving parties.

MAKES 24 CUPCAKES

CUPCAKE

1	package (18.25 oz/515 g) spice cake mix	1
3	eggs	3
1¾ cups	pumpkin purée (not pie filling)	425 mL
½ cup	water	125 mL
⅓ cup	vegetable oil	75 mL

DECORATION

1	container (15 oz/450 g) vanilla ready-to-serve frosting	1
	Orange food coloring (optional)	
	Colorful candies	

- **Preheat oven to 350°F (180°C)**
- **Line 24 muffin cups with large paper liners**

1. **Cupcakes:** In a large mixer bowl, combine cake mix, eggs, pumpkin, water and oil. Beat on medium speed for 2 minutes. Spoon batter into prepared muffin cups, filling three-quarters full. Bake for 15 to 20 minutes or until tops spring back when lightly touched. Cool for 15 minutes in pans on a wire rack, then remove cupcakes and cool completely.

2. **Decoration:** Color frosting orange if desired. Spread frosting on top of cupcakes. Decorate with your choice of colorful candies.

Variation: Omit the decorating and enjoy these muffins year-round. Add raisins or dried cranberries to the batter.

TIP
- Buy an assortment of small Halloween candies such as jujubes, candied pumpkins, jelly beans, licorice cats and bats, etc. Let kids decorate their own cupcake. Color vanilla frosting orange, if desired.

Pumpkin Cake

A moist spice cake with a mild pumpkin taste. It will be a favorite for those who don't like pumpkin pie.

SERVES 12 TO 16

1	package (18.25 oz/515 g) spice cake mix	1
1	package (4-serving size) vanilla instant pudding mix	1
4	eggs	4
1⅓ cups	pumpkin purée (not pie filling)	325 mL
⅓ cup	vegetable oil	75 mL
¼ cup	water	50 mL
¾ tsp	ground cinnamon	4 mL

- **Preheat oven to 350°F (180°C)**
- **13- by 9-inch (3 L) cake pan, greased and floured**

1. In a large mixer bowl, combine cake mix, pudding mix, eggs, pumpkin, oil, water and cinnamon. Beat on medium speed for 2 minutes. Spread batter evenly in prepared pan. Bake for 35 to 40 minutes or until a tester inserted in center comes out clean. Cool completely in pan on a wire rack.

Variation: Bake cake in two round layers for about 35 minutes.

TIPS
- A cream cheese frosting is a good choice, but a close second is a plain butter frosting with a hint of cinnamon.
- Candy pumpkins make a cute decoration.

Pumpkin 'n' Cream Cake

Even if you don't like pumpkin pie, you'll love this dessert.

SERVES 12 TO 16

CAKE

1	package (18.25 oz/515 g) white cake mix	1
1	package (4-serving size) vanilla instant pudding mix	1
2 cups	pumpkin purée (not pie filling)	500 mL
3	eggs, separated	3
1/3 cup	water	75 mL
1/4 cup	rum	50 mL
1/4 cup	vegetable oil	50 mL
2 tsp	ground cinnamon	10 mL
1/2 tsp	ground nutmeg	2 mL
1/4 tsp	ground ginger	1 mL

TOPPING

1 1/2 cups	whipping (35%) cream	375 mL
1/4 cup	confectioner's (icing) sugar, sifted	50 mL
1 tbsp	rum	15 mL
1 oz	semi-sweet chocolate, melted (see page 13) (optional)	30 g

- **Preheat oven to 350°F (180°C)**
- **13- by 9-inch (3 L) cake pan, greased**

1. **Cake:** In a large mixer bowl, combine cake mix, pudding mix, pumpkin, egg yolks, water, rum, oil and cinnamon, nutmeg and ginger. Beat on low speed for 1 minute to blend, then on medium speed for 2 minutes (batter will be thick). In another mixer bowl, beat egg whites to stiff peaks. Fold one-quarter of whites into pumpkin mixture thoroughly, then gently fold in remaining whites. Spread batter evenly in prepared pan. Bake for 30 to 35 minutes or until a tester inserted in center comes out clean. Cool completely in pan on a wire rack.

2. **Topping:** Beat whipping cream and confectioner's sugar to soft peaks. Add rum; beat to stiff peaks. Spread over cake. Decorate top with a drizzle of melted chocolate, if desired.

Variation: Change the kinds or amount of spice to suit your own taste.

TIPS

- As eggs separate more easily when they are cold, it is best to separate eggs as soon as you remove them from the refrigerator. Let them come to room temperature before using. Even a trace of yolk in the whites will prevent them from beating into stiff peaks.
- Be sure to buy pumpkin purée, not pumpkin pie filling, which has sugar and spices added to it.

Pumpkin Pie Squares

These tasty squares are similar in taste and texture to pumpkin pie but with a crunchy nut top.

SERVES 12 TO 16		
CRUST		
1	package (18.25 oz/515 g) white cake mix, divided	1
½ cup	butter, softened	125 mL
1	egg	1
FILLING		
3	eggs	3
1 cup	packed brown sugar	250 mL
3½ cups	pumpkin purée (not pie filling)	875 mL
½ cup	evaporated milk	125 mL
2½ tsp	ground cinnamon	12 mL
1 tsp	ground allspice	5 mL
TOPPING		
⅓ cup	packed brown sugar	75 mL
½ tsp	ground cinnamon	2 mL
¼ cup	butter	50 mL
1 cup	chopped pecans	250 mL
	Whipped cream (optional)	

- **Preheat oven to 350°F (180°C)**
- **13- by 9-inch (3 L) cake pan, greased**

1. **Crust:** Measure out 1 cup (250 mL) dry cake mix. Set aside. In a large mixer bowl, combine remaining cake mix, butter and egg. Beat on low speed for 1 minute or until crumbly. Press firmly into prepared pan.

2. **Filling:** In a large mixer bowl, combine eggs, brown sugar, pumpkin, evaporated milk, and spices. Beat on low speed to blend, then on medium speed until smooth. Pour over crust.

3. **Topping:** In a bowl, combine reserved cake mix, brown sugar and cinnamon. Cut in butter with pastry blender or two knives until crumbly. Stir in pecans. Sprinkle evenly over filling. Bake for 60 to 70 minutes or until set. Cool for at least 30 minutes in pan on a wire rack. Cut into squares and top with whipped cream, if desired. Store in the refrigerator.

Variations: Replace white cake mix with a yellow one. For an extra-rich filling, use whipping (35%) cream in place of the evaporated milk.

TIPS

- If you buy nuts in bulk by weight, approximately 4 oz (125 g) of chopped nuts is 1 cup (250 mL).
- Use a food processor to quickly mix the topping.

Pumpkin Pie Crunch

It doesn't have to be Thanksgiving to enjoy this dessert.

SERVES 12 TO 16		
1	can (14 oz/398 mL) pumpkin purée (not pie filling)	1
2	eggs	2
1½ cups	evaporated milk	375 mL
1⅓ cups	granulated sugar	325 mL
1 tbsp	pumpkin pie spice	15 mL
½ tsp	salt	2 mL
1	package (18.25 oz/515 g) yellow cake mix	1
1¼ cups	coarsely chopped pecans	300 mL
1 cup	butter, melted	250 mL
	Whipped cream	

- **Preheat oven to 350°F (180°C)**
- **13- by 9-inch (3 L) cake pan, greased**

1. In a large mixing bowl, stir together pumpkin, eggs, evaporated milk, sugar, spice and salt until smoothly blended. Pour into prepared pan. Sprinkle dry cake mix evenly on top. Scatter nuts over cake mix. Drizzle melted butter over nuts, moistening dry mixture as much as possible. Bake for 50 to 60 minutes or until set and golden. Cool for at least 1 hour in pan on a wire rack before serving. Serve with whipped cream. Store leftover dessert in the refrigerator.

Variation: Replace pecans with walnuts, hazelnuts or almonds.

TIP
- For 1 tbsp (15 mL) pumpkin pie spice, you can use a combination of 2 tsp (10 mL) ground cinnamon and ½ tsp (2 mL) each ground nutmeg and ground cloves.

Gingerbread People

Don't limit these to the festive season. With different cookie-cutter shapes and decorations, you can make them a year-round treat.

MAKES ABOUT 2 DOZEN 4-INCH (10 CM) COOKIES		
1	package (18.25 oz/515 g) spice cake mix	1
¾ cup	all-purpose flour	175 mL
2 tsp	ground ginger	10 mL
2	eggs	2
⅓ cup	vegetable oil	75 mL
⅓ cup	molasses	75 mL
	Raisins for eyes (optional)	
	Vanilla icing	
	Colorful candies	

TIP
- You can omit raisins and decorate later with icing. If baking ahead, don't put on the raisin decorations. Cool and store cookies in container with loose-fitting lid. They are ready to decorate when you are.

- **Preheat oven to 375°F (190°C)**
- **Baking sheets, greased**

1. In a large bowl, combine cake mix, flour and ginger. Add eggs, oil and molasses. Mix thoroughly with wooden spoon to form a smooth dough (dough will be soft). Chill for 2 to 3 hours until firm enough to roll out.

2. Roll dough out on lightly floured surface to ¼-inch (1 cm) thickness. Cut with 4-inch (10 cm) gingerbread person cookie cutter. Place on prepared baking sheets. Press raisins in dough for eyes and buttons, if desired. Bake for 8 to 12 minutes or until edges start to brown. Cool on baking sheet for 5 minutes or until firm, then remove to wire racks and cool completely.

3. Decorate if desired with frosting and an assortment of colorful candies.

Variation: Different sizes of gingerbread people cutters are available. Decrease baking time for smaller people and increase time for larger ones.

Festive Coconut Fruitcake

An abundance of colorful fruit, nuts and coconut gives this cake a festive air.

2 cups	halved candied cherries	500 mL
2 cups	mixed candied fruit	500 mL
1½ cups	golden raisins	375 mL
1½ cups	slivered almonds	375 mL
1½ cups	flaked coconut	375 mL
1 cup	diced candied pineapple	250 mL
⅓ cup	all-purpose flour	75 mL
1	package (18.25 oz/515 g) white cake mix	1
1	package (4-serving size) vanilla instant pudding mix	1
3	eggs	3
⅓ cup	water	75 mL
⅓ cup	vegetable oil	75 mL
1 tsp	almond extract	5 mL

TIPS

- Place a shallow pan of hot water at the back of the oven during baking to keep this cake most.
- If the top of the cake seems to be drying out during baking, cover it lightly with a double layer of ungreased brown paper or foil.
- Fruitcake is easiest to slice when it's cold.
- Store fruitcake at least 1 week before slicing. It will become moist and mellow, and improve in flavor. If desired, poke holes with a skewer in cooled cake and brush with warm brandy. Wrap in cheesecloth and store tightly covered in a cool, dry place.
- A shallow pan of hot water in the oven during baking helps keep the cakes moist. If the top of the cake seems to be drying out, place a double layer of ungreased brown paper or foil over the top.

- **Preheat oven to 300°F (150°C)**
- **Three 8½- by 4½-inch (1.5 L) loaf pans, greased and lined with greased brown paper or aluminum foil**

1. In a large bowl, stir together cherries, candied fruit, raisins, almonds, coconut, pineapple and flour. Mix well. Set aside. In a large mixer bowl, combine cake mix, pudding mix, eggs, water, oil and almond extract. Beat on medium speed for 2 minutes. Pour batter over fruit mixture. Mix well.

2. Spread batter evenly in prepared pans. Bake for 1½ hours or until a tester inserted in center comes out clean. Cool for 30 minutes in pans on a wire rack, then remove from pans and cool completely on rack. (If you have covered the loaves with paper or foil during baking, remove before turning out onto rack.) Wrap in airtight plastic bags and store in the refrigerator for at least 1 week or for up to 6 months. Cut into serving-size slices.

Variation: You can vary the kind of candied fruit and nuts in this cake as long as you keep the total amount the same.

Medium Holiday Fruitcake

If you make only one kind of fruitcake, this medium-colored cake is a good choice.

MAKES ABOUT 60 SLICES

2½ cups	chopped mixed candied fruit	625 mL
1½ cups	raisins	375 mL
1¼ cups	chopped candied cherries	300 mL
¾ cup	chopped candied pineapple	175 mL
1½ cups	coarsely chopped nuts	375 mL
½ cup	all-purpose flour	125 mL
1	package (18.25 oz/515 g) spice cake mix	1
1	package (4-serving size) vanilla instant pudding mix	1
3	eggs	3
½ cup	vegetable oil	125 mL
¼ cup	water	50 mL

TIPS

- When testing fruitcake for doneness, the tester may be sticky from the fruit, but it shouldn't be gooey with batter. Remember, the cake will continue to cook a little after you take it out of the oven.
- If top is becoming too brown, cover it with foil for last part of the baking.
- Brush cooled cake with warm corn syrup and decorate with candied fruit and nuts, if desired.
- Cut slices of this rich cake into halves or thirds for serving.

- **Preheat oven to 300°F (150°C)**
- **Two 9- by 5-inch (2 L) loaf pans, greased and lined with greased brown paper or aluminum foil**

1. In a large bowl, combine fruit, nuts and flour. Mix well. Set aside. In a large mixer bowl, combine cake mix, pudding mix, eggs, oil and water. Beat on medium speed for 2 minutes. Pour batter over fruit mixture. Mix well. Spread batter evenly in prepared pans. Bake for 1½ hours or until a tester inserted in center comes out clean (see tip, at left). Cool for 30 minutes in pans on a wire rack, then remove from pans, remove paper and cool completely. Wrap airtight in plastic and store in the refrigerator.

Variation: Deluxe types of mixed fruit usually contain cherries and pineapple, so you may want to eliminate these ingredients and use 4½ cups (1.125 L) of the deluxe mix.

Chocolate Fruitcake

Different and delicious. It makes a great combination on a tray with a light cake such as Light Brazil Nut Fruitcake (see recipe, below).

MAKES ABOUT 60 SLICES		
1½ cups	chopped dates	375 mL
1½ cups	chopped candied cherries	375 mL
1 cup	chopped candied pineapple	250 mL
1 cup	raisins	250 mL
1 cup	coarsely chopped pecans	250 mL
1 cup	all-purpose flour	250 mL
1	package (18.25 oz/515 g) devil's food cake mix	1
3	eggs	3
⅔ cup	water	150 mL
½ cup	sherry	125 mL
½ cup	vegetable oil	125 mL

- **Preheat oven to 275°F (140°C)**
- **Two 9- by 5-inch (2 L) loaf pans, greased and lined with greased brown paper or aluminum foil**

1. In a large bowl, combine fruit, nuts and flour. Mix well. Set aside. In a large mixer bowl, combine cake mix, eggs, water, sherry and oil. Beat on medium speed for 2 minutes. Pour batter over fruit mixture. Mix well. Spread batter evenly in prepared pans. Bake for 2¼ hours or until a tester inserted in center comes out clean. Cool for 30 minutes in pans on a wire rack, then remove cakes from pans, remove paper and cool completely. Wrap airtight in plastic and store in the refrigerator.

Variations: Replace walnuts and pecans with almonds. Replace sherry with brandy or rum.

Light Brazil Nut Fruitcake

A very attractive cake that's crammed full of large chunks of Brazil nuts and fruit, held together with a little batter.

MAKES ABOUT 60 SLICES		
2 cups	halved candied cherries	500 mL
1½ cups	golden raisins	375 mL
1½ cups	diced candied pineapple	375 mL
1½ cups	coarsely chopped Brazil nuts	375 mL
1 cup	mixed candied fruit	250 mL
¼ cup	all-purpose flour	50 mL
1	package (18.25 oz/515 g) white cake mix	1
1	package (4-serving size) vanilla instant pudding mix	1
3	eggs	3
½ cup	water	125 mL
⅓ cup	vegetable oil	75 mL
1 tsp	lemon extract	5 mL

- **Preheat oven to 300°F (150°C)**
- **Two 9- by 5-inch (2 L) loaf pans, greased and lined with greased brown paper or aluminum foil**

1. In a large bowl, combine fruit, nuts and flour. Mix well. Set aside. In a large mixer bowl, combine cake mix, pudding mix, eggs, water, oil and lemon extract. Beat on medium speed for 2 minutes. Pour batter over fruit mixture. Mix well. Spread batter evenly in prepared pans. Bake for 1½ hours or until tester inserted in center comes out clean. Cool for 30 minutes in pans on a wire rack, then remove from pans, remove paper and cool completely. Wrap airtight in plastic and store in the refrigerator. Cut in slices, then cut each slice in half or thirds.

Variation: You can vary the kind of candied fruit and nuts in fruitcake as long as you keep the total amount the same.

Dried Fruit Cake

This will be a hit with people who don't like the traditional fruitcake with candied fruit.

MAKES ABOUT 60 SLICES		
1½ cups	pecan halves	375 mL
1½ cups	chopped dried apricots	375 mL
1 cup	dried cherries	250 mL
1 cup	chopped dates	250 mL
1 cup	dried cranberries	250 mL
1 cup	diced dried pineapple	250 mL
1 cup	flaked coconut	250 mL
⅓ cup	all-purpose flour	75 mL
1	package (18.25 oz/515 g) white cake mix	1
1	package (4-serving size) vanilla instant pudding mix	1
3	eggs	3
½ cup	water	125 mL
⅓ cup	vegetable oil	75 mL

- **Preheat oven to 300°F (150°C)**
- **Two 9- by 5-inch (2 L) loaf pans, greased and lined with greased brown paper or aluminum foil**

1. In a large bowl, stir together pecans, apricots, cherries, dates, cranberries, pineapple, coconut and flour. Mix well. Set aside. In a large mixer bowl, combine cake mix, pudding mix, eggs, water and oil. Beat on medium speed for 2 minutes. Pour batter over fruit mixture. Mix well. Spread batter evenly in prepared pans. Bake for 1¾ hours or until a tester inserted in center comes out clean. Cool for 30 minutes in pans on a wire rack, then remove from pans and cool completely on rack. Wrap in airtight plastic bags and store in the refrigerator for at least 1 week or for up to 6 months. Cut into serving-size slices.

Variations: Try a yellow or spice cake mix. Omit coconut, if desired.

Frosty the Snowman Cake

Let your kids have fun decorating Frosty with their favorite candies.

MAKES 1 SNOWMAN CAKE		
1	package (18.25 oz/515 g) cake mix, any flavor	1
22	round red- or green-and-white-striped peppermint candies	22
1	container (15 oz/450 g) ready-to-serve frosting	1
	Coarse sugar (optional)	
	Assorted candies to decorate (licorice, mints, gumdrops, jelly beans, marshmallows, fruit leather)	

TIPS

- Buy a selection of candies. Don't worry about leftovers — they won't last long.
- Coarse sugar adds a nice "frosty" look, but it isn't a necessity.
- Use flaked or shredded coconut in place of coarse sugar.

- **Preheat oven to 350°F (180°C)**
- **One 8-inch (20 cm) and one 9-inch (23 cm) round cake pan, greased and floured**
- **Baking sheets, covered with foil**
- **Cake board or tray (18- by 10-inch/45 by 25 cm), covered in foil**

1. **Cake:** Prepare cake mix according to package directions. Spread in prepared pans, putting slightly more batter in the larger pan. Bake for 30 to 35 minutes or until a tester inserted in center comes out clean. Cool for 10 minutes in pans on a wire rack, then remove from pans to cool completely.

2. **Decoration:** Arrange round peppermint candies on foil-lined baking sheet to resemble a hat. Bake for about 5 minutes or just until candies start to melt and stick together. Cool completely.

3. Place cake rounds on cake board with smaller one on top for the head. Cover entire cake with prepared frosting. Sprinkle coarse sugar over frosting. Put candy hat in place. Decorate rest of snowman as desired.

Chocolate Yule Log

A normally intimidating recipe is really quite easy when you start with a cake mix. It's large and decadent — a perfect choice for the holiday season.

SERVES 12 TO 16

CAKE

1	package (18.25 oz/515 g) dark chocolate cake mix	1
4	eggs	4
1 cup	plain yogurt	250 mL
½ cup	vegetable oil	125 mL
	Confectioner's (icing) sugar	

FILLING

2 cups	whipping (35%) cream	500 mL
¼ cup	confectioner's (icing) sugar, sifted	50 mL
1 tsp	vanilla	5 mL

FROSTING

1	container (15 oz/450 g) ready-to-serve chocolate frosting	1

TIPS

- Cover a large board or stiff cardboard with foil for a serving plate. Decorate the board with plastic evergreens and holly.
- This makes a very large dessert. You may prefer to fill it and divide it in half. Frost each half separately. Use one and freeze the other for later.

- **Preheat oven to 350°F (180°C)**
- **17- by 11-inch (43 by 28 cm) jellyroll pan, greased and lined with parchment paper, leaving an overhang at the sides; grease bottom of parchment**

1. **Cake:** In a large mixer bowl, combine cake mix, eggs, yogurt and oil. Beat on medium speed for 2 minutes. Spread batter evenly in prepared pan. Bake for 15 to 20 minutes or until cake springs back when lightly touched. Dust a large tea towel with confectioner's sugar. Invert cake pan onto tea towel. Remove pan and carefully peel off paper. While cake is hot, starting from long side and using towel to help, roll up cake loosely in towel. Cool for at least 30 minutes.

2. **Filling:** Beat whipping cream, confectioner's sugar and vanilla to stiff peaks.

3. **Assembly:** Carefully unroll cake and towel. Spread filling evenly over cake. Re-roll cake. (Don't worry about any cracks; they'll be covered with frosting.) Place seam-side down on serving board. Cut a thin slice from each end to make them even. Use centers of these slices for log bumps. Attach to log with a bit of frosting. Cover log, including ends and bumps, with frosting. Run tines of a fork along icing, making lines to resemble bark. Chill until serving. Store leftover log in the refrigerator.

Variations: Flavor the filling with rum, brandy or coffee liqueur, if desired. Replace cream filling with Very Creamy Butter Frosting (see recipe, page 259).

Chocolate Candy Cane Cake

This holiday cake is simple to make but very festive.

CAKE

1	package (18.25 oz/515 g) devil's food cake mix	1
3	eggs	3
1⅓ cups	milk	325 mL
1 cup	mayonnaise	250 mL
1 tsp	peppermint extract	5 mL

FROSTING

1	container (15 oz/450 g) ready-to-serve buttercream frosting	1
¼ cup	crushed candy canes	50 mL
	Whole small candy canes to decorate	

- **Preheat oven to 350°F (180°C)**
- **13- by 9-inch (3 L) cake pan, greased**

1. **Cake:** In a large mixer bowl, combine cake mix, eggs, milk, mayonnaise and peppermint extract. Beat on medium speed for 2 minutes. Spread batter evenly in prepared pan. Bake for 35 to 40 minutes or until a tester inserted in center comes out clean. Cool completely in pan on a wire rack.

2. **Frosting:** Stir crushed candy canes into frosting. Spread frosting over top of cake. Decorate with whole candy canes.

Variation: Replace candy canes with hard mint candies to enjoy this cake year-round.

TIP
- Crush leftover candy canes and stir into vanilla ice cream.

Santa Claus Cupcakes

These cupcakes are as much fun to make as they are to eat. Kids will love to help with the decorating for a holiday party.

1	package (18.25 oz/515 g) cake mix, any flavor	1
1	container (15 oz/450 g) ready-to-serve frosting	1
¼ cup	red colored sprinkles or sugar	50 mL
48	semi-sweet chocolate chips	48
24	cinnamon candies	24
1½ cups	miniature white marshmallows	375 mL

TIP
- Have extra candies on hand because the favorites will be eaten before they get to the cupcakes.

- **Preheat oven to 350°F (180°C)**
- **Two 12-cup muffin tins, paper-lined**

1. Prepare and bake cake mix according to package directions for cupcakes. Cool completely in pans on a wire rack.

2. Spread frosting over top of cupcakes. Sprinkle top third of each cupcake with red sprinkles to look like Santa's hat. Make face using chocolate chips for eyes and cinnamon candy for nose. Cut 12 marshmallows in half lengthwise and place under sprinkles to form the rim of Santa's hat. Cut 4 marshmallows in half crosswise. Place on lower part of cupcake to form beard.

Variation: Don't limit the decorating to Santa faces. Try reindeer or other holiday favorites, such as snowmen, trees and bells.

Colorful Christmas Cream Cake

Layers of red, white and green cake under a snowy white cream cover make for a colorful conversation piece that is also delicious to eat.

SERVES 12 TO 16

CAKE

1	package (18.25 oz/515 g) white cake mix	1
3	eggs	3
1⅓ cups	water	325 mL
⅓ cup	vegetable oil	75 mL
	Green and red food coloring	

FILLING AND TOPPING

2 tsp	unflavored gelatin	10 mL
2 cups	whipping (35%) cream, divided	500 mL
3 tbsp	confectioner's (icing) sugar, sifted	45 mL
¼ cup	raspberry or strawberry jam, divided	50 mL
¾ cup	flaked coconut, divided	175 mL

TIPS

- If softened gelatin sets too quickly, you can reheat it and try again.
- Don't go overboard with the food colors. Pastel is pretty and more appealing. Also, the colors will darken during baking.
- Add food coloring gradually, a few drops at a time, until you have reached the desired shade.
- If you prefer more vibrant colors, look for paste food coloring in cake decorating supply stores.
- To color coconut, put it in a plastic bag. Add a drop of food coloring and knead well.

- **Preheat oven to 350°F (180°C)**
- **Three 9- by 5-inch (2 L) loaf pans, greased and lined with greased aluminum foil**

1. **Crust:** In a large mixer bowl, combine cake mix, eggs, water and oil. Beat on medium speed for 2 minutes. Measure 1⅔ cups (400 mL) of the batter into each of two separate bowls. Tint batter in first bowl light green with a few drops of coloring. Spread batter in a prepared pan. Tint batter in second bowl pink with a few drops of coloring. Spread batter in another pan. Spread remaining white batter in third pan. Bake for 20 to 25 minutes or until a tester inserted in center comes out clean. Cool for 10 minutes; remove from pans to wire racks. Remove foil and cool completely.

2. **Filling and Topping:** Sprinkle gelatin over ⅓ cup (75 mL) of the cream in small saucepan. Let stand for 10 minutes to soften. Then stir over low heat until gelatin is dissolved. Remove from heat. In a small mixer bowl, beat remaining cream and confectioner's sugar until frothy. Gradually add gelatin mixture, beating until stiff peaks form.

3. **Assembly:** Place green cake on platter. Spread half of the jam on top, then ½ cup (125 mL) of the cream filling. Sprinkle with ¼ cup (50 mL) of the coconut. Repeat layering with white cake, jam, cream filling and coconut. Place pink cake layer on top. Cover top and sides of cake with remaining cream. Color remaining coconut pale green with 1 drop of food coloring. Sprinkle over cake. Chill for at least 1 hour before slicing. Store leftover cake in the refrigerator.

Variations: Use different colors for other occasions, such as pink, red and white for Valentine's Day or pink, yellow and green for Easter. Color the filling a pale red or green, if desired. Decorate with candy canes or gumdrop Christmas trees.

Frostings, Glazes and Other Toppings

This book wouldn't be complete without frostings, fillings and glazes to finish your masterpieces. There's more than one to suit every cake. Mix, match, choose your favorites and enjoy!

Basic Frosting Yields

The following is a guideline to the approximate amount of frosting you'll need to cover various types of cake. This information should allow you to create different combinations of frostings and cakes, without the frustration of running out of frosting before you've finished the job. If in doubt, it's always better to have a bit too much frosting than too little. Someone will always be happy to lick the bowl!

Cake size	Frosting required (approx)
13- by 9-inch (3 L) cake, top only	1½ cups (375 mL)
13- by 9-inch (3 L) cake, top and sides	3 cups (750 mL)
2-layer (8-inch/20 cm) cake	3 cups (750 mL)
2-layer (9-inch/23 cm) cake	3½ cups (875 mL)
8- or 9-inch (20 or 23 cm) square cake, top and sides	2 to 2½ cups (500 to 625 mL)
3- or 4-layer (8- or 9-inch/ 20 or 23 cm) round cake	3 to 4 cups (750 mL to 1 L)
12 cupcakes	1 cup (250 mL)
Tube or Bundt cakes	3½ cups (875 mL)

Cake size	Glaze required (approx)
13- by 9-inch (3 L) cake	½ to 1 cup (125 to 250 mL)
Tube or Bundt cakes	1½ cups (375 mL)

TIP

- For many of the recipes, I have recommended one or two frostings that I think complement the cake. My selections are entirely personal and you may have different preferences. Feel free to experiment and, above all, have fun with your choices.

Basic Butter Frosting

A versatile frosting that lends itself to a variety of flavors.

Makes about 2¾ cups (675 mL) frosting
Enough to fill and frost an 8-inch (20 cm) round 2-layer cake.

½ cup	butter, softened	125 mL
4 cups	confectioner's (icing) sugar, sifted, divided (approx.)	1 L
⅓ cup	half-and-half (10%) cream or evaporated milk (approx.)	75 mL
1 tsp	vanilla	5 mL

1. In a large mixer bowl, beat butter and half of confectioner's sugar until light and creamy. Add cream and vanilla. Gradually add remaining confectioner's sugar, beating until smooth. Add a little more cream if frosting is too stiff or a little more confectioner's sugar if too soft to make a soft spreading consistency.

Variations

Lemon or Orange: Omit vanilla; add 1 tbsp (15 mL) lemon or orange zest and 1 tbsp (15 mL) lemon or orange juice.
Coffee: Omit vanilla; blend 1 tbsp (15 mL) instant coffee powder into the butter.
Chocolate: Add 2 oz (60 g) unsweetened chocolate, melted and cooled, to creamed butter.
Cocoa: Replace ½ cup (125 mL) of the confectioner's (icing) sugar with ½ cup (125 mL) unsweetened cocoa powder, sifted together with the confectioner's (icing) sugar.
Cherry: Decrease cream to ¼ cup (50 mL). Omit vanilla; add 1 tbsp (15 mL) maraschino cherry juice and fold in ½ cup (125 mL) well-drained chopped cherries.
Cinnamon: Omit vanilla; add ½ tsp (2 mL) ground cinnamon to creamed butter.
Berry: Omit cream and vanilla; add ½ cup (125 mL) finely chopped or crushed fresh raspberries or strawberries.

TIP

- Prepare an extra batch of this frosting to have handy for a last-minute cake. Store it in the refrigerator for up to 1 month but soften to room temperature to use.

Very Creamy Butter Frosting

This is an extra creamy, buttery variation of a standard butter frosting.

Makes about 2 cups (500 mL) frosting
Enough to frost a 9-inch (23 cm) square cake

½ cup	butter, softened	125 mL
1¾ cups	confectioner's (icing) sugar, sifted	425 mL
1 tbsp	half-and-half (10%) cream	15 mL
1 tsp	vanilla	5 mL

1. In a small mixer bowl, beat butter until creamy. Gradually add confectioner's sugar and cream alternately, beating until smooth and creamy. Add vanilla and beat on high speed until light and fluffy.

Variations

Lemon or Orange: Omit vanilla; add 1 tbsp (15 mL) grated lemon or orange zest and 1 tbsp (15 mL) lemon or orange juice.

Chocolate: Beat 2 oz (60 g) unsweetened chocolate, melted and cooled, into frosting.

TIP
- Double the recipe to fill and frost a layer cake.

Cooked Creamy Butter Frosting

This old-fashioned frosting is one of my favorites and worth the extra cooking step.

Makes about 3½ cups (875 mL) frosting
Enough to fill and frost a 2-layer cake

1 cup	milk	250 mL
2 tbsp	all-purpose flour	25 mL
1 cup	butter, softened	250 mL
1 cup	granulated sugar	250 mL
1 tsp	vanilla	5 mL

1. In a small saucepan, whisk milk and flour until smooth. Cook over medium heat, stirring constantly until thickened. Remove from heat. Cover surface with plastic wrap. Cool thoroughly.

2. In a large mixer bowl, beat butter, sugar and vanilla until light and fluffy. Gradually add cooled milk mixture, beating until light and creamy.

TIP
- There's no substitute for real butter and real vanilla.

Decorator Frosting

This is a good choice when a pure white frosting is desired. It's nice for piping as well as spreading.

Makes about 3½ cups (875 mL) frosting
Enough to fill and frost a 9-inch (23 cm) 2-layer cake

1 cup	shortening	250 mL
2 tsp	colorless vanilla	10 mL
4½ cups	confectioner's (icing) sugar, sifted	1.125 L
¼ cup	half-and-half (10%) cream	50 mL

1. In a large mixer bowl, beat shortening and vanilla until light and creamy. Gradually add half the confectioner's sugar, beating well. Beat in half the cream. Gradually add remaining confectioner's sugar and cream, beating until smooth and creamy.

TIP
- This frosting doesn't keep well, so use the cake the same day it is frosted.

Jiffy Snow Frosting

This elegant fluffy white frosting peaks like snow.

Makes about 3½ cups (875 mL) frosting
Enough to fill a 9-inch (23 cm) 2-layer cake or angel food cake

1¼ cups	corn syrup	300 mL
2	egg whites	2
1 tsp	vanilla	5 mL
¼ tsp	food coloring (optional)	1 mL

1. In a small saucepan, over medium heat, bring syrup to a boil. In a small mixer bowl, beat egg whites to stiff but moist peaks. Gradually beat in hot syrup. Continue beating until very stiff and shiny, about 5 minutes. Beat in vanilla and coloring, if desired. Spread immediately on cooled cake.

TIP
- This frosting doesn't keep well, so use the cake the same day it is frosted.

Cocoa Buttercream Frosting

Makes about 3 cups (750 mL) frosting
Enough to frost a 9-inch (23 cm) 2-layer cake

3 cups	confectioner's (icing) sugar	750 mL
¾ cup	unsweetened cocoa powder	175 mL
⅔ cup	butter, softened	150 mL
5 to 6 tbsp	half-and-half (10%) cream or milk	75 to 90 mL
1½ tsp	vanilla	7 mL

1. Sift confectioner's sugar and cocoa together. Set aside. In a large mixer bowl, beat butter until smooth. Gradually add cocoa mixture and cream alternately, beating until smooth and creamy. Add a little more cream if the frosting is too stiff or a little more confectioner's sugar if it is too soft. (Add enough cream to make a soft spreading consistency.) Beat in vanilla.

TIP
- Sifting the sugar and cocoa together eliminates lumps and blends them evenly.

Chocolate Butter Frosting

A soft, rich, velvety frosting made with the addition of egg yolks.

Makes about 1½ cups (375 mL) frosting
Enough to frost a 9-inch (23 cm) square cake

½ cup	butter, softened	125 mL
1 cup	confectioner's (icing) sugar, sifted	250 mL
2	egg yolks	2
3 oz	semi-sweet chocolate, melted and cooled (see page 13)	90 g

1. In a small mixer bowl, cream butter. Gradually add confectioner's sugar, beating until light and creamy. Add egg yolks, one at a time, beating thoroughly after each. Add melted chocolate, beating until smooth and creamy. Chill slightly, if necessary, to reach a soft spreading consistency.

Creamy Chocolate Butter Frosting

A soft, light, creamy frosting made with stiffly beaten egg whites folded in.

Makes about 1½ cups (375 mL) frosting
Enough to frost a 9-inch (23 cm) square cake

¼ cup	butter, softened	50 mL
¾ cup	confectioner's (icing) sugar, sifted	175 mL
1 tsp	vanilla	5 mL
3 oz	semi-sweet chocolate, melted and cooled (see page 13)	90 g
2	egg whites	2

1. In a small mixer bowl, cream butter until smooth. Gradually add confectioner's sugar, beating until light and creamy. Blend in vanilla and chocolate, mixing well. Beat egg whites to stiff peaks. Fold into chocolate mixture gently but thoroughly.

TIP
- Fold one-quarter of the stiff egg whites in thoroughly to soften mixture, then gently fold in remaining egg whites.

Light and Creamy Chocolate Frosting

This delicious frosting has a creamy milk chocolate flavor that looks particularly striking with a drizzle of dark chocolate on top.

Makes about 3 cups (750 mL) frosting
Enough to frost a 9-inch (23 cm) round 2-layer cake

½ cup	butter, softened	125 mL
2 oz	unsweetened chocolate, melted and cooled (see page 13)	60 g
½ cup	confectioner's (icing) sugar, sifted (approx.)	125 mL
½ cup	half-and-half (10%) cream (approx.)	125 mL

1. In a large mixer bowl, beat butter and chocolate until blended. Add confectioner's sugar and cream alternately, beating until smooth, then beat on medium speed for 1 minute or until light and creamy. Add a little more confectioner's sugar if the frosting is too soft or additional cream if it is too stiff.

Chocolate 'n' Cream Frosting

This frosting is rich, creamy and chocolaty. It is also very easy to spread.

Makes about 4 cups (1 L) frosting
Enough to frost a 9-inch (23 cm) 3-layer cake

1½ cups	unsalted butter, softened	375 mL
½ cup	whipping (35%) cream	125 mL
2 tsp	vanilla	10 mL
3 cups	confectioner's (icing) sugar, sifted	750 mL
6 oz	unsweetened chocolate, melted and cooled (see page 13)	175 g

1. In a large mixer bowl, beat butter until light and fluffy. Gradually beat in cream and vanilla. Add confectioner's sugar, 1 cup (250 mL) at a time, beating until smooth after each addition. Add melted chocolate, beating until smooth.

Variation

Mocha Fudge Frosting: Add 2 tbsp (25 mL) instant coffee, espresso powder or coffee liqueur.

TIP
- Use unsalted butter for frostings, if possible.

Chocolate Rum Frosting

A wonderful soft, creamy filling and frosting with lots of flavor.

Makes about 2 cups (500 mL) frosting
Enough to frost a 9-inch (23 cm) square cake or fill a 4-layer cake

¾ cup	butter, softened	175 mL
1¼ cups	confectioner's (icing) sugar, sifted	300 mL
2	egg yolks	2
1 tbsp	rum (or 1 tsp/5 mL rum extract)	15 mL
6 oz	semi-sweet chocolate, melted and cooled (see page 13)	175 g

1. In a small mixer bowl, cream butter and confectioner's sugar until blended. Add egg yolks and rum, beating until smooth and creamy. Fold in melted chocolate gently but thoroughly. Chill slightly, if necessary, to reach spreading consistency.

Rocky Road Frosting

This frosting, which is almost like fudge, is an ideal way to finish kids' birthday cakes.

Makes about 2 cups (500 mL) frosting
Enough to fill and frost a 13- by 9-inch (3 L) cake or 16 cupcakes

2 oz	unsweetened chocolate, chopped	60 g
2 cups	miniature marshmallows, divided	500 mL
¼ cup	butter	50 mL
¼ cup	water	50 mL
2 cups	confectioner's (icing) sugar, sifted	500 mL
1 tsp	vanilla	5 mL
½ cup	chopped pecans, walnuts or peanuts	125 mL

1. In a saucepan, combine chocolate, 1 cup (250 mL) of the marshmallows, butter and water. Cook, stirring constantly, over low heat until melted and smooth. Cool slightly. Transfer mixture to a large mixer bowl. Add confectioner's sugar and vanilla. Beat on medium speed to a soft spreading consistency. Stir in remaining marshmallows and nuts. Quickly spread over cake.

TIP
- Spread frosting while warm. It hardens quickly on cooling.

Sweet and Sour Chocolate Frosting

The subtle blend of sweet and sour makes this a favorite frosting.

Makes about 4 cups (1 L) frosting
Enough to fill and frost a 9-inch (23 cm) 3-layer cake

3 tbsp	butter, softened	45 mL
3 oz	semi-sweet chocolate, melted and cooled (see page 13)	90 g
4½ cups	confectioner's (icing) sugar, sifted	1.125 L
¾ cup	sour cream	175 mL
1 tsp	vanilla	5 mL

1. In a large mixer bowl, cream butter and chocolate until blended. Add confectioner's sugar and sour cream alternately, beating until smooth. Add vanilla. Beat on medium speed for 1 minute or until creamy.

Chocolate Sour Cream Frosting

This frosting has a light, creamy chocolate color that looks and tastes terrific on dark chocolate cake.

Makes about 2¹⁄₂ cups (625 mL) frosting
Enough for a 9-inch (23 cm) square cake

¹⁄₄ cup	butter	50 mL
3 oz	semi-sweet chocolate, melted and cooled (see page 13)	90 g
¹⁄₂ cup	sour cream	125 mL
3 cups	confectioner's (icing) sugar, sifted	750 mL
2 tbsp	warm water	25 mL
1 tsp	vanilla	5 mL

1. In a small saucepan, heat butter and chocolate over low heat, stirring constantly until melted and smooth. Cool slightly. Transfer mixture to a large mixer bowl. Stir in sour cream. Gradually add confectioner's sugar and warm water alternately, beating on low speed until mixture is smooth and creamy. Beat in vanilla. Chill slightly, if necessary, to reach a soft spreading consistency.

White Chocolate Coconut Hazelnut Frosting

An elegant choice for white, spice or chocolate cakes.

Makes about 1¹⁄₂ cups (375 mL) frosting
Enough to frost an 8-inch (20 cm) square cake

4 oz	white chocolate	125 g
¹⁄₄ cup	butter	50 mL
2 tbsp	half-and-half (10%) cream	25 mL
¹⁄₂ cup	flaked coconut	125 mL
¹⁄₂ cup	finely chopped hazelnuts	125 mL
1 cup	confectioner's (icing) sugar, sifted	250 mL

1. In a small saucepan, combine white chocolate, butter and cream. Heat, stirring constantly, over low heat until smooth. Cool for 15 minutes. Add coconut, nuts and confectioner's sugar. Mix well. If necessary, add a little more confectioner's sugar or milk to reach a soft spreading consistency.

Variation

Replace hazelnuts with pecans or almonds.

White Chocolate Buttercream Frosting

This frosting takes a little more time to make, but it is well worth the effort. It is not too sweet — just rich and creamy.

Makes about 6 cups (1.5 L) frosting
Enough to fill and frost a 9-inch (23 cm) 4-layer cake

6	egg yolks	6
¹⁄₃ cup	granulated sugar	75 mL
2 tbsp	all-purpose flour	25 mL
1¹⁄₂ cups	half-and-half (10%) cream	375 mL
8 oz	white chocolate, chopped	250 g
2 tsp	vanilla	10 mL
1 cup	unsalted butter, softened	250 mL

1. In a medium bowl, whisk egg yolks, sugar and flour until smooth.

2. In a saucepan, heat cream just to a simmer. Gradually whisk into flour mixture. Return mixture to saucepan. Cook over medium heat, stirring constantly, until mixture comes to a boil and is thickened and smooth. Remove from heat. Add white chocolate and vanilla, stirring until melted and smooth. Press plastic wrap onto surface to prevent a skin from forming. Cool to room temperature.

3. In a large mixer bowl, beat butter until light and fluffy. Beating at low speed, add pastry-cream mixture, ¹⁄₄ cup (50 mL) at a time, beating after each addition just until blended.

TIPS

- Add 1 tbsp (15 mL) of your favorite liqueur along with the vanilla, if desired.
- Unsalted butter is preferable in buttercream frosting.

Very Peanut Buttery Frosting

This creamy frosting has a great peanut butter taste. It's nice on chocolate or peanut butter cake.

Makes about 3½ cups (875 mL) frosting
Enough to fill and frost a 9-inch (23 cm) 2-layer cake

1 cup	creamy peanut butter	250 mL
½ cup	butter, softened	125 mL
2 cups	confectioner's (icing) sugar, sifted	500 mL
¼ cup	milk	50 mL
1 tsp	vanilla	5 mL

1. In a large mixer bowl, beat peanut butter and butter on low speed until blended. Gradually add confectioner's sugar and milk alternately, mixing until thoroughly blended. Add vanilla. Beat on medium speed for 1 minute or until mixture is light and creamy.

TIP

• Add finely chopped peanuts to frosting or sprinkle coarsely chopped peanuts on top to decorate the cake.

Creamy Peanut Butter Frosting

This version is very creamy with a mild peanut butter flavor. It's good on chocolate and peanut butter cakes. A good choice for kids' cupcakes, too.

Makes about 4 cups (1 L) frosting
Enough to fill and frost a 9-inch (23 cm) 2-layer cake

¾ cup	creamy peanut butter	175 mL
½ cup	butter, softened	125 mL
4 cups	confectioner's (icing) sugar, sifted	1 L
½ cup	milk	125 mL

1. In a large mixer bowl, beat peanut butter and butter until blended. Gradually add confectioner's sugar alternately with milk, beating on low speed until smooth. Beat on medium speed for 1 minute until light and creamy.

TIP

• Decorate cake with chocolate-covered peanuts, halved peanut butter cups or candy-coated chocolate peanut pieces.

Caramel Frosting

This icing is an excuse to bake a cake. I'm not sure whether I like it better on a cake or as a fudge!

Makes about 3 cups (750 mL) frosting
Enough to frost an 8-inch (20 cm) 2-layer cake

½ cup	butter	125 mL
1 cup	packed brown sugar	250 mL
¼ cup	milk	50 mL
2 cups	confectioner's (icing) sugar, sifted	500 mL
¾ tsp	vanilla	4 mL

1. In a medium saucepan, combine butter and brown sugar. Cook, stirring constantly, over medium heat until mixture comes to a boil. Add milk; bring mixture back to a boil. Remove from heat. Stir in confectioner's sugar and vanilla. Spread warm frosting immediately onto cake.

TIP

• Delicious on banana, spice, chocolate and carrot cake. In other words — almost any cake!

Quick Caramel Frosting

This smooth frosting is particularly delicious on chocolate, banana and spice cake.

Makes about 4 cups (1 L) frosting
Enough to frost a 13- by 9-inch (3 L) cake or a 9-inch (23 cm) 2-layer cake

¾ cup	butter	175 mL
1 cup	packed brown sugar	250 mL
⅓ cup	evaporated milk or half-and-half (10%) cream	75 mL
3 cups	confectioner's (icing) sugar, sifted	750 mL
1½ tsp	vanilla	7 mL

1. In a saucepan, over low heat, heat butter and brown sugar, stirring until smooth. Stir in evaporated milk. Cool slightly. Gradually add confectioner's sugar and vanilla, beating to a soft spreading consistency.

Lemon Buttercream Frosting

Well worth every calorie. It makes a lot, but some of it is bound to be eaten before it gets to the cake.

Makes about 6 cups (1.5 L) frosting
Enough to fill and frost a 9-inch (23 cm) 4-layer cake

1½ cups	butter, softened	375 mL
3 cups	confectioner's (icing) sugar, sifted	750 mL
1 tbsp	lemon juice	15 mL
1	egg yolk	1
2½ cups	prepared lemon pie filling	625 mL

1. In a large mixer bowl, cream butter until smooth. Gradually add half the confectioner's sugar. Beat in lemon juice, egg yolk and pie filling. Gradually add remaining confectioner's sugar, beating on medium speed until light and creamy. Chill, if necessary, to reach desired consistency.

TIP
- Use canned pie filling or cook a pudding and pie filling and cool before using.

Banana Butter Frosting

Makes about 3 cups (750 mL) topping
Enough to fill and frost an 8-inch (20 cm) 2-layer cake

½ cup	butter, softened	125 mL
½ cup	mashed ripe banana (1 to 2)	125 mL
4 cups	confectioner's (icing) sugar, sifted, divided	1 L
1 tbsp	half-and-half (10%) cream	15 mL

1. In a large mixer bowl, beat butter, banana and half of confectioner's sugar on medium speed until light. Add cream. Add remaining confectioner's sugar gradually, beating until smooth and creamy.

Pudding and Cream Frosting

A simple cream frosting that can be adapted to any flavor of instant pudding.

Makes about 3 cups (750 mL) frosting
Enough to fill and frost an 8-inch (20 cm) 2-layer cake

1 cup	whipping (35%) cream	250 mL
1	package (4-serving size) instant pudding mix (banana, vanilla, pistachio, chocolate, lemon or butterscotch)	1
1 cup	milk	250 mL

1. In a small mixer bowl, beat cream to stiff peaks. Set aside. Beat pudding mix and milk on low speed for 1 minute. Let set for 1 minute. Fold in whipped cream. Chill until using.

Basic Cream Cheese Frosting

This frosting is a favorite for carrot cake, but don't limit it to that. It's very versatile. I particularly like it on spice cake or chocolate cake.

Makes about 3 cups (750 mL) frosting
Enough to fill and frost an 8-inch (20 cm) 2-layer round cake

8 oz	cream cheese, softened	250 g
½ cup	butter, softened	125 mL
1 tsp	vanilla	5 mL
3 to 3½ cups	confectioner's (icing) sugar, sifted	750 to 875 mL

1. In a large mixer bowl, beat cream cheese, butter and vanilla on medium speed until fluffy. Gradually add confectioner's sugar, beating on medium speed until light and creamy. Add a little more confectioner's sugar, if necessary, to stiffen icing.

Variations

Orange: Omit vanilla. Add 1 tbsp (15 mL) grated orange zest and 2 tbsp (25 mL) orange juice to cheese mixture, alternating with confectioner's sugar.

Pecan: Fold 1 cup (250 mL) finely chopped pecans into frosting.

Pineapple: Omit vanilla. Increase confectioner's (icing) sugar to 4 cups (1 L). Fold in ⅓ cup (75 mL) well-drained crushed pineapple.

Peach: Omit vanilla. Replace pineapple above with ½ cup (125 mL) mashed and drained canned peaches.

Berry: Omit vanilla. Replace peaches above with ½ cup (125 mL) mashed and drained fresh raspberries or strawberries.

Chocolate Cream Cheese Frosting

Makes about 2½ cups (625 mL) frosting
Enough to frost a Bundt or tube cake

6 oz	semi-sweet chocolate, chopped	175 g
¼ cup	water	50 mL
8 oz	cream cheese, softened	250 g
2 cups	confectioner's (icing) sugar, sifted	500 mL

1. In a small saucepan, combine chocolate and water. Heat over low heat (or microwave in a microwave-safe bowl on Medium for 2 to 3 minutes), stirring, until melted and smooth. In a large mixer bowl, beat cream cheese and chocolate mixture on low speed until blended. Gradually add confectioner's sugar, beating until smooth.

White Chocolate Cream Cheese Frosting

This frosting is divine on chocolate cake.

Makes about 3 cups (750 mL) frosting
Enough to frost a 9-inch (23 cm) 2-layer cake

6 oz	white chocolate, chopped	175 g
8 oz	cream cheese, softened	250 g
¼ cup	butter, softened	50 mL
3 cups	confectioner's (icing) sugar, sifted	750 mL

1. In a small saucepan, over low heat, heat white chocolate until smooth, stirring constantly. (Or microwave on Medium for 2 to 3 minutes, until almost melted. Then stir until smooth.) Cool to room temperature. In a large mixer bowl, beat cream cheese and butter until blended. Beat in melted chocolate until blended. Gradually add confectioner's sugar, beating until smooth, then beat on medium speed for 1 minute, until light and creamy.

TIP
- Use very low heat for melting white chocolate. It burns more easily than semi-sweet.

Flavored Whipped Creams

This is the basic, slightly sweetened whipped cream from which you can make many different flavors.

Makes about 2 cups (500 mL) whipped cream
Enough to fill and frost a 9-inch (23 cm) 2-layer cake

Basic Cream

1 cup	whipping (35%) cream	250 mL
2 tbsp	confectioner's (icing) sugar, sifted	25 mL

Flavor Variations (Choose One)

1 tsp	vanilla	5 mL
½ tsp	almond extract	2 mL
½ tsp	peppermint extract	2 mL
½ tsp	rum or brandy extract (or 1 tbsp/ 15 mL rum or brandy)	2 mL
½ tsp	maple extract	2 mL
½ tsp	ground cinnamon	2 mL
½ tsp	ground nutmeg	2 mL
½ tsp	ground ginger	2 mL
1½ tsp	grated lemon or orange zest	7 mL
1½ tsp	instant coffee powder	7 mL

1. In a small mixer bowl, beat cream, confectioner's sugar and your chosen flavoring until stiff peaks form.

Variations

Fold ¼ cup (50 mL) crushed nut brittle, grated chocolate, chopped nuts, fruit or toasted coconut into stiffly whipped cream.

TIPS
- Chill bowl, beaters and cream well before beating.
- Double recipe as required.

Apricot Whipped Cream Frosting

Makes about 4 cups (1 L) filling
Enough to fill and frost a 9-inch (23 cm) 4-layer cake

2 cups	whipping (35%) cream	500 mL
¼ cup	confectioner's (icing) sugar, sifted	50 mL
1	jar (7½ oz/213 mL) apricot baby food	1

1. In a large mixer bowl, beat whipping cream and confectioner's sugar to stiff peaks. Fold in apricot baby food, gently but thoroughly. Chill until using.

White Chocolate Whipped Cream Frosting

This is a nice choice for a white or chocolate cake with fresh berries. White chocolate curls (see tip, page 20) make a nice garnish on the top.

Makes about 5 cups (1.25 L) frosting
Enough to fill and frost a 9-inch (23 cm) 4-layer cake

3 cups	whipping (35%) cream, divided	750 mL
2 oz	white chocolate, chopped	60 g
⅓ cup	confectioner's (icing) sugar, sifted	75 mL
1 tsp	vanilla	5 mL

1. In a small saucepan, heat ½ cup (125 mL) of the whipping cream just to boiling. Remove from heat. Add chocolate, stirring until melted. Chill thoroughly, about 2 hours.

2. In a large mixer bowl, combine remaining cream, chilled chocolate-cream mixture, confectioner's sugar and vanilla. Beat on medium speed until stiff peaks form, about 3 minutes.

Chocolate Whipped Cream Frosting

Makes about 4 cups (1 L) frosting
Enough to fill and frost a 9-inch (23 cm) 4-layer cake

2 cups	whipping (35%) cream	500 mL
½ cup	granulated sugar	125 mL
⅓ cup	unsweetened cocoa powder, sifted	75 mL
1 cup	crushed chocolate toffee bars (optional)	250 mL

1. In a small mixer bowl, combine cream, sugar and cocoa. Chill for 15 minutes, then beat mixture to stiff peaks. Fold in crushed chocolate bars, if desired.

Basic Glazes

Glazes, quick and easy to prepare, are a nice alternative to frosting. They provide a simple finish in both taste and appearance. Often drizzled over Bundt and tube cakes, they harden on cooling.

Makes about 1½ cups (375 mL) glaze

Vanilla or Almond

2 cups	confectioner's (icing) sugar, sifted	500 mL
1 tbsp	butter, softened	15 mL
1 tsp	vanilla	5 mL
2 to 3 tbsp	hot water	25 to 45 mL

1. In a bowl, combine confectioner's sugar and butter. Add vanilla and enough liquid to make a smooth pourable consistency.

Variations

Almond: Replace vanilla with almond extract.
Coffee: Replace vanilla with 2 tsp (10 mL) instant coffee powder.
Orange, Lemon or Lime: Omit vanilla and water. Add 2 tsp (10 mL) grated orange, lemon or lime zest and 2 to 4 tbsp (25 to 50 mL) orange, lemon or lime juice.
Pineapple: Omit vanilla and water. Add 1 tsp (5 mL) grated orange zest and 2 to 4 tbsp (25 to 50 mL) pineapple juice.

Peanut Butter Glaze

Makes about 1½ cups (375 mL) glaze
Enough to spread on top and drizzle down sides of a Bundt or tube cake

2 cups	confectioner's (icing) sugar, sifted	500 mL
3 tbsp	creamy peanut butter	45 mL
3 to 5 tbsp	hot water	45 to 75 mL

1. In a bowl, combine confectioner's sugar and peanut butter. Add enough liquid to make a smooth pourable consistency.

Brown Sugar Glaze

Makes about ¾ cup (175 mL) glaze
Enough to spread on top and drizzle down sides of a Bundt or tube cake

¼ cup	packed brown sugar	50 mL
2½ tbsp	half-and-half (10%) cream	32 mL
2 tbsp	butter	25 mL
⅔ cup	confectioner's (icing) sugar, sifted	150 mL

1. In a small saucepan, over medium heat, combine brown sugar, cream and butter, stirring constantly until mixture comes to a boil. Remove from heat. Cool to room temperature. Add confectioner's sugar, beating until smooth. If necessary, add a little more confectioner's sugar or cream to make a drizzling consistency. Drizzle over cake.

> **TIP**
> • Warm glazes harden on cooling, so drizzle on cooled cakes as soon as the glaze is mixed.

Chocolate Glazes

There are many recipes for chocolate glaze. Each is a little different, but all are simple to make. They are warm to spread or drizzle and firm up on cooling. Here are a few of my favorites.

Basic Chocolate Glaze

Makes about 1¼ cups (300 mL) glaze
Enough to spread on top and drizzle down sides of a Bundt or tube cake

1 oz	unsweetened chocolate, chopped	30 g
1 tbsp	butter	15 mL
¼ cup	water (approx.)	50 mL
2 cups	confectioner's (icing) sugar, sifted	500 mL

1. In a saucepan, melt chocolate, butter and water over low heat, stirring constantly until smooth. Remove from heat. Gradually add confectioner's sugar, stirring until smooth. Add a little more water, if necessary, to reach a pourable consistency. Pour warm glaze over top of cake, letting it drip down the sides.

Basic Chocolate Chip Glaze

Makes about 1⅓ cups (325 mL) glaze
Enough to spread on top and drizzle down sides of a Bundt or tube cake

1 cup	granulated sugar	250 mL
⅓ cup	butter	75 mL
⅓ cup	half-and-half (10%) cream	75 mL
1 cup	semi-sweet chocolate chips	250 mL
½ tsp	vanilla	2 mL

1. In a saucepan, combine sugar, butter and cream. Cook over medium heat, stirring constantly until mixture comes to a boil, then boil for 1 minute. Remove from heat. Add chocolate chips and vanilla, stirring until melted and smooth. Pour warm glaze over top of cake, letting it drip down the sides.

Variation
Replace vanilla with ¼ tsp (1 mL) almond extract and garnish cake with sliced almonds.

Chocolate Peanut Butter Glaze

Makes about 1 cup (250 mL) glaze
Enough to spread on top and drizzle down sides of a Bundt or tube cake

4 oz	semi-sweet chocolate, chopped	125 g
⅔ cup	creamy peanut butter	150 mL

1. In a small saucepan, over low heat, heat chocolate and peanut butter, stirring constantly, until melted and smooth. Spread evenly over cake.

TIP
• This glaze works well garnished with a sprinkling of chopped peanuts or crushed peanut brittle.

Chocolate Brandy Glaze

Makes about ½ cup (125 mL) glaze
Enough to spread on top and drizzle down sides of a Bundt or tube cake

4 oz	semi-sweet chocolate, chopped	125 g
¼ cup	butter	50 mL
2 tbsp	whipping (35%) cream	25 mL
1 tbsp	brandy	15 mL

1. In a small saucepan, heat chocolate and butter over low heat, stirring constantly until melted and smooth. Remove from heat. Add cream and brandy. Mix well. Pour over top of cake, letting it drip down the sides.

Variation
Replace brandy with 1 tsp (5 mL) almond liqueur or almond extract.

Shiny Chocolate Mocha Glaze

Makes about ½ cup (125 mL) glaze
Enough to spread on top and drizzle down sides of a Bundt or tube cake

4 oz	semi-sweet chocolate, chopped	125 g
2 tbsp	strong coffee	25 mL
3 tbsp	butter, softened	45 mL

1. In a small saucepan, over low heat, melt chocolate and coffee, stirring constantly until smooth. Remove from heat. Gradually add butter, stirring until smooth. Pour over top of cake, letting it drip over sides.

Chocolate Ganache

One of the simplest but most amazing frostings for taste and appearance.

Makes about 2 cups (500 mL) ganache
Enough to frost a 9-inch (23 cm) square cake

1 cup	whipping (35%) cream	250 mL
8 oz	semi-sweet chocolate, chopped	250 g
1 tbsp	liqueur (orange, coffee, raspberry, almond) (optional)	15 mL

1. Place cream in a small saucepan. Bring to a boil, stirring often, over medium heat. Place chocolate in a large mixer bowl. Pour hot cream over chocolate, stirring until melted. Stir in liqueur, if desired. Let stand at room temperature until desired consistency is reached.

To Use

Glaze: Let ganache stand for about 30 minutes. Pour evenly over top of cake, letting it drip down sides. Leave until chocolate sets.

Frosting: Let ganache stand for 3 to 4 hours or until a soft spreading consistency is reached. Spread over cake; leave to set.

Variation

Replace semi-sweet with bittersweet chocolate.

TIPS
- You can use ganache for a glaze or a frosting. The only difference is the cooling time. The longer you leave it, the thicker it gets.
- If ganache gets too firm, simply set over warm water, stirring to soften.

Lemon Curd

This tart, lemony filling is delicious when spread thinly between cake layers.

Makes about 1⅔ cups (400 mL)

3	eggs	3
½ cup	granulated sugar	125 mL
	Grated zest of 1 lemon	
½ cup	lemon juice (about 2 lemons)	125 mL
6 tbsp	unsalted butter, diced	75 mL

1. In a small saucepan, whisk eggs, sugar and lemon zest until thoroughly blended. Add lemon juice and butter. Cook over medium heat, whisking constantly until mixture thickens and leaves a path on the back of a wooden spoon when a finger is drawn across it. Do not boil. Pour through a strainer into a bowl. Cool to room temperature, whisking occasionally. Refrigerate, covered, until ready to use.

Variation

Replace half of the lemon juice and zest with lime or orange.

TIP
- Tightly covered, lemon curd will keep for 1 month in the refrigerator. It is delicious on toast and hot biscuits, in tart fillings and meringues or simply by the spoonful.

Crunchy Broiled Topping

Makes about 2½ cups (625 mL) topping
Enough to spread on top of a 13- by 9-inch (3 L) cake

¼ cup	butter	50 mL
¾ cup	brown sugar, packed	175 mL
¼ cup	half-and-half (10%) cream	50 mL
1 cup	flaked coconut	250 mL
1 cup	chopped pecans	250 mL

1. In a saucepan, melt butter. Stir in brown sugar, cream, coconut and pecans. Preheat broiler. Spread topping evenly over hot cake. Broil 6 inches (15 cm) below element for about 3 minutes or until golden brown. Cool cake completely in pan on a wire rack before cutting.

Liqueur-Flavored Syrup

This makes a nice addition to cakes you are serving to company. The syrup, drizzled on the cut surface of the cake layers, adds moisture and flavor.

Makes about ¾ cup (175 mL) syrup

⅓ cup	water	75 mL
3 tbsp	granulated sugar	45 mL
3 tbsp	liqueur	45 mL

1. In a small saucepan, combine water and sugar. Bring to a boil over low heat, stirring until sugar dissolves. Remove from heat. Stir in liqueur. Cool completely. Cover and refrigerate until ready to use.

2. **To Use:** Drizzle or brush 2 to 4 tbsp (25 to 50 mL) over cut surface of cake layers before adding filling or frosting.

Variation

Use your favorite liqueur, such as brandy, amaretto, kirsch or Grand Marnier, to complement the cake.

TIP

- Prepare the syrup up to a week ahead and refrigerate until you're ready to serve it.

Acknowledgments

I'd like to express my sincere thanks to the many people who helped make this book a reality. A book is very much a team effort, and without them I couldn't have done it.

First, my publisher, Bob Dees, for his patience, understanding, encouragement and guidance.

Danielle Szostak, for her endless support and encouragement, without which I couldn't have done the book. She and her family tasted cake after cake after cake, giving me valuable, detailed feedback on each one.

Brenda Venedam, who diligently typed recipe copy until I'm sure her fingers couldn't type any longer, and who, with her family, cheerfully tasted and commented honestly on many of the recipes, providing invaluable opinions from both kids and adults. I knew the dishes that disappeared overnight were winners.

My mother, Teddy, who never questioned my crazy working hours and was always willing to give me her honest opinion on just one more cake. Also for her influence, which made me appreciate and love everything "home baked" and want to carry on her tradition.

My sister and nieces, who served the recipes at every possible occasion and made a point of telling everyone their source.

All my taste testers, who critically evaluated every recipe and its revisions until we felt it was perfect.

The talented, creative team who makes all the cakes, cookies, bars, squares and desserts look amazing, yet realistic and achievable. Mark Shapiro, the photographer; Kate Bush, the food stylist; Charlene Erricson, the prop stylist; Andrew Smith, Joseph Gisini, Kevin Cockburn and Daniella Zanchetta of PageWave Graphics, who diligently worked through editorial, design, layouts and production to put it all together.

Library and Archives Canada Cataloguing in Publication

Snider, Jill, 1947–

Complete cake mix magic : 300 easy desserts good as homemade / Jill Snider.

Includes index.
At head of title: Duncan Hines.
ISBN 978-0-7788-0422-2

1. Cake. 2. Food mixes. 3. Cookbooks. I. Title.

TX763.S644 2012   641.86'53   C2012-902811-8

Index

Unless noted otherwise, all recipes are made with white cake mix.

Also Available
from Robert Rose

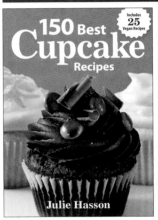
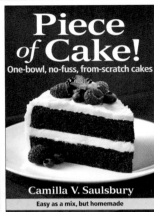

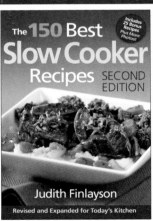

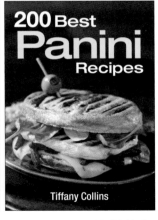

2 1982 03025 9604